Traders and Trade in Colonial Ovamboland, 1925–1990

Gregor Dobler

Traders and Trade in Colonial Ovamboland, 1925–1990

Elite Formation and the Politics of Consumption under Indirect Rule and Apartheid

Basler Afrika Bibliographien 2014

Basler Afrika Bibliographien
Namibia Resource Centre & Southern Africa Library
Klosterberg 23
PO Box 2037
CH-4051 Basel
Switzerland
www.baslerafrika.ch

Cover photo: David Sheehama's main store, Outapi. Probably mid-1970s, unknown photographer. Photo courtesy of Mrs. Jakobina Sheehama.

ISBN 978-3-905758-40-5
ISSN 2296-6986

Contents

Acknowledgment

In early 2004, I did not know anything about traders in Northern Namibia. If, ten years later, I have been able to write a book about them, it is due to the people who have shared their knowledge and experience with me, who have given me access to archival sources and who have welcomed me as a guest and a friend. My first thanks go to all my conversation partners, particularly to Matthias Hamukoto, Rose-Mary Kashululu, Julia Mbida, Oswin Mukulu, Leonard Mukwilongo, George Namundjebo, Eliakim Prins Shiimi, Jakobina Sheehama, Ras Sheehama, Erastus Shamena, Jairus Shikale, Lucia Shikwambi, Pashukeni Shoombe and Andimba Toivo ya Toivo. In many of these conversations, Joseph Ndakalako was an excellent interpreter, door-opener and co-researcher.

Over the years, many people in Namibia hospitably welcomed me in their homes and allowed me to share a piece of their lives. Among them, I am especially grateful to Peter Carolissen, Jutta and Eva Dobler and John Grobler, Nancy Robson, Erastus Shamena and Pashukeni Shoombe. Volker Winterfeldt hosted me as a guest researcher at the University of Namibia.

In the National Archives of Namibia, Werner Hillebrecht and the entire team have always been extremely helpful and welcoming. Even more enthusiastic about my research was Nancy Robson in Odibo, who has managed to gather and preserve a real treasure trove of material in the Lukenge Archives and has the deep local knowledge and experience to make sense of it. The staff at the archives of the Vereinte Evangelische Mission in Wuppertal, the Bundesarchiv in Berlin, the William Cullen Library in Johannesburg and the Zentralbibliothek Zürich have been very professional and helpful, as well, while it was a great pleasure and privilege to discuss Namibian history small and large with Pastor Peter Pauly at the archives of the Evangelical Lutheran Church in the Republic of Nambia in Windhoek.

I have written most of the manuscript while working as a lecturer at the Department of Social Anthropology and a member of the Centre for African Studies at Basel University. The atmosphere of friendly exchange, the continuous encouragement and constructive engagement with my work and the cooperation with colleagues from different subjects and with interest in different regions greatly advanced my thinking about the themes of this book.

The Swiss National Science Foundation financed a six-month research trip in 2006 in the framework of the research project "Regaining Trust and Civil Security in Post-

Conflict Societies". A university grant by the University of Basel gave me the opportunity to finish the manuscript.

Basel turned out to be an ideal place to write about Namibia, not least because of the Basel Africa Bibliographies (BAB) and the wealth of resources and services they provide to researchers. I am very grateful to the Schlettwein family for their generosity and open-mindedness in enabling and promoting research on Southern Africa, and I have learned a lot from the ongoing exchange with Dag Henrichsen, Giorgio Miescher and everybody else at BAB. Petra Kerckhoff has been an efficient, competent and patient editor.

Many colleagues provided input, encouragement or criticism. Michael Bollig, Till Förster, Robert Gordon, Dag Henrichsen, Rita Kesselring and Elísio Macamo read the entire manuscript; their comments gave me a fresh view on the material and greatly improved the book. Gerd Spittler and Till Förster have taught me what I know about anthropology and continue to inspire my engagement with the discipline, and with the world at large.

To all these individuals and institutions, and to many more who were less directly involved in the writing of this book, but shared my work and live over the last years, I am profoundly grateful.

Introduction

This book is a history of traders and trading stores in twentieth century northern Namibia. Through the prism of trade, it offers a detailed account of social and political change in the region the colonial authorities called Ovamboland. Labour migration, colonial rule in its changing forms, local social differentiation, urbanisation and the struggle for liberation were all crucially linked to the history of shops and their owners. My main focus lies on the time between 1925, when the first stores were opened, and 1990, when the former homeland Ovamboland became an integral part of independent Namibia.

Scholarly writings on Namibia's 'homelands' from 1948 to 1990 often stress political stagnation and present the period's history as a lengthy and weary path to liberation. There are good reasons for such an approach. Labour migration, apartheid policies, the brutal occupational regime and the war deeply affected Namibia's society and stifled social creativity. Hopes of independence and democracy were again and again dashed by the continuing South African oppression. The homeland administration had little legitimacy to begin with and was soon undermined by military rule, so that liberation and the transition to democracy were eventually negotiated and brought about by external actors.

But the fact that no political revolution came about in the homelands should not distract us from analysing the social history of apartheid's homelands in their own right. They were much more than dire waiting rooms to independence. Underneath the political stagnation and close to the theatres of war, social and economic developments took place that radically altered society. They laid the foundations on which post-apartheid Namibian society was to be built, and are, in different ways, quite as consequential as the country's political liberation. Without understanding these changes and their relation to the history of apartheid and oppression, we will fail to understand contemporary Namibian society.

Some such changes lie at the center of this book. In writing it, I started with an interest in the present rather than the past. In 2004, I came to Oshikango, a small but bustling trade boomtown on the border to Angola, to do research as a social anthropologist. I sought to analyse the town's international trade connections and their political implications, and I saw Oshikango as a place in which global changes affecting African countries were more visible than elsewhere. I have since written papers on trade, on Chinese expatriates, on political regulation in the new town and on cross-border dynamics.[1] But

---

[1]   See Dobler 2005, 2008b, 2008c, 2009a, 2009c for contemporary perspectives on trade in the area.

as my research progressed, a deeper and more regional history also caught my attention. I was struck by the number of rather decaying locally owned shops and supermarkets in the region's towns and villages. In every larger settlement, I saw barn-like supermarkets built by local businesspeople in the 1970s or 1980s. Almost all of them stood near empty, while South African chain stores, fruit wholesalers operated by Cape Malay families or new Chinese shops thrived next door. The old stores seemed mere relics of an earlier trade boom totally disconnected to the present one. Intrigued by this contrast of boom and bust, I became interested in the history of retail stores in pre-independence Ovamboland.

Very soon I realized how important the stores had been for the local society, not only from an economic point of view, but also for the region's social and political life. In the course of my research, I came to look at the homeland era no longer as a period of stagnation, but as formative years of Namibia's post-apartheid society – formative years, however, which took place under the very specific and decisive conditions of the apartheid state and were heavily influenced by them. My research turned into an attempt to describe social and economic dynamics in segregation and apartheid-era Ovamboland, and to show how the interplay between outside domination and local actors changed Namibian society. Apartheid and the liberation struggle cast their shadow on every scene described in this account, but under their shadow, much more happened than the limelight of nationalist history would make us suppose.

I give a detailed overview of this book and its main theses in the last part of this introduction. Before that, I set out its theoretical frame in a review of existing literature on three of its major themes – civil society, consumption and colonial domination –, provide a short overview on the region for readers unfamiliar with northern Namibia and discuss some methodological and terminological points.

A short literature review

In 1938, Isaac Schapera appealed to his colleagues to include traders in their studies of the contemporary realities of African societies. "The trading store", he wrote, "the labour recruiter and the agricultural demonstrator must be considered integral parts of the modern economic life, the school as part of the routine educational development of the children, and the Administration as part of the existing political system." (Schapera 1938: 27)

In the very year Schapera's plea appeared in Malinowski's famous collection on methods for the study of cultural change, Simon Galoua from Uukwaluudhi applied for a licence to open the first locally-owned store in colonial Ovamboland, a region in Northern Namibia. He followed the example of two larger white-owned shops established in 1925 and operated by the Chamber of Mines in Lüderitz, which wanted to promote consumption to encourage young men to look for work on the central Namibian mines. Simon Galoua's shop was short-lived, but from 1952, locally owned trading stores mushroomed all over Ovamboland.

Schapera, like many of his contemporaries, looked for a way out of a theoretical and practical impasse into which established anthropology had maneuvered itself. Anthropology's specialization on 'primitive' peoples and 'their' cultures meant that its subject matter seemed to be progressively vanishing. Some anthropologists became melancholic; Lévi-Strauss' first voyage to Brazil, later the core of *Tristes Tropiques*, had started three years earlier. Some found their niche by treating vanishing cultures as remnants of a distant past, and some tried to provide anthropology with a new rationale by serving colonial rule.

Schapera and some of his colleagues in Southern Africa instead conceived of social anthropology as a realistic social science that should describe and analyze life under contemporary colonial conditions. This new conception owed much to theoretical insights by Radcliffe-Brown and to a generational conflict with Malinowski and other established scholars, but it had more to do with the changing conditions in Southern Africa themselves. Migrant labor, urbanization, colonial domination and segregation had become too important features of social life for the anthropologist to close his or her eyes to them.

The theoretical shift for which Isaac Schapera argued in 1938 has become common ground today. Most of the topics he mentions have moved into the centre of a large body of research: migrant labor, agricultural development projects, schools and the state administration have long become blossoming sub-fields of Africanist social sciences. But that trait of contemporary African life which he mentions first is still very much neglected: the role of trading stores. Innumerable studies exist on market trade or long-distance trade routes, on smugglers or migrant traders, but we still know very little about rural trading stores and the role they have played for African societies. This is all the more surprising since two major research themes in African studies and anthropology converge in shops: the emergence of new globalised consumption patterns on the one hand, modern elites' role in civil society on the other.

Trade and consumption

There is of course a large body of literature on trade and traders in Africa.[2] Surprisingly little of it, however, deals with modern village stores. The most important strands of re-

---

[2]   For a synthesis of research in many fields, see Ellis/ Fauré 1995.

X

search concern markets and market traders,[3] the history of long-distance trade and trade routes, including the slave trade[4] and migrant entrepreneurs – Lebanese,[5] Indian[6] or today Chinese[7] traders in African countries. Most of the studies which explicitly mention store owners stem from South Africa, where businesspeople played a more prominent role in the discussions on the possible emergence of a black bourgeoisie since the 1960s and 1970s than elsewhere in Africa. While the recent interest in the anthropology of consumption has brought some very important studies on material culture and distribution in Africa, none of them has a focus on shops and shop owners. For Namibia, the topic is mentioned frequently as one deserving more interest,[8] but no serious research has yet been undertaken. The only book-length study on trade history in northern Namibia is Siiskonen's (1990) "Trade and Socioeconomic Change in Ovamboland", which covers the years to 1906.

Material culture has always been an important topic in anthropology, a discipline that was shaped at least as much by museums as by university institutes. Until very recently, however, the focus was most often on locally produced goods – on pottery, woodcraft or weavers. Aluminum pots, plastic kettles or second-hand jeans did not fascinate anthropologists working in Africa very much. This changed when the postmodern interest in diversity and incongruity spread into anthropology in the late 1980s and when globalization became a new central topic in the 1990s. The new anthropology of consumption that developed out of the old study of material culture was very much interested in global goods and their appropriation by local societies.[9] Important studies on such varied things as soap, second hand clothing, bicycles, glass beads or the adaptation of lorries to local needs broke up the old dichotomies between Western and local goods and showed how all kinds of consumer goods are appropriated by societies and integrated into their everyday life.[10] Today, consumption changes are no longer perceived as the overpowering of local societies by modern goods, but as the result of people's everyday agency and a valid expression of their own aims. Economic inequalities and political marginalization obviously play an important role for these changes, but they cannot be summed up as the

---

[3]   Bohannan/ Dalton 1965, Hodder/ Ukwu 1969, Meillassoux 1971.
[4]   Miers/ Kopytoff 1977, Lovejoy 1980.
[5]   van der Laan 1975, Leichtman 2005, Beuving 2006.
[6]   Kuper 1960, Chattopadhyaya 1970, Gregory 1993.
[7]   Haugen/ Carling 2005, Dobler 2008, 2009.
[8]   Shigweda 2006, van Wolputte 2007.
[9]   See Appadurai 1986, Miller 1995, Spittler 2001 for fundamental perspectives.
[10] Burke 1996, Hansen 2000, Beck 2001, Hahn 2004, Vierke 2006.

mere extension of Western capitalism.[11] This new approach opened the field for a broad range of studies on consumption in Africa.[12]

In many cases, however, the sheer presence of new goods is taken for granted rather than analyzed. This underplays the role distribution chains and traders play for the local appropriation of goods. The supply side obviously determines to a large degree what choices people actually have, and traders are crucial middlemen whose actions influence the local meaning of new goods. Village stores in particular have only found scant coverage in the Africanist literature, even though they have been vitally important for the changes in African consumption throughout the twentieth century.[13] They were the most important means of access to new goods for a large part of the population, and they influenced everyday life in Africa in subtle, but crucially important ways. Village stores laid the foundation for the integration of a large part of the African population into a globalised consumer society.

Modern elites

"The term élite", Dwaine Marvick writes in Kuper's Social Science Encyclopedia in 1985, "is part of a tradition which makes modern social scientists uneasy."[14] There are very good reasons for this uneasiness. The concept of elites has too often been used in a normative way, describing either an avant-garde whose ways others will follow or the group which, for good or bad, really matters in a society's trajectory. The social sciences (particularly anthropology, more interested in the powerless than in the rulers) have learned to be skeptical of such ascriptions. To define a group as elite immediately provokes the question of perspective and power: in whose perception is a group defined as an elite, and whom does this definition serve? This is accentuated by the often rather intuitive use of the word. Where other terms to designate social groups – from class to milieu – are clearly definable, 'elite' remains vague and underdefined.

Even though I share these misgivings, I have decided to use the term 'elites' in this book to describe an emic category of unclear boundaries but high practical importance. 'Elite' in this sense are the people who, in a political meeting or a public gathering under a tree, are offered chairs by the organizers; who are invited to eat in the homestead of the host of a feast where others are given food outside; who get the seats next to the

---

[11] Spittler 1991, Verne 2006.
[12] The best overview on these discussions, Hahn (2005), is unfortunately only available in German; see Hahn 2008 for a short form.
[13] See Burke 1996, Verne 2006, 121–140, Spittler 2008 and Dobler 2008 for some exceptions.
[14] Marvick 1985, 243.

driver if they take a local bus. Their status can derive from very different sources and vary considerably according to the context. A village headman or a school teacher can be an important member of a rural elite, but s/he usually does not get a VIP invitation if the State President opens a public building; a wealthy businessman might be well-respected in town, but disregarded in a village. In a given context, most people would roughly agree who should and who should not get a privileged chair, but this does not turn the 'elite' into a homogenous group who share pre-defined qualities. Instead, the different possible sources of elite members' status can lead to a recognized inner differentiation of the elite and to conflicts over social and political power.

Such a power struggle was the background of African studies' first interest in elite groups. In the 1950s and 1960s, scholars became more and more interested in 'modern' elites, members of a new high-status milieu which often stood in conflict with the 'old' elites of village headmen. The 'new elite' owed their status more to their school education, their formal-sector profession or the political leadership they sought to provide in the modern state than to any traditional legitimacy. Scholars saw the new elites as both the driving force and the product of economic, political and social modernization. Development studies and political analyses of liberation movements and post-colonial states often ascribed a positive role to them.[15] Researchers more interested in class analysis in contrast often regarded them as a new petty bourgeoisie with a less positive role. Within the general framework of capitalist underdevelopment, they argued, the new elite's ascent masked existing injustices and contributed to the exploitation of the rural masses.[16]

In spite of this interest in ascending groups in the modern-sector economy, only scattered evidence in the literature concerns trade as an independent source of income for developing nationalist elites.[17] It was one of the few occupations in the modern sector open to Africans – together with that of the teacher, the preacher, the nurse, the government clerk or in rare cases the physician or lawyer, all of which necessitated more formal schooling than trade. African store owners were an important part of the social groups that contributed to independence and profoundly changed African societies between the 1950s and 1970s. Still, I am not aware of a single book-length study on African village storeowners.

The early interest in African elite groups more or less faded away in the 1980, when a new focus on everyday life, popular culture and democracy made the earlier studies look

---

[15] See Cole 1975, Nafziger 1977 for West, Marris/ Somserset 1971 for East, Kuper 1965 for South Africa.

[16] Mamdani 1976, Fauré/ Médard 1982, Hudson/ Sarakinsky 1986, Lubeck 1987, Randall 1996, Berman/ Leys 1994. For the exceptions, see Kuper 1965, Hart 1972, Southall 1979, Boone 1993.

[17] Allusions to traders' role are found for example in Rich 2004 for Gabon, Wild 1991 for Rhodesia and Dumett 1973 for Ghana.

under-differentiated and too intent on modernization. Elites continued to play an important role in the discussions on the African state, but instead of analyzing the elites themselves, most studies were merely interested in their role in political structures.[18] When the topic re-emerged in anthropology in the early 2000s, it was emphatically presented as a new research field.[19]

My use of the term elite reflects these earlier debates and tries to avoid their pitfalls. I use the term to describe people who had a high status in the respective local society, be it in a village, a town or the entire region. 'Elite' thus is not yet a functional ascription. It is true that elite members often influence political decisions. Through their social recognition, elite members have more access to political power; politicians, both through their resources of power and patronage and through their office's charisma are more likely to be regarded as part of the elite. Even so, elite status is only typically, but not necessarily connected with political or economic power. The term 'elite' was the best word I have found to describe traders' role as an ascending group whose economic and social success challenged earlier ways to define social status, and I hope that the teleological confidence with which much of the 1960s literature used it has not entirely corrupted it.

Civil society

Civil society – societal groups organized around common interests and interweaving into a web of civil relations that channels and frames political engagement – has played a formative role in the institutionalization of European (and North American) states. By using economic, cultural and social capital to engage regents in a constant discussion about the right way to govern, civil society has acted as a counterweight to monarchical power and has helped to bring about both the strong institutionalization and the constant checks and balances characteristic for modern European states.[20]

The importance of civil society in Europe is the background for a lasting debate on its role in Africa.[21] Can civil society in Africa play a similar role as it did in Europe?

Although with many differences between times and regions, all empirical data suggest a lower degree of civil society organization in African than in European countries.

---

[18] Swainson 1980, Bayart 1989.

[19] Shore/ Nugent 2002, Fumanti 2003, Rich 2004. – Newer literature often prefers the term "middle class" to describe traders, but the urban and bourgeois connotations the concept brings with it do not really fit my context, while there is no local upper class above the traders which could justify such a designation.

[20] For a synthesis of different strands in this discussion, see Cohen/Arato 1992, Putnam 1993, Reinhard 1999, Warren 2000.

[21] Bretton 1994, Harbeson et al. 1994 and Comaroff 1999 probably are the most important reference points of the ongoing discussion.

If the emergence of modern state institutions was linked to a specific form of politicized civil society, can these institutions be successful in a completely different social setting? Is the weak institutionalization of bureaucratic state power in many African countries the consequence of this missing civil society – and if so, can stronger institutions and better governance be reached by strengthening civil society?

These questions are in the centre of the debates on statehood and good governance in Africa. One side – often connected to the more practical work of democracy building – sees civil society institutions as part of the solution. By strengthening civil society structures and empowering interest groups, donors hope to build up the in-country awareness of good governance that is instrumental for the emergence of sustainable control and democracy. Many political analysts on the other hand – especially those critical of the liberalist framework on which a large part of civil society proponents base their reasoning – question the very idea of an African civil society as counterforce to the state. In their eyes, the very fragmentation of African societies combined with a close interweaving between state and society[22] prevents the emergence of civil society structures which could act as a counterweight to government power.[23] In weak economies based on rents from commodity exports or from donor transfers, bargaining power of the relatively few interest-based groups is low, and access to those in power – not opposition to them – is their most important resource. This effectively prevents the emergence of civil society groups opposed to the state.[24]

On both sides in the debate, empirical studies of the actual role of existing civil society groups are rarer than theoretical statements. Most studies concentrate on NGOs' work in the present and either stress the immediate role of civil society groups as lobbyists for transparency, democracy or economic deregulation or focus on their integration with state hierarchies which effectively undermines their role as a counterweight. But in the study of political mobilization, social networks and institution buildings, the most important effects are necessarily long-term and only become visible in a longer time perspective, which often lacks in the existing literature on civil society in Africa. This book is also an attempt to analyze the role an identifiable professional group played in civil society organization over time and through several fundamental changes in the political regime.

---

[22] Migdal 2001.
[23] Chabal/ Daloz 1999, Daloz 2003.
[24] Allen 1997.

Structures and agency in domination

Pour ce coup je ne voudrois sinon entendre, S'il est possible, & comme il se peut faire, que tant d'hommes, tant de Villes, tant de Nations, endurent quelques fois un Tyran seul, qui n'a puissance, que celle qu'on luy donne ; qui n'a pouvoir de leur nuire, sinon de tant qu'ils ont vouloir de l'endurer : qui ne sauroit leur faire mal aucun, sinon lors qu'ils aiment mieux le souffrir, que luy contredire.

Etienne de la Boëtie, 1548 (1727, 75 f.)

There are few places in Africa in which indirect colonial rule was driven to such smooth perfection as in Ovamboland during the time of Native Commissioners Hahn and Eedes between 1920 and 1954. One senior and one junior administrator, with the help of less than a handful white and a small number of local staff ruled over roughly 200.000 people in an area much larger than the Netherlands. There was no rebellion and no really serious unrest during this time; even the military deposal of the unruly Uukwambi King Iipumbu ya Shilongo in 1932 did not lead to any bloodshed, although his homestead was bombed after his flight. I can think of few places where Etienne de la Boëtie's question is as much to the point: How is it that so few administrators with grossly insufficient resources could bring so many people under colonial domination? Why did people accept their overlordship?

This, of course, has been one of the major topics in African studies over the last thirty years. Historians, anthropologists or sociologists have started to break up the category of domination and look at the inner workings of colonialism, at the ways in which colonial power became meaningful in practice. One of the constant findings from all over Africa is a blatant insufficiency of colonial means of domination. Even though military conquest and sporadic symbolic violence played an important role in the establishment of colonial rule, the normal situation was the lone white administrator in an area much too large to control it by himself.

This had been a practical problem for colonial administration before turning into an analytical conundrum for social scientists. Colonialism's main solution had been the cooption of local rulers in a system classically formulated by Lord Lugard in his "The Dual Mandate in British Tropical Africa", published in 1922. Lugard's manual of course only served as a model for British colonialism, but in practice, similar means were a necessary part of many European states' colonial administration.[25] Lugard advocates a system of rule which integrates local resources of domination into the chain of command. If a colonial power manages to co-opt local rulers, Lugard argues, they can be integrated into

---

[25] On indirect rule's in the different versions of European colonialism, see e.g. Crowder 1964 and 1970, Kiwanuka 1970, Geschiere 1993, Miles 1994.

a single system of indirect colonial rule, in which domination is all the more effective because it is decentralized. Instead of controlling the entire population, the colonial power only has to influence a few central figures. Local rulers pay the price of becoming subject to colonial rule, but if they do so, they gain new resources of domination towards their own subjects.

The workings and consequences of indirect rule have been thoroughly analyzed in African studies. Over the last twenty years, it has become clear that indirect rule was one of the major avenues on which local authority and colonialism were intermingled in practice and colonial authority became relevant on an everyday level.[26] Indirect rule has thus become a favorable domain for the analysis of larger questions in the sociology of domination. How is a formal system of government translated into practices of domination? What is the nature of the link between the apparatus of domination and individual agency? Or, in de la Boétie's fundamental formulation: why do the many accept to be governed by the few? These questions constantly hover in the background of this book. What answers I provide will remain on the concrete level of a historically framed, socially bounded analysis of a case study. As this analysis is, or so I hope, guided by a theoretical outlook on practical workings of domination, it might be useful to briefly outline my approach on a more fundamental theoretical level.

My basic assumption is that the explanation of social phenomena has to be grounded in human agency. The concept of 'structures' can be used as an often handy abbreviation, but it is not a theoretically satisfying explanation of social order. Social structures only matter, only exist, as far as human agency produces them.

But agency is never without preconditions. It is framed in three fundamental ways: First, it finds its limits by the mundane conditions of the world we live in. For Alfred Schütz, the fundamental bounding of agency in time and space was the starting point of any analysis of the conditions of the lived world given, *vorgegeben*, to us. Space and time form easily acceptable limits: we cannot be in two places at once, we can only meet people who are our contemporaries, and death will put an end to our agency. But these are just the most obvious examples for the limits our agency finds in the 'objective' structures of the world we live in. Many of these 'objective' structures are socially created and might be changed over time, but this does not make them less real in any given situation: crossing social boundaries is not always easier than walking through a concrete wall.

Secondly, agency is never completely our own. Whatever we do is a social phenomenon. This is true on the very fundamental level on which our very subjectivities are

---

[26] For some of the most influential studies in which much of the older literature is summed up, see Asiwaju 1988, Mamdani 1996 and Berman 1998.

shaped by our engagement with the social world; Pierre Bourdieu has used the metaphor of *habitus* to describe this. But even if we take the formation of subjectivities as granted, it is also true in everyday life, simply because we do not base our every action on identifiable conscious decisions. We rely on normalized practices in what Giddens describes with the Husserlian term 'durée'.[27] These normalized practices structure the world and thus produce social institutions, but they are inseparable from the social world we live in.

Thirdly, our knowledge of the given world as we experience it, including of the social institutions we perceive as relevant, forms the background of our motives and the precondition of our interactions, and it structures the factors we include in our conscious decisions. While strategic plans and conscious (sometimes even rational) decisions are not easy to separate from normalized practices, the difference exists, and our perceptions of the outer world influence both types of agency in slightly different ways.

These three ways in which individual agency is framed by the outer world are also the paths by which domination is produced in practice. Domination is based on the ability to form the objective structures surrounding an individual, in the capacity to shape the subjectivities and normalized practices of his or her everyday life and in the aptitude to influence social actors' perceptions of relevance and concsequently their strategic decisions.

I think that most of the literature on domination which is interested in agency at all can be allocated to one or several of these three levels. Three examples cannot prove, but at least illustrate this: When Heinrich Popitz stresses the power to set data – building roads and walls, furthering or withholding knowledge, inventing new tools of war – as one of the crucial ways to transform power into domination, he describes the first point: the ability to change structures with which people have to engage.[28] When John and Jean Comaroff use Gramsci's concept of hegemony to analyze how missionaries contributed to the acceptance of colonialism by changing African subjectivities, they stress the second point: the power of influencing social actors' motives and their perceptions of relevance.[29] And when social historians talk of the 'strategic use' people made of the colonial administration, they look at the third point: the conditions of conscious decisions by social actors.

In its analysis of traders' agency under colonialism, this book, then, is an attempt to describe how domination was produced through agency on all three levels: by setting objective conditions people had to deal with, by changing structures of relevance and practice, and by providing a new frame for conscious decisions. At times, I will use abbreviations. I will talk of 'apartheid', of 'the homeland system' or of 'government' to denote

---

[27] Bourdieu 1979; Giddens 1995.
[28] Popitz 1999.
[29] Comaroff 1991.

a combination of practices which took on an objective form in the everyday perceptions of people who came into contact with them. But these 'structures' only existed through agency. They were not always created from above, neither – not always based in conscious strategies of powerful actors. If they were, they only became socially relevant in so far as other people accepted them as conditions for their actions; such acceptance did not always look like the strategists intended.

Ovamboland: a short geographical and historical outline

"Ovamboland" is the colonial designation of a region in northern Namibia. In 19th century sources, the term described the territory of thirteen independent polities whose inhabitants spoke closely related languages (collectively called Oshiwambo[30]) and shared many economic, cultural and political traits. When Germany and Portugal drew a line between their spheres of influence in South-Western Africa in 1886, it cut this area in half. Five polities and half of the largest kingdom, Oukwanyama, fell on Angolan territory. As a consequence, "Ovamboland" became an administrative designation of the South West African part of the settlement area alone. It still covered the areas of eight polities: Oukwanyama, Ondonga, Uukwambi, Ongandjera, Ombalantu, Uukwaluudhi, Uukolonkadhi and Eunda. Uukolonkadhi and Eunda were later merged into one tribal authority under the system of indirect rule. Map 1 shows the polities as the German missionary Bernsmann depicted them in his 1896 map, with the addition of the colonial border between Angola and South West Africa.

As a term in physical geography, Ovamboland describes an endorheic basin fed from the Cuvelai River in Angola. Except for the Kunene, whose rand mountains form the geographical border of the basin, no permanent rivers flow in Ovamboland, but an extensive system of temporary watercourses (Oshanas) is fed by floods from the Cuvelai during the rainy season between January and April. In years with exceptional rains, their water drains into the Etosha salt pan and evaporates there, but more often the watercourses simply dry up after the rainy season. This floodplain does not extend over the entire Ovamboland basin. In the areas not watered by Oshanas, permanent settlement was only possible close to clay pans which function as water storage.

Before the first towns developed since the 1950s, people lived in homesteads dispersed over the settled territory, and which usually housed between one and fifteen people. Sorghum and millet fields lay around the homesteads. Cattle were kept close to the

---

[30] See below for a remark on orthography and terminology.

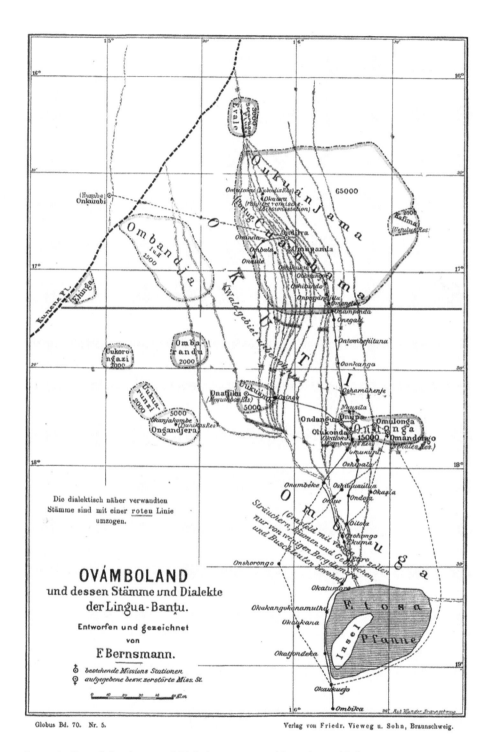

Image 1: Ovamboland in 1896. Today's international boundary added.

homesteads outside of the planting season and were moved to cattle posts, often in the wilderness areas between the polities, during the agricultural season.

In precolonial times, the different polities were self-ruling entities separated by large stretches of wilderness. After the official demarcation of the international border to Angola in 1927, differences in British and Portuguese colonial rule led to a mass movement of Oshiwambo speakers from Angola to South West Africa. Due to this migration and natural population increase, the settlement areas expanded until they had merged into one continuous inhabited area covering the entire area in which the availability of water made settlement possible. Map 2 shows the boundaries of the local polities after they had been transformed into administratively mapped realities, and the boundary of the continuous settlement area in 1970.

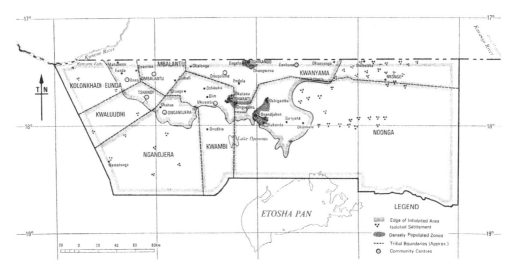

Image 2: Administrative Map of the Homeland showing 'tribal' boundaries in 1970.

South West Africa was declared a German protectorate in 1884, but Ovamboland remained largely outside the grasp of German colonialism. The region was connected to European rule through mission stations and through early labor migration of mostly young men to the farms, towns and mines of central Namibia, but no permanent government post existed in Ovamboland before World War I. In 1906, Germany declared the area a Native Reserve and introduced pass laws regulating travels to and from Ovamboland. When South Africa defeated the German troops in 1915, took control of the territory and was later given the League of Nations mandate over South West Africa, this system remained in place. The first permanent administrative posts were established in the reserve, and between 1915 and 1932, the new colonial power subjugated the independent polities under colonial domination and integrated the chiefs and headmen into a system of indirect rule. A white native commissioner governed the area through the chiefs, who were backed by the colonial power if they kept to its rules, and displaced if they did not.

When the National Party came to power in South Africa in 1948, South West African administration started to move from segregation to apartheid. Amidst growing internal and external opposition, Ovamboland was transformed from a reserve into a 'self-governed' homeland in 1968. Chiefs and headmen of the seven 'tribal groups' within Ovamboland were appointed as ministers in the new homeland government; later, partial elections replaced the appointment system. The homeland system never brought any real measure of self-determination and was fiercely contested by the growing liberation movement.

In 1966, when South Africa did not accept the final revocation of the League of Nations mandate by the United Nations, the largest liberation movement Swapo (South West Africa People's Organisation) started armed guerilla attacks in Ovamboland. With Angolan independence in 1975, Swapo could use bases in that country and intensified the sporadic war. South Africa reacted with a massive expansion of its military and paramilitary presence in the area and strict emergency regulations. From the mid-1970s, Ovamboland became an occupied country under de facto military rule. Actual fighting in South West Africa remained sporadic and of low intensity, but its repercussions and the violence linked to the military oppression severely affected life in the area.

After a long process of reforms, negotiations and warfare, the first democratic general elections were held in 1989 and Namibia became independent in 1990. The liberation movement Swapo turned into a political party and has won a vast majority in every election since. In 1992, the country was portioned in 13 regions and Ovamboland ceased to exist as a political unit. The four regions Omusati, Oshana, Ohangwena and Oshikoto roughly cover its former area.

Terminology, Methods, Sources

When writing about segregation and apartheid era Southern Africa, it is sometimes unavoidable to use terms that were important instruments of apartheid policy. No analysis of apartheid can do without such terms, but in using them we always run the danger of unwittingly reproducing categories the analysis intends to deconstruct. I do not think that there is any way to avoid this conundrum, unless our analysis contributes to a world in which racist categories have lost their credibility to a degree that they we can use them purely in a critique of past ideologies.

The problems already start with the region about which I write. For very good reasons, many people in the area resent the term "Ovamboland". It is too closely linked to the South African homeland policy and its attempts to base the political order on institutionalized ethnicities. Independent Namibia has opted for a different way of institutionalizing political belonging, and created regions which do not match the former homeland boundaries. For these reasons, I do not use the term for the region today. But from 1906 to 1990, Ovamboland was an administrative unit with a distinct legal and political reality, which makes it necessary to use the term when writing about this period.

In much the same way, terms like "black", "native" or "white" described the realities of life under a racist administration. These categorization where obviously fictive and sometimes arbitrary, but they had important consequences for the subjects of a state which used them. To avoid them would rob us of the possibility to analyze the workings of this state.

In the administrative terminology between 1915 and 1990, "Chief" denoted the head of an independent polity; the term corresponds to today's "King" or "Queen". "Headman" is the title of the principle of a tribal sub-unit. Ondonga, Ongandjera, Uukualuudhi, Oukwanyama before 1917 and Uukuambi before 1932 were governed by central Chiefs, while the remaining polities were ruled by headmen or councils of headmen. To avoid too much confusion when citing sources, I have decided to keep the administrative terms and talk about "chiefs and headmen" wherever the highest 'native' authorities in the system of indirect rule are concerned.

Although "Namibia" replaced "South West Africa" in the international discourse since the late 1960s and the UN and the OAU adopted the new name in 1973, I use the country's official name, South West Africa, until March 1990. This corresponds to the realities of colonialism, and the claim for independence which was connected with the contrafactual use of "Namibia" fortunately is no longer necessary.

Orthography of local languages is not wholly standardized. I have spelt Oshiwambo words according to Tirronen's Ndonga dictionary. For the toponymy, I have kept to today's standard usage as reflected in The Namibian's and New Era's Oshiwambo[31] pages, typographically treating class prefixes as part of the noun (thus writing Uukwambi instead of uuKwambi etc.).

The oral history data for this book was gathered during fourteen months of fieldwork in northern Namibia. While my main research interest lay in present-day trade

---

[31] As the standardizing grammars and dictionaries were mostly written by German or Finnish missionaries, the language is usually called Oshiwambo (with a w), while the region Ovamboland is written with a v, as British colonial officers called it.

and politics, I soon began to be interested in the history of shops, as well. The relatively long stay in Namibia allowed me to go back and forth between archives and interviews. My knowledge of archival material was a very good opening for interviews. Especially a nominative traders' list of 1969 proved an excellent entry-point, as most of the older traders were immediately interested in it and, remembering, started to tell stories about people they knew. I conducted most of the formal interviews with former traders towards the end of my second longer stay, between August and October 2006. Most interviews were done in English; if the interviewee preferred to speak in Oshiwambo, Joseph Ndakalako from Okatope, who also worked as manager in a supermarket owned by Usko Nghaamwa, the governor of Ohangwena Region, proved an excellent and untiring co-researcher and translator.

Apart from the formal interviews, informal talks, gossip and everyday interaction taught me a lot about life under apartheid and about shops' and traders' roles. My fieldwork in today's shops brought many occasions to talk about trade in earlier times, look back on the history of shops or compare the historical situations. But a large part of my data comes from archival sources. Of foremost importance were the collections of the National Archives of Namibia in Windhoek and the Lukenge Archive at Odibo. For the German period, crucial material is found at the German Federal Archives in Berlin, the Archives of the Vereinte Evangelische Mission in Wuppertal and the ELCRN Archives in Windhoek. Fewer, but equally important data came from the ELCIN archives in Oniipa, the William Cullen Library in Johannesburg and the collections of the Basler Afrika Bibliographien in Basel.

The latter also provided my most important access point to the extensive scholarly literature on Ovamboland. I could not have written this study without learning from the excellent studies already in existence. I will not attempt to review them here, but I would like to point out some of the works which have been most important for me. At the same time, I will address some trends in the literature which have had consequences for the structure of this book.

As often in colonized African countries, the earlier works dealing with Ovamboland were written by missionaries, anthropologists or colonial officers, while much of the newer literature has an historic interest. After the first travelogues in the nineteenth century, the missionaries Hermann Tönjes and Carlos Estermann, the colonial officer Carl Hugo Linsingen Hahn and the anthropologist Edwin Loeb have written the most important reference works on 'traditional' society.[32] They shared a tendency to reify paternalistic

---

[32] The most important travelogues are Galton 1853, Andersson 1856, Hahn 1981 [1857], Schinz 1891. The other works mentioned: Tönjes 1911, Estermann 1976, Hahn 1928, Loeb 1962.

structures, masking change and idealizing a self-sustaining agricultural society, but used carefully, all of these works can provide crucial information on twentieth century societies in Ovamboland.

After the end of South African occupation and Namibian independence made it again possible to conduct research in the area, a new wave of scholars worked there, often combining archival research with oral history and mostly interested in the early colonial and segregation era. Thanks to the excellent work done by scholars like Martti Eirola, Patricia Hayes, Meredith McKittrick, Emmanuel Kreike, Harri Siiskonen and others, we know a great deal about Ovamboland before 1950.[33] They all built on more or less the same corpus of written sources. Especially the NAO (Native Administration Ovamboland) and A.450 (Accessions C.H.L. Hahn) series in the National Archives in Windhoek have been extensively used, and no monthly report has been left uncited.

The time after 1954, however, has barely found any coverage in the literature on Ovamboland. After Native Commissioner Eedes retired and Native Affairs in Ovamboland came under the control of the South African Ministry of Native Affairs in 1954, the archival situation becomes more difficult (the relevant material is split between the archives in Pretoria and Windhoek, and much has been lost or has never been archived in the first place). Scholarly interest on the era concentrated on the beginning liberation struggle, but internal politics and social change have never been studied thoroughly. Almost nothing is known about the implementation of the Odendaal plan, about administrative changes in Ovamboland, let alone about social developments in the region.

This uneven distribution of scholarship on northern Namibia leads to a certain unevenness in my own study. For the years to World War II, I was able to concentrate on the history of trading stores and their social role alone. While the history is new – the only study focusing on trade in the region, Harri Siiskonen's "Trade and Socio-Economic Change in Ovamboland", stops before the first stores are opened –, its background is well known. I disagree with the existing literature in some important points, but the ground is sufficiently cleared that such debates become meaningful. For the time after World War II, however, especially for the 1970s and 1980s, it was not possible to write a history of traders and stores without simultaneously giving at least a tentative image of the social, political and economic background. Here, my study had to broaden its perspective and give more background information. For this, I could rarely rely on academic

---

[33] Siiskonen's (1990) is a fundamental monograph on trade before 1906; Eirola (1992) has worked on the German government's policy towards Ovambo polities before World War I; Patricia Hayes (1992) has written the pioneering comprehensive history of the area before 1930; Meredith McKittrick (2002) has looked at conversion and generational conflict before 1960 and Emmanuel Kreike (2005) has studied environmental change and agriculture in relation to colonialism.

studies, but had to use a large amount of propaganda publications, development plans and annual reports on the one hand, solidarity newsletters and anti-apartheid eyewitness accounts on the other.

I often spent a frustrating amount of time gathering information which might seem irrelevant to a reader not specifically interested in Ovamboland, but which was crucial in order to come to an understanding of the situation. The dates of office of a Bantu Affairs commissioner, small changes in the delegation of authority or biographical details of key politicians might not be of immediate relevance for the general reader, but in the absence of more specialized literature, they will be useful to future researchers. I have tried to relegate such data to the extensive footnotes.

The book's storyline

Trade in Ovamboland obviously has a much longer history than European colonial expansion. Chapter 1 gives an outline of this history and presents the background of the first stores' foundation. Long-distance trade routes had connected the different Ovambo polities to their southern and northern neighbors for centuries when European trade caravans began to regularly visit the region around 1850. Long-distance trade had largely been under the control of local rulers, who managed to integrate the new traders into the existing system of trade and largely monopolize the new trade goods. As guns and horses – excellent instruments of rule by force – were among the most important goods of European traders, the new trade made a stronger centralization of domination possible. As economic resources could now directly be converted into resources of domination, the gun trade encouraged rulers to extract higher taxes from their own subjects and to raid their neighbors more aggressively. Early colonial trade thus led to higher insecurity and to a redistribution of wealth and power in favor of chiefs and headmen. This was one reason for the military strength of the local polities which kept the region relatively free from colonial rule until World War I, but also for the depletion of resources which made the subsequent integration into the colonial economy through migrant labor more attractive.

European caravan trade from the south dried up when the new colonial power Germany controlled the gun trade more tightly, and above all when veterinary regulations following the rinderpest in 1898 prevented the exportation of cattle, until then the main exchange commodity, from Ovamboland to central Namibia. After the shock of the 1904 war, Germany declared Ovamboland a native reserve in 1906 and tried to avoid all disturbances which could dry up labor supply or lead to political or military trouble. The colonial government would have liked to increase trade, but it saw traders as a potentially disruptive element and prevented caravans from entering the area. It therefore wanted to open a store on one of the mission stations, which had long bartered European goods for services and local goods, but the attempt came to nothing.

South Africa took over colonial control in South West Africa in 1915. For the first time, the administration established permanent stations in Ovamboland. It established its military supremacy by subjugating the largest polity Uukwanyama and killing its King Mandume. Since migrant labor was the most important resource Ovamboland had to offer, the new government tried as carefully to avoid 'disturbances' in Ovamboland as the old one. But South Africa, as well, regarded trade as a means to induce more young men to work in the colonial economy. When the Chamber of Mines in Lüderitz asked leave to establish a trading store in Ovamboland in connection with a reorganization of labor recruitment, the administration saw this as a welcome opportunity for a closely controlled store to be opened, one for which mere profit would not be the most important guideline.

Chapter 2 relates the history of the two stores opened by the Chamber of Mines in Ondjodjo in Ondonga and Omafo in Uukwanyama in 1925. They were the only stores which existed in the reserve and soon became important points of reference for the local society. People who had come into some money and wanted to buy clothing, a plough or just a bag of tobacco walked for several days to reach them. Returning migrant workers spent a large part of their wages in the new shops and took the goods they had bought to the villages to barter for cattle or grain. As cash, a necessary precondition of buying in the shops, was very scarce before roughly World War II, the migrants could exchange European goods at very favorable rates, which increased the value of their income and made migrant work more attractive.

In 1937, when the share of diamond mining in the national economy had greatly diminished due to the world economic crisis, and the political leverage of the Chamber of Mines had become smaller, its stores were accused of monopolistic gains. A report came to the conclusion that the stores' prices were indeed too high, even if no excessive profits had been made. As a signal to the Chamber of Mines, a third trading licence was granted to a German trader who opened a store in Endola in southern Oukwanyama in 1938. Five years later, however, labor recruiting was put on new grounds with the founding of the South West African Native Labour Association SWANLA. The new organization was now responsible for recruiting in the entire territory, and it took over Ondjodjo and Omafo stores, as well. Although it was a private institution, it had close links to the government, and when the private store owner mistreated a senior headman in 1947, he was expelled from the reserve and his licence given to SWANLA. In 1952, finally, the organization opened a fourth store in Ombalantu.

In the history of these stores, the encroachment of colonial rule and the increasing interlinkage between local and colonial economy become tangible. As more cash became available locally, the stores' turnover increased continuously. The shops were always closely watched by the colonial administration, but had much more leeway than private stores would have had.

The four SWANLA stores, together with shops in the Police Zone, also became models for the first locally owned stores which are the topic of Chapter 3. The first store was founded by Simon Galoua in Ombalantu in 1939, but it soon had to close down due to supply problems during the war and trouble with the local headman. When more people applied for licences to open shops in the early 1950s, chiefs and headmen were at first opposed to their plans. Instead, they opted for cooperative stores under their own supervision, a model then Native Commissioner Hahn favored, as well. This would also have allowed them to regain control over trade and play an important role in the cash economy. But in a mixture of free trade ideas and skepticism towards locals' ability to run larger stores, the colonial administration decided in favor of individual stores.

The first store owners were either migrant workers who had earned a starting capital in the south and wanted to establish themselves at home, or teachers or preachers who could invest a part of their local income and capitalize on their professional status. In the following twenty years, storeowners became an economically successful and socially important new elite. They were literate, used to industrial wage labor and increasingly politicized. For them, 'modern' goods and 'modern' ways of life became a way of self-assertion and a means to carve out new social spaces for themselves. But most of them remained anchored in the village society and saw their main role on the local level, not in nationalist politics.

From the 1950s, trade in Ovamboland is more directly linked to the specific conditions of public life under the developing social order of apartheid. As Ovamboland's administrative history of the formative years between 1948 and 1978 is not well known, it was necessary to dedicate Chapter 4 to the political and economic changes in the region. From a native reserve, the area was gradually transformed into an officially self-governed homeland. These political transformations were accompanied by massive state-organized development efforts. The idea of 'separate development' of the homelands was put into practice in Ovamboland with higher energy and more success than in many South African homelands. This was partly due to the better conditions in Ovamboland, which had not been subject to the forced resettlements and fragmentation that characterized 'native' areas in South Africa; and it was partly caused by the anxiousness of the South African government to prove to an increasingly hostile world that its mandate rule was good for South West Africa. This, of course, was not how most South West Africans saw it. From

1966, the conflict between liberation movements and the government resulted in war and the occupation of Ovamboland by South African troops.

Against this background, Chapter 5 looks more closely at the development of stores and at the social role of the new traders. Between 1956 and 1972, the number of licenced shops in Ovamboland grew from 28 to 1.524; most of the shops were scattered over the entire area, so that in the early 1970s, almost every cluster of homesteads had a licenced store. These stores obviously differed much in size and turnover. When analyzing the traders' role in the local society, I concentrate on the more successful traders who played a more important role in the supralocal organization of civil society. Starting from three biographies of traders, I treat trade organization, credit networks and most importantly the ways in which traders gained social importance and status within their spheres of influence.

As the first public meeting places under local control, stores also became the nuclei of new towns that partly supplanted, partly complemented mission stations and chiefly courts as the old centers of social gravity. This change, which is the topic of chapter 6, is most visible in the example of Ondangwa and Oshakati. Ondangwa simultaneously was an administrative centre as the seat of the Native Commissioner, an important passage point as the labour recruiting centre, and the biggest shopping centre due to Onjdodjo wholesale. A large number of shops, bars and eating-places developed around these landmarks and provided services for the people who passed through on the way to and, with fuller pockets, back from contract work. In the early 1950s, this was the first urban centre which developed in northern Namibia. Oshakati was founded in the 1960s as the new homeland capital and quickly developed into the largest town in the area. Just like Ondangwa fifteen years earlier, it was perceived by many as a hotspot of social change, as a social frontier on which the accepted rules of practice could be changed.

On a lesser scale, villages in the entire area transformed with the establishments of shops. The new concrete buildings, necessary due to the licence regulations, became meeting places, bars and occasions to exchange local gossip, and slowly the old structure of scattered homesteads was complemented by new village cores. In some cases, especially where government offices, a mission station or a hospital provided employment for non-agrarian workers, this led to the small-scale urban development that today is so characteristic for the densely populated central northern regions.

As Chapter 7 shows, the shops and the new towns were also places of political exchange, and traders were increasingly drawn into politics. In the 1960s, a process of differentiation began in which a part of them left business – and usually the country – to become professional politicians, while most remained professional traders with a part-time interest in politics. Professional politicians in exile took an increasingly radical stand towards the South African government, while professional traders were more willing to compromise and cooperate with the colonial regime. They were, however, among the most active civil society groups. Much of their business life was affected by state regulations which they experienced as constraints in their economic freedom; backed by their high status in their own society and their economic success, traders began to actively lobby for their own interests. They were the first professional group to organize their interests as a counterweight to the administration. Since the later 1950s, several associations of local businessmen or shop owners were founded. They were not openly (party-)political, but voiced their concerns wherever their group interests were affected by government decisions. Some of the associations also became shields for opposition work and contributed to Swapo's internal organization. Overall, a very complex pattern of political alliances emerged that can neither be summarized as "alliance between the white ruling class and the subordinate African petty-bourgeoisie [...] intended both to facilitate an outward appearance of a de-racializing economy and to deprive the African mass of political leadership by allowing for a degree of upward mobility",[34] nor seen in the terms of racial opposition the struggle between apartheid policy and the liberation movement would suggest. Instead, the traders emerged as an active political group that tried to further their common interests through organization, while simultaneously pursuing very different political agendas in other forums.

Their situation became much more difficult during the war. In the interest of their business, traders had to appear neutral and to cooperate with everybody, which drew both sides' suspicions to them. Many shops were burned down and a number of traders killed during the war. But the war also led to an unprecedented boom of local shops, as the soldiers' wages represented a steady inflow of capital in the area, of which a large percentage was spent in local pubs and shops. Politically well connected traders were in the best position to profit from this boom, which lay the grounds for some of the largest fortunes in today's Namibia.

All in all, the political role traders played in pre-independence Ovamboland had many facets and cannot simply be understood in the categories of collaboration or resistance. Far from being passive victims of, in Mamdani's term, a "decentralised despotism" which fragmented the public and prevented political organization in the rural areas,[35] traders were strategic actors who actively pursued their own agendas.

---

[34] Southall 1980, 41.
[35] Mamdani 1996.

1 The early years: from itinerant traders to monopoly stores

All over nineteenth century Africa, explorers, missionaries and traders have been witting or unwitting forerunners of colonial administrations and external agents of social change. Due to their rather small numbers and their weak integration with the political apparatus of domination, they were not able to exert domination and force important changes on societies; but their presence changed the conditions under which local people reproduced and reinvented their own lives, adding new possibilities and new constraints and linking local actions to the larger structures of European expansionism and its consequences.

This book is not concerned with missionaries or explorers (even if both appear from time to time), but with traders and trade. Its main focus is on shops founded and run by Africans between 1939 and 1990. In order to understand the history and significance of these shops, however, it is necessary to look at the earlier history of trade in northern Namibia. In the second half of the 19ᵗʰ century, trade expeditions by European traders provided local societies with horses and guns and thus created the preconditions for more efficient and more extractive centralized political domination. The resulting violent conflicts between different polities furthered migrant labor, Christian missions and finally colonial expansion, which in turn was the background for the establishment of white trading enterprises in the first half of the 20ᵗʰ century. These new shops acquainted people living in Northern Namibia with the concept of trading stores and provided the institutional model on which later shops were based.

The first trading store in Ovamboland only opened in 1925, ten years after the area was brought under South African control and five years after the mandate by the League of Nations ended military rule in South West Africa. European goods had been traded in the area for a considerable time, however – mainly by itinerant traders who visited the area sporadically to buy cattle, ivory or ostrich feathers, and by missionaries who imported goods to pay for services and for locally produced goods. In this chapter, I will give a short overview of early trade organization, relate aborted attempts to open stores prior to 1925 and analyze the background of the establishment of the first store in 1925.

The era of trade expeditions and mission trade (1850–1925)

European trade expeditions

Pre-colonial trade in Ovamboland – and in Africa in general – is most often analyzed as a precursor of colonialism, as the first major linkage between local societies and capitalist modernity.[1] In the long process of colonial expansion, traders and missionaries prepared the ground for soldiers and administrators. They opened up new areas to Europeans, and they encouraged consumption aims in the local population that became one of the foundations for new alliances between colonialists and local elites.

This perspective linking trade and colonialism is certainly valid, but it offers an analysis after the fact. In the second half of the nineteenth century, trade could not have been perceived by locals as the precursor of a new regime. If we want to understand why people accepted to be integrated into a system that slowly took away large parts of their ability to control their own lives, we have to try to put aside our knowledge about the consequences, and instead look at what made trade attractive. The presence of traders created new options for local societies and endowed local political leaders with new power resources. It helped to strengthen the very domination that, for a time, permitted local leaders to effectively domesticate and control trade.

When the first European traders arrived in Ovamboland from the Cape, their presence was integrated into a well-established pattern. Pre-colonial trade between the different Ovambo polities had been organized on the household level – individuals or small groups of people travelled to other polities to exchange surplus goods –, while trade between Oshiwambo-speaking groups and their Herero, San or Nama neighbors had relied on small caravans of twenty to thirty people.[2] Caravans often followed established routes and schedules, but they did not generate market places in the ordinary sense of a specialized site for regular and organized exchange of goods.[3]

Both regional and long-distance trades were controlled by the local kings or chiefs.[4] Trading parties had to seek permission to enter a kingdom, and bring gifts to the king;

---

[1]   For Ovamboland, see mainly the major studies by Clarence-Smith 1979 and Siiskonen 1990; for central Namibia, Dag Henrichsen's (1997) excellent study is the most important work on pre-colonial trade.

[2]   Siiskonen 1990, 70ff.

[3]   See Henrichsen 1997 for markets in central Namibia.

[4]   In scholarly literature and in contemporary usage, 'king' is used for the ruler of an entire polity (which in precolonial times were clearly identifiable as they were separated from each other by broad stretches of uncultivated land). 'Chiefs', 'senior headmen' or 'councilor headmen' only rule a smaller area within a polity. As not all polities were governed by kings in the late 19th and early 20th century – the last Ombalantu king had been killed somewhere in the first half of the 19th century, and the country was since ruled by several more or less independent chiefs; the last Oukwanyama king was killed by the British in 1917 and replaced by a council of seven headmen –, I will mostly use "kings and chiefs" to designate the most important rulers. – Coquery-Vidrovitch 1977, 87 stresses the importance of the control of long

when they came back from a trading trip, they had to pass a part of their proceeds on to the king as a present. Traders from the neighboring areas had to present their wares to the king before trading with commoners.

Trading trips of other groups to Ovamboland seem to have been rare, however; most long-distance trade expeditions were sent out from Ovamboland. In the South, they sold iron goods – tools, spearheads, knives or beads – to Herero groups in exchange for breeding cattle and egg shells used for bead-making, and traded different handicrafts for copper ore mined by San groups in the Otavi area. To the North, Ovambo groups traded salt, metal products and ivory for cattle, tobacco and glass beads.[5]

When European traders came to the area, they were at first simply regarded as a different source of trade goods. Kings treated them as they would have treated African traders who came with coveted goods, and they did their best to monopolize trade relations with them. This was an easier task in Ovamboland than in many African areas. From the south, only two trade routes (east and west of Etosha) provided enough watering holes to travel with ox wagons; from the north, Portuguese authorities tried to restrict trade to one route[6], which was all the more effective since wagons could only cross the Kunene at a few fords.[7] Water holes on the way were often also cattle outposts, and word could be sent ahead of the traders. Whenever Europeans entered the settlement areas from the wilderness between the polities, a local headman would welcome them and either send to the king or have the entire party accompanied to the king's court.

European traders constantly complained about the impossibility to escape the chiefly supervision, and were frequently nettled by a need to obtain the rulers' goodwill through presents. Even before European traders became a common sight, Charles Andersson and Francis Galton had to seek the Ondonga king's authorization before trading with commoners.[8] Botanist Hans Schinz, who spent more time at one place than most traders did, constantly mutters in his diary about the demands for goods made to him by Ondonga nobles.[9]

The control local rulers exercised over European trade was not only motivated by commercial interests and by the wish to restrict the access to status goods. Even more im-

---

distance trade for domination, a point which since has become a commonplace in African studies.

[5] Siiskonen 1990, 77–83.

[6] Pelissier 1977, 139–150, Clarence-Smith 1975, 59–61.

[7] For an account of the attempts by Hans Schinz's party to cross the Kunene, see the letter to his mother, dated 24 October 1884 (Zentralbibliothek Zürich, Ms. Z IX 319.1). I am very grateful to Dag Henrichsen who allowed me to use his transcription of Schinz's correspondence.

[8] Galton 1890 [1853], 130.

[9] See his unpublished diary in the Central Library in Zürich, e.g. the entry of 14 and 22 August 1885 (Zentralbibliothek Zürich, MS Z IX 656 Tagebuch Schinz, 1884–1886); now also Henrichsen 2012.

portantly, it was an attempt to centralize resources of domination: firearms and, slightly later, horses. Firearms seem to have been largely unknown in Ondonga (and probably most of Ovamboland) in 1851.[10] The first guns were traded in small quantities from Mossamedes in the late 1850s and early 1860s.[11] During this decade, trade both from the north and the south intensified. In the north, elephant herds had become scarce in the more easily reachable coastal areas after the Portuguese government had abolished the ivory monopoly in 1834. In the south, due to the restriction of cattle movement Jonker Afrikaner imposed in his territory after the outbreak of lung sickness, cattle was replaced as an export commodity to the Cape by ivory and ostrich feathers in the early 1860s. By 1870, elephants had become so scarce in Hereroland that commercial hunters had to extend their operation areas to the north, and firearms and ammunition became more important as an exchange commodity.

On the demand side, the threat posed by Afrikaner raids also increased the urge of Ovambo rulers to have access to firearms and ammunition. Other goods, from to-bacco to alcohol, were still the most important trade commodities, but around 1870, Ondonga King Shikongo already possessed at least 20 firearms, which were kept in his own storeroom.[12] More guns will probably have come into the other Ovambo polities from Portuguese trading expeditions.[13] Throughout the 1870s, the number of firearms increased greatly. This had important social and political consequences, to which I will come back later.

Trade between Ovamboland and Walvis Bay declined sharply in the early 1880s. Most elephants and ostriches in the area had been killed, leaving Ovamboland with only scarce resources to pay for imports, and the insecure situation in the central parts of what today is Namibia made trade caravans dangerous and more expensive.[14] In 1892, the German governor Leutwein prohibited arms trade throughout the colony, a regulation that was enforced through control of the harbours.[15] It affected the most coveted trade goods and

---

[10] Andersson 1856, 192; Galton 1890, 129f.; see also Siiskonen 1990, 99ff. McKittrick (2002, 53) puts the arrival of firearms in the 1840s or earlier, but does not substantiate this by any sources.

[11] See Siiskonen 1990, 100ff. for more details.

[12] Een 1872, 105.

[13] In the 1860s, muzzle-loading rifles imported from Mossamedes had the largest market share; their importance decreased with the arrival of more modern guns from Walvis Bay. Gun trade was hampered by the Cape Colony's embargo on arms trade through Walvis Bay after the outbreak of the Nama-Herero war in 1880 (Siiskonen 1990, 132). On the Angolan side, trade in guns and ammunition was proscribed in the 1880s, as well, but, according to the German missionary Wulfhorst, even Portuguese officers frequently traded in these goods in exchange for slaves and cattle (Wulfhorst, Kaukugua (Noah), RMG 2636, p. 16).

[14] Siiskonen 1990, 141ff.

[15] Deutsches Kolonialblatt 1892, 484f.

combined with depleted resources, new taxes and duties and a tighter administrative control to bring caravan trade from Walvis Bay to Ovamboland almost to a standstill in the 1890s.[16] It was partly replaced by a revival of trade between Mossamedes and Ovamboland by Portuguese traders; even Axel Eriksson, the most important trader in South West Africa, traded between Ovamboland and Mossamedes for some time.[17] From 1896, ox wagon trade between Ovamboland and the rest of South West Africa was effectively severed due to quarantine regulations connected to the rinderpest epidemic. These quarantine regulations marked the end of the epoch of caravan trade in Ovamboland.

In its half century of existence, caravan trade with European goods to Ovamboland changed substantially in extent and nature of traded goods, but its organizational patterns remained fairly stable. Walvis Bay traders usually travelled in an ox wagon caravan with one to five white traders and a substantially larger native retinue. Trade goods and the necessary provisions, tools, weapons and spare parts were stowed in the wagons, each of which was usually drawn by twenty oxen. The hardest part of the journey was the "thirst belt", a very arid stretch of land around the Etosha saltpan. During the dry season, water was only obtainable at few and far distant watering holes. Humans could usually reach the next resting place in time, but train animals frequently died of thirst, especially if a broken axle or other obstacles slowed the wagons down. Travelling between Walvis Bay and Ondonga could take anything between two weeks and three months; the average time seems to have been around six weeks. In spite of the difficult conditions, more than ten trade expeditions reached Uukuambi annually in the early 1870s.

The larger trade caravans established base camps in Ovamboland, usually near the respective king's palace. The king of Uukuambi had special huts built to house traders during their presence; in other kingdoms, traders lived in one of the king's guesthouses. The most important trade goods, ivory and ostrich feathers, were obtained both by hunting and by bartering. Those traders who also were hunters spent several weeks on hunting trips, coming to the depot in between trips to store their goods and re-provision. Some successful traders – Charles Andersson and Axel Eriksson among them – also permanently employed professional hunters who roamed the areas between settlements and regularly brought ivory and ostrich feathers to the trading posts.

The traders obtained all cattle and a part of the ivory and ostrich feathers through barter. When traders arrived at a chiefly court, they exchanged presents with the local ruler and started bartering for specific goods. When the rulers' demands had been met, his entourage and finally the common people were allowed to barter for the remaining goods.

---

[16] Siiskonen 146.
[17] Johansson 2007, 145f.

When all exchange goods had been spent, the caravan travelled back to Walvis Bay to sell their acquisitions. A trading expedition could take up to two years; in the 1880s, when the pattern was well established and trade routes were travelled by more frequently, an average trip seems to have taken around six months. Larger trips needed substantial investment in wagons, oxen and trade items; possible profits were good, but the risk was high, as well, and the initial outlay could only be recovered after the expedition's return.

Due to the trade's organization, kings were able to control both the profits made from trade and the distribution of European goods.[18] Trade thus directly brought new resources to the powerful and increased social stratification. It did so indirectly, as well: trade created a new possibility to accumulate wealth and to exchange in into means of domination. Prior to the arrival of European traders, cattle had been the most important means of accumulating and storing wealth. Large chiefly cattle herds were a sign of power. They could be used as a resource to gain followers through patronage, and they were a focal point for a division of labor according to political status. But prior to the arrival of European firearms, cattle herds could not be directly converted into means of coercion. What is more, available grazing, water and manpower put limits to the useful size of even a kingly herd. Under these conditions, there was not much scope for the accumulation of wealth and power by extraction.

Trade in firearms now made it possible to convert excess cattle into means of coercion. As kings and senior headmen could use their position to monopolize trade, this deeply affected the relations between rulers and subjects.[19] Domination became more effective and extraction more interesting. In the interior, it led to higher taxes; towards

---

[18] In the contemporary travel literature, there are many descriptions of the reception of traders. All of them show how trade caravans were monopolized by the chiefs and kings upon arrival, and the following two quotes stand for many. Missionary Hugo Hahn writes in 1857: "On exiting Otjikohondra, we met an Ovandonga (Ovambo) party going to Otjorukuko. They came towards us from their campsite. The leader, by name of Tjizumba, an especially handsome man, told us that he had come to meet our emissaries halfway, and that he himself would bring us to Ondonga. It was his office to accompany all travelers from the South. He spoke very good Otjiherero." (Hahn 1980, 29; my translation). Gerald McKiernan relates a typical welcome to a trade caravan in 1876: "That evening, we reached the first Ovampos and were halted at the habitation of Savora, a headman of the Ovaquamba (Okomba, Uukwambi) tribe. He enquired who we were, where we came from and where we were going, and immediately dispatched a runner to the chief with a request for permission to enter his territory, we to remain till the return of the messenger. [...] Early in the morning we were informed that the messenger had returned in the night, and that we were to proceed immediately; Savora himself volunteered to guide us. [...] Arrived at the chief's place, we were directed to stop under a tree set apart for whites, about a quarter of a mile from the residence. Not long after, Necumbo the chief paid us a visit, accompanied by a guard." (McKiernan 1954, 100ff.)

[19] In early 20th century, firearms were no longer a monopoly of chiefs. Old muzzle loaders were freely sold to commoners by Portuguese trades in Oukwanyama. Modern guns, however, were only sold secretly to senior headmen and kings. (Wulfhorst, Erastus Omulundu, RMG 2636, p. 235).

the exterior, raids became more frequent. While the respective political weight of senior headmen and king differed widely between polities and rulers, their behavior towards their subjects did not.

"When traders came into the land", a German missionary writes of Oukwanyama king Ueyulu ya Hedimbi (r. 1884–1904), with whom he was very well acquainted, "he sent his senior headmen to steal cattle wherever they found them. Nobody was sure that his cattle would not be robbed from the pasture. As king Uejulu was doing this, his senior headmen did not want to stand back. There were five senior headmen at the time, and all tried to pay their commercial debts with their subjects' cattle; so there was much grief and misery. […] As he got his cattle so easily, he liked often to use large amounts of them. There were traders who exported more than 500 heads of cattle at once to Angola. Once he paid 70 oxen for one – admittedly very beautiful – stallion. But the land became poor in this time."[20]

The greater power resources for the chiefs and kings also led to a stronger centralization of the society. More efficient central rule, all the more since it was not uncontested, needed a greater enforcement staff.[21] For young men, going to a king's court as a warrior or guard became an easy way to achieve status and wealth. (This established a pattern and was the precursor of a quite different practice: only a few years later, those young men who did not succeed to achieve a place at court, or had no interest in it, started to look for new resources by leaving as migrant workers.) Kings expressed their enhanced status in consumption, as well. In a country in which even 'salted' horses often died of sleeping sickness, they rode through their country on horseback, accompanied by their followers; they built bigger houses, sometimes close to European style; they wore European clothing, drank champagne,[22] adorned their wives with special glass beads and generally showed a weakness for various kinds of European luxury goods, from accordions to easy chairs.[23]

New trade routes, new trade goods and new ways of trading have always been catalysts of social change by providing new resources for societal creativity and for the articulation of power relations. In pre-colonial and early colonial Ovamboland, however, trade brought about a much more radical social change. Trade was the first modus of local society's integration into the system of colonial expansion; missionary endeavors followed slightly later, then war and finally administrative integration. Trade in European goods

---

[20] Wulfhorst, Kaukugua (Noah), RMG 2636, p. 18 (my translation).

[21] I use this term as the regular English translation of Max Weber's (1921) concept of Erzwingungsstab, but the German original, literally staff of coercion, is much closer to the realities of late 19th century Ovamboland than the more bureaucratic enforcement staff.

[22] As again Wulfhorst tells us of Oukwanyama king Nande (r. 1904–1911). Wulfhorst, Kaukugua (Noah), RMG 2636, p. 18v.

[23] For more details see McKittrick 2002, 59–65.

thus opened up an entire new field of resources and linked the local society to a new system of power relations which were more radical, more globalised and more totalizing than those in the neighboring societies linked with earlier trade routes had been. Due first to the remoteness of Ovamboland, later to the administrative seclusion of the area, trade continued to play this role of providing the most important connection to economic, social and cultural resources in the outside world well into the twentieth century.

Missionary trade

After the traders arrived the missionaries; and unlike the traders, they came to stay, with the explicit aim of changing local society. The first mission stations in Ovamboland were established in the 1870s. Over the next 50 years, 21 stations were founded by Protestant, Catholic and Anglican missionaries.[24] Missions not only provided access to new cultural patterns and new ideas about social organization; they also became important sources of European goods. This seems to be one of the main reasons why some chiefs and kings allowed, even encouraged missionaries to settle in their area.[25] They rarely showed much inclination to be converted. Many used the missionaries as a new (and at first easily controllable) source of firearms, ammunition, tobacco and other European goods, and some liked to spend idle time discussing theological questions or hearing tales about Europe.

From the beginning, missionaries were involved in trade. The scope and extent of missionary trade varied greatly both over time and between missionary societies and localities.[26] It never even remotely reached the dimensions of, for example, Basel Mission trade in West Africa, and always remained an accompanying activity necessary to reach the missions' more spiritual aims. But it did bring a lot of European goods into the local society, and it laid the material ground for many missionary activities.

---

[24] For the history of missions in Ovamboland, see, among others, Hayes 1992, McKittrick 2002, Miettinen 2005.

[25] The relation between chiefs and missionaries was by no means smooth; the reactions reached from enthusiastic welcome to the killing of two catholic missionaries in 1908, and they often changed with new rulers or new advisors. For more detail on this, see McKitrick 2002, Miettinen 2005.

[26] Siiskonen 1990, McKittrick 2002 and Miettinen 2005 mainly cover Finnish missionaries. For the Rhenish Mission Society, I use some of the material in the archives of the Vereinte Evangelische Mission in Wuppertal (cited as RMG) and in the ELCRN archives in Windhoek. Nancy Robson has succeeded in bringing together most of the material on the Anglican Mission in Odibo; the early material in the Odibo archive often consists of photocopies from various sources, which I can only quote without reference to the original archival shelf numbers. The material on Roman Catholic missionaries in Ovamboland has, as far as I know, not yet been systematically used; it is spread over the archives in Döbra and Windhoek and the Oblate (OMI) archives in Mainz (Germany) and Rome.

The early missionaries started to trade out of necessity. Their salaries were low and the costs of purchasing goods at the coast and bringing them to Ovamboland were very high. Their ability to bridge the distance between European markets and local consumption became an important asset for missionaries, and one that made missionary activities financially sustainable. In the 1870s, Finnish missionaries went onto trade expeditions in the more remote parts of Ovamboland; this was both a means to familiarize themselves with areas in which missionary presence was proscribed by the chiefs and a way to gain new resources.

At first, Finnish missionaries were very critical of the gun trade, which they saw as disruptive and dangerous. They soon started to trade guns and ammunition themselves, however. Their main partners in the arms trade were, of course, the chiefs. Providing guns to Chiefs not only helped mission finances, it also secured the missionaries' position in the country. They bartered arms for cattle, ivory or ostrich feathers. The cattle were partly slaughtered; ivory, feathers and the remaining cattle were sold on to traders.[27] In the 1870s and 1880s, German missionaries further south even imported guns directly from Germany to avoid the Cape Colony's customs duties.[28]

At first, so, the missionary's presence further increased the chiefs' control over the distribution of European goods. But with time, control over missionaries and the goods they brought slipped from the grasp of the chiefs. The missionaries' idea was not to serve their king, but to teach and convert the people. They slowly managed to expand their sphere of influence, often in conflict with the local rulers. Where chiefs often wanted schooling to be restricted to their own children, missionaries were trying to teach as many children as possible; where chiefs wanted to control access to European goods, missionaries strategically kept a few exclusive items as gifts or trade goods for the rulers and freely bartered things they saw as more common. Chiefs were able to largely retain control over firearms, ammunition and horses, but access to strategically less important European goods by and by eluded them. By the end of the 19th century, mission stations had probably become a more important source for European goods than trade caravans.

Missionaries' did not only engage in barter and trade for strategic and economic reasons. It was of course much cheaper to keep missions running by using European goods to barter for local items and paying native workers in kind. Cereals, eggs, meat and vegetables were bartered for small quantities of cloth or tobacco. Payment for casual work was also mostly given in kind – most important were building work, transport, herding

---

[27]   Siiskonen 1990, 128ff. According to Siiskonen, cattle were used for the missionaries' own consumption. From at least the turn of the century, however, Rhenish missionaries kept cattle herds for sale, as well.

[28]   Büttner 1884, 283.

or threshing and grinding the missionaries' corn. Only local aids permanently employed by the missions, teachers, catechists, nurses or servants, received a small salary in cash in the early 20ᵗʰ century. But while goods were used as a cheaper substitute for cash in these cases, missionaries also actively promoted the use of some European goods as outward signs of conversion and civilization. Especially clothing and religious books were, in the beginning, distributed among parishioners on credit or as payment for small services. Only when missions were more firmly established (and more expensive to run) did the missionaries begin to ask payments for clothing, hymn books or bibles from their converts. The German Rhenish missionaries were strongly encouraged to do so by the central mission authorities in Barmen, who feared the extra expense of providing a growing number of converts with clothes and books. The missionaries only agreed to sell books and clothing in 1911. They fixed cash prices, but expected that most of the people would pay for the goods by working for the missionaries. In that case, the price equivalent was doubled. The price in work for a woman's dress was fixed at 3 marks, for a girl's dress at 2 marks. Women's and girls' shirts were 1.50 marks. If people wanted to pay in kind, one large cup (*Becher*) of millet was evaluated at 0.15 mark.[29]

Migrant workers

In the last quarter of the nineteenth century, a new source of European goods became more and more important. Instead of waiting for traders or missionaries to bring goods into the country – goods they could not purchase anyway, for want of means or status –, young men started to look for work in central Namibia and South Africa. They spent six months or a year on contract work and used the money they had earned to bring back European goods from the shops in the South or to buy cattle and other goods in order to establish themselves in their home villages.

This is not the place to write a history of migrant labor and its consequences for northern Namibia.[30] But trade in Ovamboland, most of all the establishment of shops, is so closely linked to labor migration that it is necessary to describe some of its major trends.

---

[29] ELCRN, Konferenzbuch Ovamboland, 19 October 1911. For earlier discussions, see ELCRN, Letters from RMS W.-Barmen to the RM Ovambo Missionaries. – In 1903, Wulfhorst had written: "We give as many clothes as we have to our Christian women, so that they can come clothed at least to the service and to us. If they are without clothing while working in their homesteads, that does not hurt, especially since we never have sufficient clothes, and have to strongly recommend them to spare their clothing." RMG 2630, Referat Wulfhorst 1903: "Gibt es in unserer Ovambomission eine Frauenfrage?", p. 85v f.

[30] There is no comprehensive history of labor migration from Ovamboland. Important elements can be found in most of the literature covering the area, mainly in Cooper 2001, Gewald 2003, Gordon 1977, Hayes 1993, Kreike 2001, McKittrick 2002, Moorsom 1997.

We do not know the name of the first young man who decided to try his luck working for a white employer in the South. He probably had come into contact with employers more or less by chance. A number of young men, even prior to the emergence of a pattern of migrant labor, had regularly gone to the Herero areas as far as Okahandja and beyond – on trade expeditions, while hunting, as medical or ritual specialists or on cattle raids.[31] Some had also worked as herders for Herero cattle owners in the 1870s.[32] European trade caravans employed others as porters, herders or servants, and some were captured in Nama raids and brought south. Shikepo, an omulenga (senior headman) of Oukwany-ama King Uejulu, went to Hereroland with the trader Eriksson in the early 1890 to get to know these foreign parts.[33] In short, there were possibilities for individual young men to learn about new opportunities, and perhaps to test out temporary employment. Between 1890 and 1905, their example slowly grew into a cultural pattern, a more or less normal station in a man's life course.

Many scholars have overlooked this early migration. Even Jan-Bart Gewald, an excellent historian, writes that "prior to 1915, Ovambo speakers were virtually non-existent in central and southern Namibia. Ovambo migrants only started moving into these areas following the labour shortage engendered by the genocide perpetrated by the German military on the Nama and Herero populations of central and southern Namibia." The hardships which migrant workers were subjected to in Karibib during a particularly difficult period induce him to continue: "Even so, given the extreme nature of lengthy migrant labour – absences from home, brutal abuse and abominable living conditions – one wonders why people first started moving south in search of employment. Here, Richard Moorsom has detailed the role of Ovambo chiefs, intent on self-improvement through the remittances of migrants, as the push factor in driving migrants south. Yet, of greater importance was the collapse of sustainable living conditions in Ovamboland as a whole."[34] Jürgen Zimmerer writes in the same vein, situating the reasons for migration mostly in "traditional Ovamboland agriculture's enormous vulnerability to crises" and in the elite's attempts to get a share in the salaries.[35] Similar explanations are found in much of the 'struggle era' literature on migrant labour. It seems to be inconceivable for many scholars that people start to work on farms or mines out of their free will. If

---

[31]   RMG 2630, Referat Wulfhorst 1905: "Was können wir tun für die zum Hereroland ziehenden Ovam-bojünglinge u. Männer, insbesondere für unsere Gemeindeglieder?".
[32]   Henrichsen 1997, 211f.
[33]   RMG 2600, Rückblick auf 25 Jahre Ovambomission, p. 26f.
[34]   Gewald 2003, 211f. He cites Moorsom 1980.
[35]   Zimmerer 2001, 214f.

they leave their homes and look for work, they have to be driven by cruel necessity or by the effects of domination.

This fits into a common interpretation of migrant labor in Southern Africa. Due to its massive effects in later years, labor migration is often interpreted as socially and economically disruptive, and as part and parcel of a system of colonial exploitation that forced people to leave their homes.[36] In recent decades, however, some fundamental works have shown that labor migration almost always originated in the energy and initiative of the workers who were looking for ways to better their own situation.[37] In Ovamboland, labor migration predated the existence of any form of colonial administrative control, let alone taxation, by decades. The most important agents in the early history of labor migration were the migrants themselves. Far from being forced to leave against their will, they saw labor migration as an important element in the planning of their own life course, and they tolerated considerable risks and hardships to find work.

But labor migration can, of course, neither be seen as independent from the social and political changes linked to European traders and their goods nor from the cultural changes triggered by missionary activities. Internal and external raids left many people destitute. They redirected resources from household reproduction to the production and reproduction of political domination, and wealth could no longer reliably be transferred from generation to generation. Young people's ascent through the ranks of society thus became less predictable.

At the same time, raids brought considerable wealth to the raiders. The spoils were partly spent on conspicuous consumption by members of the chiefs' entourage. Social differentiation was increasingly expressed in consumption patterns. This was not a completely new phenomenon, of course. Even before the arrival of European traders, a large share of long distance trade in Ovamboland had been in luxury goods expressing wealth and status, and certain elements of dress or adornment had been efficient markers of social status or class. But the violent reshaping of social structures, which had become possible as soon as material wealth could be transformed into new means of coercion, also brought a new degree of social mobility. With many young people moving to the chiefly courts and surrounding the powerful, status differences became more fluid. They were as much defined by as expressed in consumption patterns. The political changes linked to the availability of guns thus made material wealth both more precarious and more desirable.

---

[36]   E.g. SWAPO 1981, Katjavivi 1988, Clarence-Smith/Moorsom 1995, Cooper 2001, Zimmerer 2001.
[37]   See, among others, Beinart 1982, Delius 1984, Manchuelle 1997; for Ovamboland, Kreike 2001, McKittrick 2002. For a similar perspective on the labor migration of European sailors, cf. Dobler 2002.

As long as raids and wars brought sufficient income for a warrior class that was able to absorb most young men, migrant work was not seen as an interesting alternative – even if poorer young people who either did not want or did not manage to 'go to court' felt increasingly marginalized. (Many of the early converts came from this group.) Towards the end of the 19th century, however, the unsustainability of a political system that used a large part of a country's resources to import weapons seems to have become strongly noticeable. Natural resources in ivory and ostrich feathers were largely depleted, and the remaining cattle herds were often brought out of the country by their owners.

Oukwanyama and Ondonga concluded a peace treaty in 1890;[38] other polities followed. It consequently became more difficult to gain access to wealth through raids, and the warrior lifestyle young men in the chiefs' entourage had acquired was threatened by a lack of resources. They had to find new resources to establish their own homestead, to found a family and to get access to social status in their own society. Some still found such resources at the chiefly courts, some on the mission stations – but most had to look elsewhere.

The general situation further declined when the rinderpest pandemic killed a large number of cattle in 1897 and the following years. Temporary employment in the South now became an interesting complement to local sources of income, and sometimes a vital economic alternative. Until well into the 20th century, however, it remained integrated into a mixture of economic activities in the household from which people could strategically choose, and whose aim was a combination of immediate consumption opportunities and long-term investment in agriculture.[39]

There were, of course, waves of labor migration linked to natural or social disasters, as the 1914 famine Gewald writes about. But such episodic migration occasioned by drought is structurally different from the normal pattern of labor migration we find in Ovamboland. In normal years, labor migration was not a sign of destitution, but of relatively good resource endowment combined with insufficient markets. Barren land in the northern floodplain needed high initial input of labor to become productive, but the amount of labor needed for everyday production on agricultural land was rather low. This made labor migration (and warriordom) possible. Agriculture was largely women's work.

---

[38] Wulfhorst, Kaukugua (Noah), RMG 2636, p. 16. For more details on the border demarcation that happened on this occasion, see Dobler 2008.

[39] The relative importance of these two aims varied, of course, but a large percentage of money seems to have been invested on long-term aims. There are many accounts of workers coming back with European goods, but many of them were expressly bought to barter for cattle. (See, for example, RMG 2630, Referat Wulfhorst 1905: "Was können wir tun für die zum Hereroland ziehenden Ovambojünglinge u. Männer, insbesondere für unsere Gemeindeglieder?", p. 259v.)

Young men sometimes helped planting or harvesting, tended cattle and kept up the water infrastructure, but their labor was usually not essential for local subsistence.

As there was no nameable market for agricultural products other than cattle, it did not make sense to expand the agricultural surface, even though both the labor and the land would have been available. Quite contrary to the conventional wisdom in African studies, labor was not the scarcest factor of production in Ovamboland. As a use for surplus labor, migrant work was thus economically much more interesting than warfare or 'loitering and lazing around', as missionary Wulfhorst described his view of young men's usual activity.[40]

Whatever the motivation for migrant work, it is only possible if it meets with demand for workers. Employment opportunities in late 19th and early 20th century's colonial economy in central Namibia increased even faster than the number of young men searching employment. The first migrants who started working in the South in the 1880s found work on farms or as servants, transport workers or store hands. After the area was declared a German protectorate in 1884, more German settlers started to arrive, and the demand for 'native' labor increased; but employment was still largely non-industrial, decentralized and often casual. The only notable exception seems to have been guano production on the Namibian coast, but the numbers of workers from Ovamboland employed there remain uncertain.[41] There might also have been some workers going to the Cape Colony or to the gold and diamond mines in Transvaal before 1900, but I have found no information on them.[42]

In 1892, explorations of the Tsumeb copper deposits started, and the first copper ore was brought to Swakopmund on ox wagons in 1900. In order to solve the transport problem, the private Otavi railway line was built between 1903 and 1906. Industrial exploitation of the mine started in 1906. While not many workers from Ovamboland will have been employed during the exploration phase, both the construction of the railway line and the copper mines needed a large number of workers. Finnish missionary

---

[40] For a more nuanced picture, see Dobler 2009. The discussion on factor relations in Africa has brilliantly been summarized by Gareth Austin (2008).

[41] Dove writes (1903, 179) that "Schwabe lauds them [Ovambo workers] for being much more industrious than other coloreds and states that, for example, almost exclusively they had done the work on the guano fields at Cape Cross."

[42] For the early history of South West Africans working in South Africa, see Henrichsen 2008. Axel Eriksson, in 1883/84, brought 2.500 head of cattle from Ovamboland to the Transvaal, accompanied by herders from Ovamboland. After the venture proved successful, he repeated the journey until 1894 (Siiskonen 1990, 159). It is quite possible that some of the herders from Ovamboland stayed on the Rand to work in the mines, and those who came back will certainly have spread the tale of the gold and diamond boom.

Rautanen speaks of 2.000 workers from Ovamboland working on the railway projects alone in 1905.[43]

This was just one of a number of important railway projects in the colony. From 1897 to 1902, the German government built the railway from Swakopmund to Windhoek, and between 1906 and 1914, further lines were constructed to Lüderitz, Keetmanshoop and Grootfontein. Between 1899 and 1902, a new harbor was built in Swakopmund. Government architect Laubschat, who travelled to Ovamboland in 1903, casually mentions in his account that he "was known to very many Ovambos from Swakopmund".[44] This clearly implies that Ovambo workers were routinely employed in government projects.

Labor demand sharply increased with the colonial war 1904–1907, in which a large percentage of workers from the central parts of Namibia were killed, interned or displaced, while many of the remaining workers turned away from employment by the oppressors and murderers of their relatives and friends.

In South Africa, as well, the Anglo-Boer war had brought a severe shortage of labor in the mines. In 1903, the German colonial government in South West Africa authorized the Witwatersrand Native Labour Association to recruit an unlimited number of workers in South West Africa. Under this authorization, which could be revoked at any time, WNLA had to pay the workers' passage back after the end of the contract and deposit 20 marks per worker with the German South West African government as a guarantee of their return.[45] This sum was deducted from the workers' salary and only paid out after their return. Around 900 workers went to Johannesburg on a two-year contract, among them around 300 from Ovamboland.[46]

In 1908, finally, diamonds were discovered in South West Africa, and very quickly, diamond mining developed into an important and labor-intensive industry that attracted many workers from northern Namibia.[47] After World War I, the labor demand of the

---

43 Eirola 1992, 214.

44 Laubschat 1903, 644.

45 Süd-Afrikanische Wochenschrift, 28 November 1902, p. 170. The article has "200 marks", which probably is a misprint; Gewald 1999, 25, who uses the government sources in the NAN (which do not mention Ovambo workers), has 20 marks. – In its number of 15 March 1903, p.133, the Deutsches Kolonialblatt incorrectly signals that Mr. Hewitt from WNLA had left Swakopmund without recruiting any workers.

46 The workers thought they had engaged themselves for 20 months, but they later realized that their contracts were for 20 periods of 30 working days, not including Sundays, so that the actual time was closer to two years. These and many other issues complementing and partly correcting Gewald's (1999) sources can be found in the correspondence of Ovamboland missionary Bernsmann, who stayed for six months with his children in Johannesburg in 1904/05 and frequently visited the South West African workers on the Rand. (Here: RMG 1613d, Briefe Ernst Bernsmann. Letter by the missionary Bernsmann to the mission principal, 27.4.1905)

47 On the role of migrant laborers from Ovamboland on the diamond fields, see also Strassegger 1988.

diamond mines became decisive for the establishment of the monopolist labor recruiting agencies, but prior to the war, labor recruitment was decentralized and relatively unregulated. Larger companies or government officials sent labor agents to Ovamboland. "Early this year [1905], the Outjo Bezirkschef wrote a letter to [Oukwanyama king] Nande asking for workers. At the same time, two gentlemen wanted to make a contract with Nande granting them the right to recruit workers in Oukwanyama. Now someone is here recruiting laborers for the Otavi railway. […] Natives, as well, are frequently sent from Hereroland to fetch new workers."[48]

The war radically increased the German presence in the country. The attempts to re-establish 'law and order', to increase the German hold over the territory and not least to regain some of the costs of the war led to increasing settlement of Germans in South West Africa and to the intensification of economic activities in general. It also brought more attention to Ovamboland, which until then had remained very much at the margins of colonial administration.[49] In January 1906, the "Verordnung betreffend den Verkehr in und nach dem Ambolande" ("Regulation concerning the traffic in and with the Amboland") was the first administrative act to treat Ovamboland as a separate entity and to regulate access to it. It laid the foundation for the policy of separation that should become one of the defining features of northern Namibian history throughout the 20th century. In a wholesale manner, it forbade access to Ovamboland by all but "members of the native tribes living in Ovamboland, members of the existing mission stations and such persons who for special reasons have been provided by the governor with a permit". Import of guns, ammunition, horses and spirits into the area was forbidden, trade by outsiders and labor recruitment were linked to a special permit, and recruited laborers had to pass through the police posts in Okaukuejo or Namutoni, to be registered and provided with a pass mark. This was the first attempt to regulate and control the movements of migrant laborers between Ovamboland and the South. Although it was not strictly enforced in the first years, the regulation established the pattern of organized migration that would more or less remain in place until Namibian independence in 1990.

---

[48] RMG 2630, Referat Wulfhorst 1905: "Was können wir tun für die zum Hereroland ziehenden Ovambojünglinge u. Männer, insbesondere für unsere Gemeindeglieder?", p. 257. The labor recruiter might have been one of the German traders Haag and Lenssen, who came to Ondonga in 1904/05 (see Eirola 1992, 214).

[49] The first direct intervention of colonial personnel in Ovamboland had been by Lt. Franke in 1899; since then, about one official delegation came to Ovamboland per year. For more detail, see Siiskonen 174ff. and Eirola 1992, 100ff.

One minor consequence of that new regulation is that we are better informed about the flows of migrant workers between Ovamboland and the rest of the colony. Although it is clear that many workers had left Ovamboland since 1895, figures for earlier times are hard to come by. Missionaries usually vaguely talk of "thousands of young men" leaving the country. The first concrete number is mentioned by Dernburg. According to him, 1700 people from Ovamboland were working in the farm zone in 1907.[50] This is already a very substantial number, more than one per cent of an Ovamboland population officially estimated at the time at roughly 150.000 people,[51] but the official numbers continue to grow. The police posts in Namutoni and Okaukuejo issued around 4.000 passes in 1908, 9.253 in 1910 and 8.094 in 1911.[52] In 1913, partly due to a drought, the number had risen to 12.025.[53] Most of these came from the eastern polities, and almost none from the western parts of Ovamboland. Even if we assume population figures of twice the official number, almost the totality of young men in some areas must have looked for work in the South at one time or the other – and this in a region with no administrative infrastructure, no taxes, no permanent labor recruitment office and an economy that was, in spite of the rinderpest shock, relatively healthy. These numbers can only be explained through the agency and initiative of the workers themselves and the advantages they sought to gain.[54]

For the colony's economy, workers from Ovamboland were irreplaceable even before World War I. A British consular report declares in 1912 that "practically all the Protectorate natives, other than Ovambos, are employed as domestic servants and farm labourers. Other industries, such as the copper mines at Tsumeb, the diamond mines at Luederitzbucht and works of all kinds, are dependent upon Ovambo labour. From 3.000 to 4.000 is the present complement of the diamond industry and from 1.000 to 1.500 of

---

[50] Dernburg 1909.
[51] Population figures for this time are, of course, far from reliable; judging on later official numbers, they might have been higher by 50 or 70 percent. I would however estimate that the numbers of migrant workers given are fairly low, as well.
[52] Nitsche 1912, 133. The figures are from July of the previous year to June of the year cited. A different source puts the number of workers recruited from Ovamboland at 9.295 for the calendar year 1911. 6.969 people returned home during the same year after having completed their contract. At the end of 1911, 5.728 workers from Ovamboland were still in contract. (Müller 1912, 8). – Registration was not very efficient, however. When Major Manning after 1915 tried to establish the inheritors of deceased labor migrants, he found that only one out of fifty laborers had given particulars that allowed finding his relatives. He was informed by King Martin that "this false information was given as a matter of course to avoid arrest for breach of contract." (NAN RCO 2/1916/I: Manning to Herbst, 24.9.1917.)
[53] Müller 1914, 7.
[54] In 1907, an extraordinary locust plague annihilated a good part of the harvest, but migration figures do not seem to be significantly affected. They are too unreliable, however, to base any further reaching theoretical interpretations on them.

the copper industry."[55] One year later, Consul Müller also provides a reason for the mining sector's dependence on labor from Ovamboland: "Under the old scheme of taxation, only the cheapest labour available could be employed with advantage". As labor supply rarely met the demand, the colonial government sought to secure the in-migration of new laborers by improving transport infrastructure, sinking wells along the migration routes, sending labor commissioners to Ovamboland to negotiate with the chiefs, and by employing a special commissioner (*Eingeborenenkommissar*) to survey labor condition and workers' treatment on the mines.[56]

Early attempts to open stores

Before World War I, colonial control of Ovamboland was precarious at best. The German colonial government constantly saw Ovamboland as a dangerous, untamed area which would be difficult to subject to colonial rule. The experiences of the war in central Namibia made the prospect of a colonial war with the well organized, well armed and populous Ovambo polities look even less attractive – especially since King Nehale's troops had managed to defeat the Germans at Namutoni in 1905. On the other hand, Ovamboland had become an important labor reserve, and both peace and some measure of control seemed necessary to keep up the labor influx.

The reserve regulation that was passed in early 1906 is the outcome of these conflicting sentiments. It was meant to contain the potential threat by controlling movements from and to Ovamboland, while at the same time refraining from potentially disruptive interference. The implementation rules by Governor von Lindequist make for almost comic reading in their scrupulous insistence on avoiding "any possible disturbance" in Ovamboland by police patrols, excessive controls or generally by any appearance of becoming a nuisance to prospective workers. He stresses that the regulation "is not aimed at curtailing the traffic with the Ovambo, but on the contrary, to increase it and to preserve it from dis-

---

[55] Müller 1912, 8.

[56] Müller 1912, 12. Even if the term literally means "Native Commissioner", the role of the Eingeborenenkommissare was very different from the Native Commissioners' under British colonial rule. They had more the character of Ombudsmen for native affairs, controlling the application of existing laws on the mines, whereas the later native commissioners were de-facto rulers of their territory. (See Zimmerer 2004, 120ff.) The role laborers from Ovamboland played for the mining industry can also be deduced from the choice of the first Eingeborenenkommissar, Hermann Tönjes, who had started his career as a long-time missionary in Oukwanyama. He had written an ethnography of the Ovakwanyama and had gone to Berlin to teach languages at the Seminar für Orientalische Sprachen, where he published an Oshikwanyama grammar and dictionary. From there, he went back to South West Africa in November 1911, in the employ of the colonial government. About the frictions between Tönjes and the mining companies over labor questions, see Zimmerer 2004, 222f.

turbances" and that the guiding principle for the authorities in the border districts had to be "to gain the trust of the Ovambo who pass their stations and to make them ever more useable for the service of whites, as well as to habituate them to the communication with whites." To further this aim, von Lindequist envisages the establishment of markets in Okaukwejo and Namutoni twice a year, in which the former Ovamboland traders could meet their customers from Ovamboland "without causing any disturbance".[57]

This is the first appearance of a pattern that was going to rule official trade policy in Ovamboland over the next thirty or forty years. Trade as such was seen as positive by the colonial governments. By showing possible migrant workers what they could buy with the money they earned, the presence of European goods in the reserve was thought to further labor migration. This reasoning looked sound enough; there were, after all, not many possibilities to spend money north of Tsumeb or Grootfontein. So why work for wages you could only spend in the south, bringing the goods back home after a perilous and burdensome voyage? The flaw in the argument was that precisely the scarcity of European goods in northern Namibia made it attractive to work for low wages. Even low wages provided access to goods that could, at home, be exchanged for an important amount of resources. So at this early time, the better availability of European goods might well have resulted in an increasing reluctance to leave. By the time trading stores were well enough established in Ovamboland to test the theory, the use of money had spread much more widely, and labor migration had become an established pattern.

The second important element behind colonial policy on trade in Ovamboland was the fear of 'disruptive influences'. Independent white traders were difficult to control. They brought arms, ammunition and alcohol to areas of potential unrest, and their good and steady relations to local rulers sometimes gave them the status of middlemen interpreting colonial policies to the kings, thereby gaining rather more power than the colonial government could wish for.

The administration liked trade, but it distrusted traders. This is one of the factors behind the Amboland-Verordnung in 1906, and it is the rationale for von Lindequist's idea of establishing regular markets in Okaukuejo and Namutoni – the two northernmost police posts of the German colonial government. As long as traders acted under surveillance, they were very welcome.

The colonial government soon had to realize that by barring access from the south, the regulation did not prevent the presence of European traders. It just opened the field for 'Portuguese' traders from Angola (most of them long-established settlers of mixed Angolan

---

[57] Ausführungsbestimmungen zur Verordnung betreffend den Verkehr in und nach dem Ambolande. 25.1.06. Deutsche Kolonialgesetzgebung 10 (1906), 27–30.

and Portuguese heritage) who were even less easy to control than traders from central Namibia. During the drought in 1908, for example, Angolan traders brought 6000 to 8000 head of cattle from German Ovamboland to Angola, which they had bartered for food.[58]

All German officials traveling in the area urged the Colonial Office to allow traders into the area to keep resources in the territory, but Windhoek and Berlin were very reluctant to act. In the eyes of most higher colonial officials, itinerant traders could not be allowed in the area without a permanent government presence. "I cannot utter a sufficiently serious warning against the authorization of traders in Ovamboland", Oskar Hintrager wrote to the Colonial Office in 1910. "He who allows itinerant trade to Ovamboland before a German administration is established in the area plants the first seed of warlike disturbances, just like it happened in Hereroland. […] Even through a careful selection of the most reliable traders, we will not be able to avoid the dishonesties, deceits and violations which experience shows will always be present in itinerant trade, as the people who lease themselves to this office in the service of the large companies are, without any exception, no angels. As experience has shown in Hereroland, all of them have to suffer it for business' sake that natives lay them over the wagon pole and thoroughly beat them up, which again undermines the white man's reputation."[59]

For their double aim to further trade without losing their semblance of control, colonial authorities instead turned towards the only Europeans whose continued presence was allowed by the new regulation, and who were conceived of as being less likely to cause disturbances and strife: the missionaries. In 1909, Governor von Schuckmann wrote to the Finnish missionary Rautanen asking his opinion about allowing reliable persons into Ovamboland to establish trading stores. Rautanen replied positively, hoping that the presence of German traders would stop the Portuguese liquor trade, create further mediators between the colonial government and the local rulers and strengthen local markets. He even reported that he had secured the support of the four relevant local leaders for the idea.[60] When the German representative Görgens came to Ondonga in September

---

[58] BA R1001 2161, Aufzeichnung zur Ovambofrage [Memorandum on the Ovambo question], unsigned, undated (early 1910). The memorandum, which was based on H. Görgens' travel report, called on the Colonial Office to allow German traders into Ovamboland, argueing that "if at that time German traders had been active in Ovamboland, this great mass of cattle would still stand on German soil or would at least have been processed for German entrepreneurs." The same Görgens, however, downplayed trade to Angola in slightly later memorandum (BA R1001 2162, Görgens, Report 27 January 1910).

[59] BA R1001 2161, Letter Hintrager (for the Governor) to Colonial Office, 22 March 1910. The deciding administrator commented on the differences between Governor Schuckmann's and Hintrager's opinions on trade ("Rin in die Kartoffeln – raus aus den Kartoffeln", a slightly surprising official marginal note) and decided that things should be left as they are until further notice. This was officially sanctioned by Permanent Secretary Lindequist in summer 1909 (BA R1001 2162, Notice 3598, 13 September 1910).

[60] Eirola 1992, 253; see also BA R1001 2160, Vorbericht über Mission Frankes im Ovamboland [Pre-

1909 and suggested to establish a military post, a permanent store and a labor recruiter in Ondonga, however, King Kambonde kaMpingana rejected all permanent German posts in his area. Four weeks later, Kambonde died, and his successor Kambonde kaNgula accepted a German police post in his country, probably to secure his own throne against rivaling relatives. The Colonial Office, however, hesitated to establish such a station – until the succession troubles were over and Kambonde changed his attitude in early 1910.[61] While the plans to establish a permanent police post and a Resident Commissioner in Ovamboland were abolished, the idea to establish a shop was not. In 1911, the colonial government asked the German missionaries from Barmen who were established in Oukwanyama if they could imagine opening a trading store there. The administration saw this as a relatively safe and promising way of inducing men to look for work. Missionaries were present anyway, and they would not risk compromising their position by illegally selling weapons, ammunition or liquor.[62]

The concerned missionaries were surprisingly open to the plan. The earlier reluctance to compromise missionary work by worldly endeavors is no longer echoed in the conference minutes. But they opposed the government's plans in two important points of commercial relevance. First, in order to induce men to look for work, Streitwolf had insisted that goods in the new shop should only be sold for cash. This, the missionaries argued, was impossible, as cash was still far too scarce in the land. Secondly, they would only agree to open a shop if the ban on cattle movement between Ovamboland and the rest of the colony was lifted. Only then, they argued, would a store have a reasonable chance of success, as cattle was the only local product suitable for barter that was likely to find good enough a market in the colony to pay for trade goods.

This ban on cattle movement had first been introduced in 1906 to protect the settler economy by preventing the spread of lung sickness.[63] It was the beginning of the partition of South West Africa into a 'Police Zone' and the native reserves.[64] The missionaries saw the ban as a temporary measure and very much hoped it would soon be lifted. The German government, however, did not like to risk the backbone of the settler economy after

---

report on Franke's Mission to Ovamboland], 6 July 1908, where Franke already mentions that the five independent headmen in Ovamboland "directly and urgently asked for German traders".

[61] Eirola 1992, 257–275.

[62] The demand seems to have come from two directions: at home, the Colonial Office approached Dr. Spiecker, the head of the Rheinische Missionsgesellschaft, who in turn asked the missionaries. They had already been informed about the plan by Ltn. Streitwolf who had visited Ovamboland in 1911. (ELCRN, Konferenzbuch Ovamboland).

[63] Eirola 1992, 191f.

[64] On the history of this partition and the 'red line' separating Ovamboland from the rest of the country, see Miescher 2011.

the traumatic experiences with the rinderpest epidemic in 1897: the ban remained in place throughout the entire colonial period and is still kept up in independent Namibia today.

So the missionaries were reluctant to comply. Contrary to Streifwolf's assurance that only missionaries would be allowed to open a store, the German administration asked the trading firm Hälbich in Karibib to open a store at a Finnish mission station in Ondonga, whose ruler was friendlier towards Germany than Oukwanyama's rather self-assured King Mandume ya Ndemufayo. The Hälbichs were one of the oldest German colonial families in South West Africa; Johann Carl Eduard Hälbich had come to the mission station Otjimbingwe in 1864. The family had bought Karibib from Chief Zeraua and established important shops in central Namibia. Eduard Hälbich travelled to Ondonga to establish a store in December 1911, but to the administration's consternation, Chief Kambonde did not authorize the business, and Hälbich had to leave without success.[65] Some further discussions between the administration and the German missionaries followed, but no shop was established in Ovamboland before the British/ South African victory in 1915 and the Versailles Treaty in 1920 ended German colonial rule in South West Africa.

The establishment of the first stores

When the Austrian crown prince was shot in Sarajevo in June 1914 and Austria decided to take this as the reason for a war, the consequences were felt all over the world. War between the European powers brought war to their colonies, as well, and the German protectorates in Africa were drawn into the fighting. In South West Africa, troops from the British dominion South Africa soon gained the upper hand.

After the German capitulation in August 1915, the new military government sent a delegation under Major Pritchard to Ovamboland with the aim to establish relations with the local chiefs and to further migrant labor. Pritchard decided that the moment was favorable for the establishment of a permanent colonial presence, and Major Charles Manning was made Resident Commissioner for Ovamboland in November 1915. A representative in Namakunde and two officers, Captain Bowker and Lieutenant Hahn, completed the new Administration.[66] The latter, Carl Hugo Linsingen Hahn,[67] called 'Cocky' by his friends and colleagues and 'shangolo' ('whip') by his subjects, a grandson

---

[65]   BA R1001 2162, Letter Hintrager (for GSWA Governor) to Colonial Office, 2 January 1912.

[66]   For a detailed account of colonial officers in Ovamboland from 1915 to 1935, see Kotze 1984.

[67]   7 January 1886 to 27 September 1948. His third given name is in fact the reminder of another powerful colonial presence in his upbringing: it's the maiden name of his mother Anna von Linsingen (1861–1938), whose father had been Baron Major Wilhelm Carl Ferdinand von Linsingen, C.M.G. (1831–1880), a German immigrant from Northeim who fought and died in the South African frontier wars. For biographical details on the latter, see Hummel 1989, 20.

of the very German missionary Carl Hugo Hahn who had been one of the first Europeans in Ovamboland, came to dominate the Ovamboland administration and ruled as a bureaucratic autocrat for the next decades. He became Representative in Namakunde in 1919, and when Manning left the area in 1921,[68] he was made Native Commissioner.[69] He had played rugby for the Springboks,[70] was an excellent sportsman, an amateur ethnographer and photographer, and a full time administrator. When he came to Ovamboland, he was twenty-nine; by the time he retired from his post as native commissioner in 1946, he was sixty and had passed most of his life in Ovamboland. He married Alyce, one of the daughters of Nelson Fogarty,[71] the first Anglican Bishop in South West Africa, in 1926; another daughter of Fogarty, Lorna Mary, had married Rupert Stephen Cope, who then was Officer in Charge Native Affairs in Windhoek and later worked for a long time as the first labor recruiting agent in Ovamboland. In the old system of personalized indirect rule, Hahn was actually a very successful administrator and came to be widely known. His obituary in African Affairs was written by Lord Hailey, whose praise of Hahn is symptomatic for both men: "He was an ideal Native Commissioner, for he conducted the administration mainly by means of his personal influence, with practically no staff and no police."[72]

He managed to please his chiefs in Windhoek by successfully maintaining the colonial order and the steady flux of migrant workers. His reports were exemplary and combined

---

[68] Major (later Colonel) Stanley Archibald Markham Pritchard (born 1874 in Madras) was the first Officer in Charge Native Affairs in South West Africa and commanded the conquering force against King Mandume until December 1915. He had started his career at the Cape Mounted Rifles and moved on to the Native Affairs Department. In 1914, when being called to South West Africa, he was Director of the South African Native Labour Bureau (Koetze 1984, 19); later in World War I, he was appointed Deputy Controller of Labour in France and awarded the C.M.G. – Charles Nicholas Manning (1877–1944) had started his career as police commander in Pretoria location; from 1904 to 1914, he was Sub-Native Commissioner in Tshanowa. He became Resident Commissioner in Ovamboland from 1915 to 1920, when he was promoted to Chief Native Commissioner in Windhoek. In 1926, he was transferred to Benoni as Native Commissioner (Leverton 1987, 488).

[69] To avoid confusion, I am using the title of 'Native Commissioner' throughout, except when directly citing from the sources. The office was called "Officer in Charge Native Affairs" prior to the Native Administration Proclamation (15 of 1928), in force from 1.1.1930.

[70] His rugby career, which fits very well with his reputation of being a man's man, is mentioned in most biographical notices on him. While he had indeed played very well for a colonial officer, he only made it into three official Tests, all against Britain, in August and September 1910, and scored one try. (This rather ephemeral information is found on the South African rugby site www.scrum.com, accessed in August 2009.)

[71] Nelson Fogarty was born in 1871 in Canterbury, England. He served as army chaplain during the South West African campaign and was appointed Archdeacon of Damaraland in 1916. When the missionary diocese of Damaraland was formed in 1924, he became its first bishop (Boucher 1981, 159). After his death in 1933, George Tobias, who had founded Odibo Mission in Ovamboland in 1924, succeeded him.

[72] Hailey 1949, 74.

the intelligence officer's eye for political details with the administrator's ordered mind. He had the reputation of – and was indeed – a good anthropologist, whose familiarity with local factions and 'customs' was only matched by the longer-serving missionaries. All this kept Windhoek and Pretoria off his back and enabled him to rule the area according to his own lights. His style of ruling was, on the other hand, very compatible with the auto-cratic government of local chiefs. They understood each other's power games and shared an interest in maintaining an order that secured their domination.

Hahn became Native Commissioner one year after military rule in South West Africa was replaced by the League of Nations mandate in 1920. Like his two successors before 1955, when Native Administration was reformed and put under direct responsibility of Pretoria,[73] he governed Ovamboland with the help of one Assistant Native Commissioner in Namakunde (from 1927 in Oshikango) and a very limited number of staff. In his system of indirect rule, most decisions in local matters were left to the chiefs, who were controlled by Hahn. The administration imposed itself as representation of the "supreme chief" in Windhoek or Pretoria. Just like the king let his senior headmen act according to their wishes as long as his own interests were not threatened by it, Hahn did not in-terfere in everyday tribal affairs. He made it very clear, however, that he could choose to intervene at any moment, and that he expected to be obeyed if he did. The potential use of a military power which had been very visible in the campaign against Mandume in 1917 always remained in the background, and it was indeed realized in 1931, when Chief Iipumbu of Uukwambi was deposed and his homestead destroyed by air bombs.

Hahn also saw eye to eye with the chiefs in his aversion to social change. He preferred his own version of traditional society to the modern changes it was subject to, at least for 'the Natives', and he sometimes spoke strongly against missionary influence. Much of his energy was devoted to keeping Ovamboland 'intact' and safe from outside influences. As Agnes Winifred Hoernlé – who had been a co-founder of the liberal Institute of Race Relations and at that very time taught anthropology to Max Gluckman, Hilda Kuper and Eileen Krige at the University of the Witwatersrand – wrote to him in 1935 after a meeting in Windhoek, "it was splendid to hear you say that you would refuse to see any changes introduced into the social structure of the Ovambo, which had not been carefully

---

[73] Harold Lionel Pritchard Eedes (1899–1975) became his successor in 1947. He had started his career as Resident Commissioner for Oukwanyama in 1918/1919 and as Assistant Native Commissioner from 1923 to 1930. In 1932, he was promoted to the post of Native Commissioner in Kavango (Nkurunkuru 1932–1936, Rundu 1936–1946), before returning to Ovamboland from 1947 to 1954. After a short vacancy during which Assistant Native Commissioner A. Bourquin filled the job, Bruwer Blignaut be-came his successor. In his retirement, Eedes lived in Grootfontein as farmer and acted as consultant for the copper mining company Tsumeb Corporation (NAN NAO 51 3/2, Address NC Eedes to Chief Kambonde 24 June 1954).

considered by the organized administrative units of the people themselves. […] I feel that you are the anthropologist's ideal administrator."[74]

But Hahn was not in danger of going native; he was also convinced that certain changes were necessary and beneficial to the local societies. Tribal administration had to be rationalized and conducted among legal principles, social unrest had to be quelled, and a certain amount of economic modernization was necessary. While traditional matters were left to the chiefs, all things 'modern' had to be under the control and authority of the administration. We will later see that the line became blurred very soon, and that Hahn's vision of a good life in a traditional patriarchic society clashed with the administration's aim of economic development. But this conflict, which often is visible in a paradoxical attitude of the colonial government towards local traders, only really broke out after World War II.

The establishment of an administration in Ovamboland after 1915 has to be seen in the context of the labor shortage the new South West African government had inherited from the Germans. Major Pritchard's mission to Ovamboland had had as its main aim to renew labor agreements with the Chiefs, and only his analysis of the situation led to the establishment of a permanent post there. Far from trying to establish an all-encompassing administration, Manning and Hahn first concentrated on eliminating possible sources of 'disruption'. This, however, included the military subjugation of local rulers who would not ally. Most importantly, Oukwanyama King Mandume ya Ndemufayo was killed in a military expedition in 1917. As the administration feared a united revolt in Oukwanyama, no new king was allowed to be chosen. Instead, Oukwanyama was governed by a number of senior headmen who, from 1930, regularly met in a Council of Headmen 'counseled' by the Assistant Native Commissioner.

The campaign against Mandume successfully established colonial military domination. Quelling smaller sources of disruption by seizing firearms and preventing the sale of alcohol proved much more demanding and took several decades. By the early 1920s, however, a very indirect form of colonial rule had become the normal situation in Ovamboland and no further rebellion was to be feared. This left more room for the organization of the interest for which pacification had only been a necessary precondition: labor migration.

After much experimentation with different forms of administration, from early 1918 on all workers wishing to be employed in the South had to pass through Ondangwa, where they were issued individual numbers and group passes to Tsumeb, where the railway line started. This turned Ondangwa into the main thoroughfare, even for workers

---

[74] NAN A.450 4-1/30, Letter Hoernlé to Hahn, 9.6.1935. On Hoernlé see Carstens 1987 and Gillespie 2011.

from Oukwanyama or from the Portuguese areas. The government office in Ondangwa was responsible for issuing the passes and supervising the movement of migrant laborers.

In spite of these efforts to smoothen and organize migrant labor, the number of workers from Ovamboland dropped from a high point of 7000 in 1920 to 3000 in 1922.[75] The Administrator discussed the establishment of a regular motor transport from Ovamboland to Outjo, but the mining companies did not want to invest the necessary funds. They agreed, however, to reorganize the recruiting system, which had so far entirely relied on government officials. In 1924, the Native Affairs office which organized the distribution of labor was moved from Tsumeb to Ondangwa and put under Hahn's authority, and the Chamber of Mines in Lüderitz[76] stationed a privately paid medical officer at Ondangwa to examine prospective workers.[77] In 1926, the system was re-organized and two private bodies, the Northern Labour Organisation (NLO) and the Southern Labour Organisation (SLO) were formed. Their task was the recruitment of labor for the diamond mines (SLO) and for the northern mines and the farms (NLO). Ovamboland and Southern Angola were given over to SLO as their recruiting area. Government affairs and labor recruiting in Ovamboland were separated organizationally. As a consequence, a new private labor recruiting office was opened in Ondangwa. The administration seconded Rupert S. Cope, Hahn's brother-in-law, who had worked as Officer in Charge at the Windhoek headquarters of Native Affairs, to the SLO as new recruiting officer.[78]

Parallel to the move from Tsumeb to Ondangwa, government and the Chamber of Mines in Lüderitz fell back on an old plan to increase the number of workers. The mining companies felt that without any possibility to spend earnings at home, the incentive

---

75 Kotzé 1984, 97–104 with a further discussion of possible reasons. Between 1917 and 1925, the number of registred workers from Ovamboland usually was between 3000 and 4000; 1920 had been an exceptional year.

76 The Chamber of Mines was the organisation of the South West African diamond mines. When South Africa took over the administration of South West Africa, eight mining companies had mining quota in the area. The five largest were acquired by Ernest Oppenheimer's new enterprise Consolidated Diamond Mining South West Africa (CDM) as of 1 January 1920. The remaining companies vanished from the market until the 1930s, but the Chamber of Mines remained in existence.

77 NAN SWAA 1057-135/22 Letter Drew, Native Affairs Windhoek, to Hahn, 6 September 1924.

78 NAN SWAA 1057 135/22, Letter OiC Hahn to Secretary, 16 January 1927. Cope was some years Hahn's senior, being born in 1875 in Bredasdorp, South Africa. Even though they had been brothers-in-arms during the South West African campaign and became brothers-in-law later, he was in frequent conflict with Hahn, who repeatedly reported about his lack of loyalty during Cope's time as a labor recruiter. Just like Hahn, Cope lived in Grootfontein after he retired in August 1948, aged 73 (NAN NAO 51 3/2 Letter Vlok, SWANLA Secretary, to CNC Windhoek, 10 August 1948). It seems that his retirement was provoked by a conflict with Hahn's successor Eedes over Angolan migrants settled by Cope in Ondonga. Eedes reported to his superiors that "Mr. Cope has at last definitely retired" (NAN SWAA 1057 135/22, Extract of monthly report September 1948).

for men to look for wage labor was too weak, and applied for a licence to open a trading store in Ondangwa.

Until 1924, government had always regarded private trade to Ovamboland as possibly disruptive, and had turned down all applications for trading licences. Both Manning and the Secretary for South West Africa argued that colonial rule was still too weak in Ovamboland to tolerate the presence of traders likely to illegally sell alcohol and firearms. Furthermore, trading could generate disputes between Black and White which could bring the administration in the difficult obligation to take sides.[79]

In September 1924, however, it was decided to grant a trading licence to the Chamber of Mines.[80] This decision, which was hotly contested by several government agencies, shows once more to what degree colonial policy of the time was concentrated on migrant labor. Where possible economic advantages of trade were no reason to accept the risks of disturbances, the promise of increasing numbers of migrant workers was a different matter. The Secretary for South West Africa wrote to Hahn in 1924: "If a serious shortage of labour occurs on the diamond fields at the present juncture, it may have serious consequences on the Revenue of the Administration, and the whole Territory will in consequence suffer."[81] Hahn reacted to this in his annual report for 1924, expressing the hope that "a properly controlled store should indubitably have a good effect on prospective recruits or natives who have never been away from their homes to earn wages. It would raise the value of money and increase the wants of chiefs and headmen who would interest themselves more and more in the labour requirements of the country and send their boys to work, it would also keep trade and large sums of money in our country which at present goes to unscrupulous Portuguese traders across the border. Returning Ovambos also would specially benefit by it since they would be able to buy their requirements nearer their homes instead of having to do so in the South and then carry their purchases up to 20 and more miles through difficult country ere they reach their kraals."[82]

This aptly sums up the hopes the Administration set into the first store in Ovamboland. And indeed: the stores brought all the changes Hahn hoped for. But their effects would not remain contained to migrant labor; by and by, trade changed the economic, social and political landscape in Ovamboland.

---

[79] NAN ADM 2425-2; RCO 2/1916/1. Instead, Manning suggested in 1916, and again in 1918, that the administration should establish a trade depot in Okaukuejo, where returning workers would be able to buy supplies under government control, but this suggestion was not taken up by his superiors – see Kotzé 1984, 144f.

[80] NAN SWAA 1057-135/22 Letter Drew, Native Affairs Windhoek, to Hahn, 6.9.1924

[81] NAN NAO 3, 2/1: Letter Secretary to Officer in Charge, Native Affairs, Ovamboland, 14.1.1924.

[82] NAN A450 7 2/18, Annual Report 1924.

2   The monopoly stores, 1925–1952

In January 1925, the first trading store in Ovamboland opened at Ondjodjo, close to the Native Affairs office in Ondangwa. It was operated as a Limited Company, the Ondonga Trading Company, wholly owned by the Chamber of Mines in Lüderitz.[1] Half a year later, the same company opened a second store in Omafo, in Oukwanyama near the border-to-be to Angola. Both stores were named after their venues, 'Ondjodjo' and 'Omafo Store'. They, and two other white-owned stores which followed later, not only established a new trading pattern in Ovamboland. They crucially influenced the social, political and physical landscape of twentieth century Ovamboland. They became important elements in local social life, models for a new elite economic activity and nodes of urbanization. In the closed reserve economy, they were the first points of contact to a modernizing colonial society, and images of modern consumption were first developed in relation to them. This chapter will look at their history during the time of their trading monopoly; my focus will be on the economic, social and political role of the shops and on their relation to the administration.

The concept of trading stores was not completely new to the area. The old caravan trade almost ceased after Ovamboland was declared a Native reserve in 1906, and stationary trading posts took over the distribution of long-distance trade goods. Mission stations were crucial for the commerce in clothing and tobacco, sometimes also in furniture or household goods. Returning migrant laborers spent their wages on goods in the southern towns or in Okaukwejo, often with the aim of selling them at a profit in their home villages. Finally, Portuguese traders from Angola illegally came to Ovamboland to buy and sell goods, and people went to their stores north of the border.

Before the border was demarcated in 1927, and for some time after the demarcation, this was a very common practice. When two Portuguese traders came to South West African Ovamboland in 1924, the resulting enquiry made it clear that they were well known to the local headmen. Headman Andreas of Omafo, for example, made the following statement (in Eedes' English version): "I know these men. They are Portuguese traders and live at a place called Omatemba in Angola, near Namakunde. I once visited

---

[1] OTC was registered in 1925, with the statuary meeting on 10 February. The share capital was £ 1000 in 1000 shares, of which Hans Härlin, the General Manager of CDM, held 998, two other CDM directors one each "in a representative capacity on behalf of the Lüderitz Chamber of Mines", as a letter from OTC explained to the Registrar in 1943. OTC was constituted as a Private Limited Company, so that no balance sheet had to be submitted (NAN COM 40). The Ondjodjo store opened on 8 January 1925. (NAN NAO SWAA 1056 135/22, Letter NC Hahn to Secretary, 10 May 1938).

their stores there and found that these men lived with native women. […] If I send a native from Omafo to Omatemba he can purchase any amount of wine from these traders at 10/- per bottle, and bring it to Ovamboland."[2] Eedes commented on this: "During my last tour of the Ovakwanyama area I was frequently offered Portuguese wine by the headmen. I enquired from them as to where they obtained it and they informed me that any native could go across the line and purchase it at the stores of the Portuguese traders."[3]

This trade continued well into the 1930s.[4] The Angolan traders risked detention as illegal foreigners, seizure of their goods and expulsion if they came to South West Africa without authorization – but the risk seems to have been small enough to take it, as several such cases are reported over the years.[5] The traders were detested by the Native Commissioner (he saw them as "an irresponsible and slovenly class of wine and liquor sellers and absolutely unscrupulous in their business methods"[6]), but neither the local population nor later the storekeepers at Omafo and Ondjodjo had any reservations about doing business with them.

So when the stores in Ondjodjo and Omafo opened, they did not bring an entirely new concept of trade to Ovamboland. But for the first time, they made modern goods locally available on a continuous basis, at a fixed place and at transparent cash prices. And, more importantly, the new shops were no longer located in the outside world, but in the hearts of Ondonga and Oukwanyama. They started to become part of the local society, not an external influence. The most important consequences of the appropriation of shops by the local society only became visible after 1950 and will be the topic of Chapters 4 to 7: opening a shop became a business model for an emerging new elite, and small stores spread over the countryside. They brought modern goods into everyday life, and they formed both the spatial cores of new settlements and the ideological cores of new individual and collective aspirations. Their success would not have been possible without the model of the early monopoly stores.

Institutional history of the monopoly stores

Official discussions about the establishment of a trading store started in 1924 in connection with the reorganization of labor recruiting (see Chapter 1). At this time, the administration was very suspicious of European trading in Ovamboland, and certainly

---

[2]   NAN NAO 16 10/2, May 1924.
[3]   NAN NAO 16 10/2, Letter ANC Eedes to NC Hahn, May 1924.
[4]   See NAN NAO 26 20/2 for further references.
[5]   See e.g. NAN SWAA 1057 135-22/2.
[6]   NAN SWAA 1057 135-22/2, Letter OiC Hahn to Secretary, 7 October 1929.

no ordinary profit-seeking trader would have been allowed to establish a store in the area. When trading was re-interpreted as a policy measure and the establishment of a store linked to labor recruiting, however, government was suddenly keen on having the store. From the start, the shop was thus a hybrid venture: privately owned but close to the government, run on business lines but justified by its political and social role. It was more tightly controlled than normal trade firms, but it also had a much wider leeway towards its shareholders and towards the administration. For its customers, the shop took the same double character. On the one hand, it was just a store, the only place to buy things you needed if you had the necessary money. But it was a store located near the Native Commissioner's and the recruiting agent's offices, was owned and partially run by white people, and was generally regarded as being close to the government.

The site of the new shop was strategically chosen to be relatively easy to reach and close to the administration which, in 1925, was still responsible for sending migrant laborers south and for paying out the guarantee sum on their return. The location was a dry, sandy spot North of the road from Namutoni to Ondangwa, about a kilometer from the Native Commissioner's office. A plot of 300 by 200 yards (ca. 182 by 275 meters) was fenced in with the consent of Ondonga King Martin, who received £50 as the "customary payment for the allotment of a piece of land".[7]

This plot came to be the economic centre of Ondangwa for the next fifty years. The organizational structure under which the shop was run changed several times, but the shop continued to play an important role in the local economy. It was taken over by the newly founded South West African Native Labour Association (SWANLA) in 1943 and by the Bantu Beleggings Korporasie (Bantu Investment Corporation, BBK or BIC) in 1969. The BIC closed down the retail store from 1 June 1971[8], and only continued to operate Ondjodjo Wholesale. Its buildings are still standing today, partly occupied by a foam rubber factory, but the actual shop was taken over by a local trader after independence in 1990 and closed down in the late 1990s. For most inhabitants of Ovamboland who grew up between the 1920s and the 1960s, Ondjodjo came to be the ideal type of a trading store. Well into the 1960s, it had the widest selection of goods available anywhere between Grootfontein or Tsumeb and the Angolan inland towns, and the largest turnover of any store in the area.

---

[7]   NAN SWAA 1057 135-22/1, Letter NC Hahn to CNC F.P. Courtney-Clarke, 23 December 1938.
[8]   NAN OVE 44 9/4/4, Letter BBK to Hoofdirecteur Ondangwa, May 1971.

Imgage 3: Omafo Store, ca. 1929.

Imgage 4: Colonial high tea on the Omafo store's terrace, 1930s. Store manager Arends seated in the middle, together with mission personnel from Odibo.

In the 1920s, Ondonga (the polity in which Onjdodjo is situated) was still separated from the other Ovambo polities by a stretch of wilderness, and people rarely travelled from one polity to the other. The main labor reservoir, however, lay in Oukwanyama, the largest Ovambo polity, that stretched both north and south of the border to Angola. In order to reach possible ovaKwanyama workers, the Ondonga Trading Company opened its second store in Omafo in late 1925. For the Native Commissioner, this was also a possibility to "counteract the activities of the Portuguese traders" and "keep cash within our borders"[9] – a measure to increase South African sovereignty in Ovamboland.[10]

The Omafo store, too, lay close to a government station. It was opened in rondavels originally erected as home for a district surgeon, only a few kilometers south of the Assistant Native Commissioner's office in Oshikango.[11]

The initial closeness to the Administration had obvious advantages for the company, but it also implied a stricter control than businesses in the 'Police Zone' – the central areas not subject to reserve regulations – had to face. The regulations on trade in Ovamboland stipulated that "in the event of any complaint being received from Chiefs and/ or Natives that excessive prices are being charged, the Native Commissioner, or duly authorized person, shall, subject to the approval of the Administrator, have the right to examine the books, records, stock-lists etc., of any trader and any trader who is proved to be charging excessive prices shall, after having been duly warned and repeating the offence, have his licence cancelled."[12]

---

[9] NAN SWAA 1057 135/22, Letter NC Hahn to Secretary, 5 August 1929.

[10] In 1932, the Chamber of Mines stopped recruiting in Ovamboland, as CDM (taken over by De Beers in 1929 after Ernest Oppenheimer, founder of Anglo American, had become De Beers' chairman) was hit hard by the Great Depression. As a consequence, the Ondonga Trading Company closed its store in Omafo from 10 September 1932. Labor recruiter Rupert Cope, who found himself temporarily unemployed (if paid), took over the shop in Ondjodjo. In 1932 and 1933, no Ovambo workers were recruited by the two labor organizations, and recruiting was only resumed after Native Commissioner Hahn proposed to send workers from Ovamboland to the Rand gold mines (NAN NAO 4 211/11. Letter NC to Secretary Courtney Clarke, 25 July 1934). As wages were much higher in South Africa than in South West Africa, CDM felt its long-term interests sufficiently threatened to resume recruiting for 1935. Cope was again employed as labor recruiter, and the Omafo store re-opened from 23 August 1935 (NAN SWAA 1057 135/22, Letter CoM to Secretary, 13 June 1935; Letter NC Hahn to Secretary, 10 May 1938).

[11] The ANC's office moved from Namakunde to Oshikango when the new border was drawn in 1927. – The store originally was located on today's main road B1, about a hundred meters north of the turnoff to Engela; it was housed in three small houses which had served as a government building. The plot is still surrounded by a dense hedge of prickly pear cacti today. In 1952, the administration reclaimed the buildings, and the shop was moved towards Oshikango, opposite today's "Michael Jackson Drive" to the Namundjebo family's lodge and former store (NAN NAO 63 17/1). Its buildings are still standing; they were taken over from ENOK by Johannes Hamtumwa in 1975 and, when he went into exile, by Eliakim Namundjebo, in whose family they remain today. In 2008, they served as a storeroom for a Pakistani plastic factory nearby.

[12] NAN SWAA 1057 135-22/1, Regulations framed under the provisions of section 14 of ordinance No. 13 of 1935, as amended by ordinance No. 1 of 1936, and relating to trade in Ovamboland.

In 1938, complaints of excessive prices became vocal enough to actually lead to an official inquiry by the Additional Native Commissioner. The results were ambivalent, if hardly flattering for the company. Prices charged, the Additional Native Commissioner stated, were very high: "the average gross margin of profit is at present 50% on the cost prices *landed in Ovamboland.*" Under similar circumstances, traders in the Transkeian Native Territories could make a comfortable living on a margin of about twenty percent. But, the report continued, "even if the prices are abnormally high, the Administration is only empowered to interfere if […] it can be *proved* that he is charging *excessive* prices." This was not possible in the present case. "Although the business methods of the Company may perhaps be criticized, the fact remains that the Company was run at a loss until 1935 and that only moderate nett profits have been made for the last two years." This was rather strange, as "the proposition of a virtual cash trading monopoly over the whole of Ovamboland with its 107.000 inhabitants is one which *should* pay."[13]

In short: the Company was exploiting its monopoly by charging very high prices, but it still managed to run at a loss. The reason for this only appears between the lines of the report, when it mentions "excessive rent payments", "administration fees" and "high salaries": a good part of the shops' profit was transferred to the Chamber of Mines in Lüderitz, disguised as necessary expenses. To mask the profit as costs allowed maintaining high prices without causing too much suspicion on the part of the Administration – after all, the shops were operating at a loss. What is more, the shops' losses could simultaneously be charged to the employers of migrant workers as recruiting costs.

In order to understand this better, we have to have a closer look at the organization of labor recruitment in South West Africa before 1943.

The labor recruitment agreement of 1924 had created two recruiting organizations, the Southern Labour Organisation (SLO) and the Northern Labour Organisation (NLO). This was a government-facilitated compromise between the diamond mines, the Northern mines and the farming interests. SLO was granted the exclusive right to recruit workers in Ovamboland, which at the time already was an important labor reservoir with a working recruitment infrastructure. This advantage, which was always regarded as unfair by the employers represented by the NLO, was given to SLO because the difficulties in obtaining sufficient workers for the diamond fields threatened the entire economy of the mandate territory – in the financial year 1923/24 the South West African Administration had collected more than £443.000 in diamond revenues.

---

[13] NAN SWAA 1057 135-22/1, Trading in Ovamboland: Ondonga Trading Company, Limited (23 September 1938).

While NLO, which represented a multitude of employers, was soon institutionalized with headquarters in Grootfontein and the Okavango as its main recruitment area, SLO was never properly set up. It represented the interests of the companies that came together in the Chamber of Mines in Lüderitz (CoM), and the Chamber acted as if it were the SLO. With the rapid concentration in South West African diamond mining, the Chamber itself soon became synonymous with Consolidated Diamond Mining Corporation South West Africa (CDM). SLO letters were written on CoM letterheads, and the sources often mention SLO, CoM and CDM interchangeably. Hahn even calls his brother-in-law Cope "the recruiting agent of the Consolidated Diamond Mines" in an official report.[14]

After a general slump in labor demand in the early 1930s, employment in the northern mines and on the farms picked up in the mid-1930s. Labor demand for the diamond mines, however, remained very low.[15] SLO still had the exclusive right and the infrastructure to recruit in Ovamboland, but it no longer needed the recruited workers. Its solution was to pass the workers on to NLO and to charge the organization according to their operative costs per worker. In 1939, SLO recruited 229 workers for the diamond mines and more than 6.000 for the NLO.[16] This implied that almost all of SLO's recruiting costs were actually paid for by the NLO. Not surprisingly, the NLO felt that they were overcharged, and could recruit in Ovamboland at much lower costs if allowed to do so. After long negotiations, this led to the amalgamation of both organizations in the South West Africa Native Labour Association (SWANLA) in 1943, which also took over the stores in Ovamboland from January 1943.[17]

---

[14]   NAN NAO A450 7 2/18, Annual Report 1935. As the literature has so far seen SLO as a real institution comparable to NLO, it might be good to cite a few further sources: In the 1930 transport agreement with Hermann Tietz, Lüderitz Chamber of Mines is mentioned as direct counterpart of the Northern Labour Organisation. The account of the recruiting expenses was titled "Lüderitz Chamber of Mines – recruiting expenses" in 1940, "Recruiting Expenses Southern Labour Organisation" in 1939. Letters regarding the amalgamation of SLO and NLO were, in SLO's name, written on the letterhead of CDM in Kimberley (all NAN A450 7). When representatives of NLO and SLO met in 1940 to discuss a possible amalgamation, NLO noted that "although under the 1925 agreement the recruiting rights in Ovamboland were granted to the S.L.O., there appears to be no record of this organization having ever registered themselves as such, in other words they apparently do not legally exist." At the same occasion, the NLO reported that the SLO representatives were very surprised to hear that "NLO was obliged to operate as a non-profit making concern, for which they could see no justification and which in the event of amalgamation they wished to alter" (NAN NAO A450 7 2/17, Memorandum by NLO on talks with SLO). Finally, the official Memorandum of Association of SWANLA registered on 10 November 1943 in Windhoek was concluded between the Consolidalted Diamond Mines of South West Africa Ltd and the NLO, each taking one share. SLO is not mentioned once in the document (NAN KNL 1, Commission on Native Labour).

[15]   The Administration's diamond revenue was at an all-time low of £2.604 in 1932/33; it picked up to reach £23.549 in 1934/35, but that was still less than 5% of the 1922/23 figure. See Cooper 1999, 132.

[16]   NAN NAO A450 7 2/17, Memorandum by NLO on talks with SLO.

[17]   NAN NAO 25 17/1, Letter Administrator to Secretary of SWANLA, 26 January 1943. The Northern La-

The Ondonga Trading Corporation Ltd., the company running the stores in Ondangwa and Omafo until 1943, was wholly owned by the Chamber of Mines in Lüderitz. The Chamber tried to apportion the losses connected to the trading store to recruiting costs charged to NLO since 1928. It argued that the store "was inaugurated in 1925 for the sole purpose of stimulating recruiting, and has proved a valuable link in our recruiting scheme by steadily draining the country of its surplus cash and thereby indirectly benefitting the labour market."[18] The NLO at first refused to accept liability for the store's losses, but at least from 1935, the loss was added to the recruiting costs and thus taken charge of by the employers of migrant workers.

This meant that the Ondonga Trading Company had no need to make profits. Any loss incurred could be charged to the migrant workers' employers. Furthermore, a part of the loss consisted in payments to the mother company: the annual rent paid by the shop was a very high 14% of the capital invested by CoM in the buildings, with maintenance charges taken over by the Ondonga Trading Company; a yearly administrative charge was paid to CoM for keeping the Company's books; all furniture and such was written off over a mere ten years…[19] The resulting 'losses' served to justify high prices in the shops, to deflect suspicions of profiteering and to convince the Administration that the rationale behind the stores was political, not commercial.

This image was damaged by the 1938 report. The political climate had shifted between 1925, when the Lüderitz diamond fields had been of paramount importance for South West Africa, and the late 1930s. The colonial administration in Ovamboland had now become more settled, labor migration was routinised, and the overall balance was more in favor of the NLO and the northern mines. The Administration was much less willing to give the Chamber of Mines all possible advantages, and in the central government, liberalist preferences for free trade once again prevailed over mining concerns. In order to break the OTC's monopoly and further healthy competition, a second trading licence for

---

bour Organisation had had a hawking licence in Okavango, which was equally transferred to SWANLA.

[18] NAN SWAA 1057 135-22/1, Letter CoM to NLO, 18 September 1928.

[19] NAN SWAA 1057 135-22/1, Trading in Ovamboland: Ondonga Trading Company, Limited (23 September 1938). To cite just one example of the sums involved: the Company paid an annual rent of £975 for the buildings it hired from the Chamber of Mines; at the same time, the South West Africa Company charged the NLO £72 per year for more extensive buildings (NAN NAO A450 7 2/17, Memorandum on the proposed amendment to, or cancellation of, the 1925 agreement). When the Administration decided in 1941, after long hesitation, to charge a rental fee for the land the OTC occupied, that rent was fixed at £60 per year for Ondjodjo (NAN NAO 25 17/2, Letter NC to CNC, 3 June 1941). The rent for the government buildings in Omafo was £30 annually from 1941 (NAN NAO 25 17/2, Contract of Lease between CNC and CoM, 20 October 1941). All rents were payable to the Tribal Trust Funds.

Ovamboland was advertised and, from August 1939, granted to Erich Beersmann (called Amunyela by the locals). He opened his shop in Endola in southern Oukwanyama.[20]

Beersmann's store, which he operated with his wife and her sister, one white assistant and several local store hands, soon became well known, even if it was smaller than OTC's Ondjodjo store. Although his store was farther removed from the administrative centers, he did not escape official scrutiny. After SWANLA took over the stores from the Ondonga Trading Company, which was liquidated in 1943, the Administration's attitude towards the stores in Ondjodjo and Omafo changed. The amalgamated recruiting agency was responsible for all labor supply to the colony. Contrary to the SLO, it was not seen as a proxy for CDM, but as an important factor in government policy. In late 1944, the Secretary for South West Africa P. R. Botha wrote that "seeing that SWANLA is a semiofficial body and all their trading profits go into reducing recruiting charges, it does not seem desirable to grant private trading concessions in Ovamboland. […] SWANLA has already mooted the question of cancelling Beersmann's concession in Ovamboland to clear the entire field for SWANLA."[21] When the choleric shopkeeper manhandled Uukwambi senior headman Silas y'Ipumbu[22] in 1947 and tied his hands with a piece of string for 'loitering' in his backyard and keeping his hands in his trouser pocket while talking to Beersmann, the Administration took the opportunity to revoke his licence, and the shop was taken over by SWANLA from December 1, 1947.[23] European trading once again became the monopoly of the recruitment agency.

---

[20] Beersmann was a naturalized British of German descent and language who ran one of three garages in Okahandja in the 1930s. Shortly before the war, he was "ostracized by the Germans as he does not share their political views" (NAN NAO 25 17/3, Telegram Secretary to NC, 7 June 1939). When his application for a licence was successful, he sold his garage for £ 1000 and moved to Endola (SWAA 1056 135/22, Letter NC to CNC, 2 June 1939). He had been one of only two applicants, the other being Hermann Tietz, who lived on a transport contract for people and goods to Ovamboland and was in danger of losing his living with the opening of the railway bus service in late 1938. Beersmann's shop was opened in September or October 1939.

[21] SWAA 1057 135/22, Letter Secretary SWA to NC Hahn, 14 December 1944.

[22] Fikameni Silas y'Ipumbu, son of Uukwambi King Iipumbu ya Tshilongo, who was deposed by the colonial government in 1932 and sent to exile. He was born in 1912 and became one of the senior headmen of the area after his father was banished from the area. From 1968, he was a member of the Ovambo Executive Council, the homeland cabinet. In 1973, he founded the Ovamboland Independence Party which represented the interests of the headmen cooperating with South Africa. He had six wives and about sixty children (Tötemeyer 1978, 64); his son Herman Ipumbu today is the chairperson of the Uukwambi Traditional Authority.

[23] NAN NAO 95 42/6, Complaints against European Traders; NAN SWAA 1057 135/22 (ii); NAN NAO 63 17/1, Agreement of Lease between Administration and SWANLA, 20 May 1948. The new rent was £12 per year; SWANLA had bought Beersmann's buildings and inventory when taking over the shop.

The last SWANLA store was finally opened in Ombalantu in 1953.[24] These four stores remained the largest and most important shops in the area well into the 1970s.

Trade organization and shopping

Even today, many villagers in northern Namibia spend months without entering a shop or buying anything. State pensions to people over 65 are the main regular source of cash income for many families, and provisions are often bought once a month at the mobile markets which form around pension payout points. But today, even the remotest villages have a shop within less than an hour's walking distance, everybody is informed about the selection of goods available in village stores and town supermarkets, and buying goods in stores has become a routine activity. The four stores at Ondjodjo, Omafo, Endola and Ombalantu introduced the population of Ovamboland to this activity at a time when the act of buying things for money was far from an everyday occurrence.

All transactions at the shops had to be done in cash. Barter was proscribed by the licence regulations, and giving credit to 'natives' was strictly forbidden. This regulation was meant to protect the local population from the exploitative practices prevalent in many areas of South Africa, where ticket sales and credit on expected wages had led many people into lasting dependence of one trader.[25] The only exception was that storekeepers were allowed to barter for large stock.[26] However, due to veterinary regulations, the cattle thus obtained could only be sold locally or in Angola, and profits were not very high, so that the traders only looked for slaughtering cattle for their own needs or for direct sale.

Before World War II, a visit to one of the four stores was virtually the only occasion at which most people needed money at all. Between villagers not involved in migrant labor (and more often than not between those who were), goods were exchanged by barter or for services.[27] Missionaries very often obtained necessary services and goods – mostly

---

[24] "The Ombalantu Council of Headmen agreed to the granting of a site to the SWANLA for trading purposes in the Ombalantu tribal area. The headmen expressed satisfaction with the proposal to establish a store in their country." (NAN NAO 63 17/1, Letter NC to CNC 18 December 1950). The licence had already been granted by the Administrator in August 1950, the contract of lease was signed on 7 May 1951 to start from October 1951. In the Annual Report for 1952, however, the Native Commissioner mentioned the shop as "not yet built" (NAN NAO 61 12/2).

[25] E.g. Kuper 1947, 136ff. – A German trader in Kamanjab became the focus of a police investigation in 1938. For years, he had paid representatives to buy sheep in Kaokoveld against tickets which could only be used for purchases at his own shop. By 1938, he had bought a herd of 930 sheep. NAO 31 24/23 Trading in Kaokoveld.

[26] See e.g. the licence regulations for Beersmann in NAN NAO 25 17/3.

[27] The natural economy was probably slightly overstated when local administrators tried to prevent measures by the central government, but local people's memories match with the following excerpts. Arguing against charging 'natives' for timber, Hahn stated in 1941: "It must be remembered that the only cash

grain, cattle or eggs – through barter. Cash only played a role for migrant laborers and in the stores.

The cash economy made a big leap forward during World War II, when many young men from the area enlisted for military service in the South African army and received war gratuities.[28] After demobilization, many of them used the knowledge and contacts they had gained in the army to work on the Rand mines in South Africa for better wages than the South West African mines paid. Due to the better postal service and increasing alphabetization, they were in better contact with their relatives at home than the workers had been in the 1920s. Relatives' pleas for money could reach them more easily, and many were more willing to send money home, as closer contacts gave them a modicum of control over how their wages were spent. All this increased the influx of money and spread its use at home.[29] In 1946, Hahn even reported that "in a few years the change-over to a money economy has almost been complete."[30] This was certainly an overstatement, but in the memories of many local people, as well, the need to have money started at around this time.

Even after World War II, shopping remained a special occasion for most people, which needed planning, saving and often enough travelling. Three of the four stores were built at strategic places near administrative centers, Mission stations and chiefly courts, but the population of early to mid-20th century Ovamboland was still fairly evenly scattered across the fertile landscape. Homesteads were politically organized in wards under a sub-headman, several of which again were under the authority of a senior headman, but this organization did not correspond to a clear clustering of homesteads. Villages and towns in the modern sense only slowly began to develop towards the middle of the twentieth century. For most people, visiting a shop involved at least a day of walking.

---

circulating in the country is that brought by returning labourers. The economic life of the Ovambo is not based on a monetary system." (NAN NAO 25 17/3, Letter NC Hahn to CNC, 2 June 1941.) When the Administration wanted to proscribe barter in 1948 to prevent exploitative trade and to simultaneously stimulate a cash economy linked to migrant labor, Assistant Native Commissioner Crossman described the situation in Oukwanyama: "As between Native and Native the barter system is the only form of currency. It is an age-old custom and its prohibition will result in hardship as the Native who, in the remote parts of the area, offers his services to another in return for grain etc., has no practical use for money." (NAN NAO 64 17/7, Letter ANC to NC, 28 June 1948.)

[28] According to official sources, 2676 recruits were accepted into the SADF between 1941 and 1943 – see Gordon 1993, 156. Gordon calls his article "a prospectus for a study" (147), but it is still the best source on World War II recruiting and the impact the War in Namibia.

[29] In 1942, Hahn reported that the "turnover of both [trading companies] has increased considerably since last year. This is due to the fact that so much more money has been paid to natives in connection with military allotments." NAN NAO 20 11/1 Vol. 15, Annual Report 1942.

[30] NAN NAO 20 11/1 Vol. 19, Annual Report Ovamboland 1946.

The first store, Ondjodjo, had an obvious advantage: it was build only one kilometer from the recruiting agency's office, where prospective migrant workers were examined, received their passes and were organized into transports. Migrants waiting for the next bus often spent several weeks in the area. While they rarely had much money left, the returning migrants' collective journey ended here, as well, and the shop was the best occasion to spend wages without having to transport the goods from the South. This turned Ondjodjo into the largest and most important store in Ovamboland.

All four stores were behind-the-counter shops. From an inventory drawn up when Beersmann planned to sell his store in 1945, we are best informed about Beersmann's store in Endola, but the other shops seem to have followed the same pattern. The Endola store was housed in a rondavel of ten meters circumference; the floor was laid in linoleum, the roof was made of wood. Entering the shop through the wooden door after taking the few steps onto the small verandah, you found yourself in the salesroom. The shop attendants stood behind a large counter with drawers opening to their side; a display cabinet, a cash box and the balance with its weights were arranged on the counter. Behind the counter, a large shelf holding textiles and rolls of cloth stood next to four smaller shelves with shirts in the first, undershirts and socks in the second, shoes, blankets and hoes in the third and soap and haberdashery in the fourth. Patent medicine was arranged in a smaller corner cupboard.[31] Sugar, rice and coffee, which customer could buy without seeing them, were housed in a shelf with lided boxes. Besides the counter stood a larger and a smaller closed cupboard with glass fronts as further showcases.

Goods the customer wanted to see were placed on the counter to be examined and compared, and when someone had chosen a piece of cloth, its length was measured there with the help of a wooden ruler. If the attendant had to reach the upper shelves or the clothes and tools that hung from railings on the ceiling, s/he could use one of the two stepladders. All in all, the room was rather packed, but somewhere space for a wall clock had been found.

The counter barred the entrance to an office separated from the shop by a cellotex wall. It had enough space for a desk, two cupboards and three tables, not to mention two strongboxes. Here, Beersmann or his wife kept the books and wrote commissions.

A back entrance led to the courtyard, which was off limits to customers. The owner's family's living quarters, their kitchen and bathroom were arranged around the court, just as the shop's auxiliary buildings – storerooms, cooling room, garage, workshop and shed.

---

[31] Selling patent medicine, pre-packed pharmaceuticals tradeable outside of pharmacies, was only allowed with a special licence in addition to the general trading licence.

Slightly further afield, smaller rondavels housed the families of the local store hands and household personnel.[32]

The stores were open all year from morning to late afternoon; from 1947, they had to close on Saturday afternoons, Sundays and Public Holidays.[33] The shops were obliged to have printed price-lists in both the local language and English displayed at their shop. Prior to 1938, these lists were frequently ignored by employees who overcharged illiterate customers;[34] after the issuing of a second licence showed the dangers of contravening the regulation, this practice seems to have stopped. People came into the shop, waited in front of the counter (where in some shops chairs or benches were placed) and asked for the goods they wanted to buy. In the case of standardized goods – like salt, sugar, paraffin or tobacco tins – the desired quantity was measured and handed to the customer after payment. When the customer wanted to buy textiles, clothes or other non-standardized goods, different items were brought to the counter for inspection and testing. The smaller shops seem to have been rather quiet on normal days, but Ondjodjo was often crowded, so that people had to wait before being served. Often, young boys and girls were sent to the shops to buy minor items, especially foodstuff or tobacco. Headmen and other important people sent dependents with shopping lists, or they went to the shop to choose their goods and later sent a servant to pay and pick up the wares.

It is difficult to establish how often people visited a shop in the 1930s and 1940s. Ordinary village household heads with some money to spend probably went to a shop once or twice a year, and sent somebody to buy minor items from time to time. Senior headman Silas y'Ipumbu came to the Endola store "approximately once a month" in 1946 and sent dependents to buy things in between.[35]

Even people who did not have a regular income knew about the stores and the possibilities they offered. They had heard about the storekeepers and had a rough idea about the assortment of goods and prices in the shops. Whenever somebody needed to buy anything, s/he knew where to go. People came to Endola and Ondjodjo from as far as Ombalantu. Namibian President Hifikepunye Pohamba remembered how, when he needed a new pair of shoes as a young man in the early 1950s, he first walked from his home village to Omafo. As he did not find shoes that fit him there, he walked a further sixty kilometers to Ondjodjo in the hope of finding a suitable pair.[36] This shows how exceptional it was to

---

[32]   NAN NAO 25 17/3, Verzeichnis Endola Store, Ovamboland, 31 August 1945.

[33]   NAN NAO 25 17/2, NC to SWANLA Manager, 6 December 1947.

[34]   NAN SWAA 1056 135/22 Letter NC Hahn to Secretary 10 May 1938.

[35]   NAN SWAA 1057 135/22 Statement Karl Vollmer, Statement Ernst Beersmann.

[36]   Namibian Economist, 18 March 2005.

Image 5 and 6: Two white-owned "over the counter"-stores: Wecke & Voigts in Windhoek, 1926 (above) and Zetzmann in Swakopmund, 1963.

Image 7: Women returning from Omafo store (1940s photograph. Caption: "Three Kwanyama beauties who have been to the local store.")

make any larger purchase at a store, but also how well anchored the stores were in the mental maps of people living in the area.

Since 1948, SWANLA also sent hawkers to the western parts of Ovamboland and to the Kaokoveld. The company had experience with hawking in Okavango and applied for a hawking licence in Ovamboland in 1947, mostly to forestall Beersmann who had started delivering clothes on command to other parts of Ovamboland.[37]

---

[37]   NAN SWAA 1056 135/22, Memo on discussion between Native Affairs and SWANLA, 5/6 June 1947.

The first hawking trip to the Kaokoveld in 1948 was described by the Officer-in-Charge Native Affairs Kaokoveld as "successful from the natives' point of view. [...] Especially the Hottentots expressed their satisfaction at being able to buy supplies, clothing etc. again and wished to convey their thanks to the Administration for making it possible. They also intimated that they thought the prices charges for the different commodities

Image 8: Crowd waiting in front of Ondjodjo Store in 1953.

were reasonable. I have already had several enquiries as to when the hawker's next visit will take place."[38] This sounds like official propaganda in favor of trade, but SWANLA's letters indicate it might be very close to the truth. The hawker reported from Kaokoveld that "the Zesfontein Hottentots arrived, without money, but with roll tobacco for sale, which was purchased from them at the request of the Native Commissioner. This enabled them to buy our goods." He bought more than 1.500 pounds of tobacco, which proved very difficult to sell around Ondangwa as it was judged too try and of inferior quality.

So while the trip had given access to new goods to people in remote areas, it had not brought much profit to the traders, and only the administration's threat to give a hawking

---

[38]   NAN NAO 31 24/23, Letter Officer-in-Charge Native Affairs Kaokoveld to NC Ovamboland, 12 June1948.

licence to somebody else induced the company to make further trips.[39] Business turned out to be better in the following years, however. From 1949 to 1952, four trips a year were made to Kaoko or Ombalantu, usually with stops in Eunda, Uukwambi, Uukwaluudhi and Onkolonkathi. On each trip, up to one thousand Pounds were realized; the most popular items were textiles, ironware, beads, matches, sweets, soap, coffee and sugar.[40]

Another local alternative to the licenced stores were shops over the border in Angola. A number of traders had established stores there, mainly selling cotton textiles imported from Brazil and different alcoholic beverages.[41] In South West Africa, the League of Nations mandate of 1920 ruled that "the supply of intoxicating spirits and beverages to the natives shall be prohibited",[42] and shops were not allowed to sell alcohol to non-Whites. As border controls were virtually absent outside of Oshikango, many people instead bought alcohol in Portuguese stores over the border. When South Africa slowly ceased to see the League of Nations mandate as the source of its power, controls became even laxer, until every village had its "Cuca Shop" selling the eponymous Angolan beer.[43]

All four stores sold roughly the same goods. Goods and prices were the same at all OTC/ SWANLA stores. The assortment differed, though; Ondjodjo had the widest selection of goods available. About 180 different goods are mentioned on the price lists from the 1930s and 1940s, plus a further 65 marked as "for Europeans" on the 1941 price list (see annex). The most expensive goods were saddles for £4.7/- in 1941 – more than three months' wages of a mineworker towards the end of his contract. On the other extreme, a pound of salt cost one pence, the same as a darning needle or a piece of washing blue.

The most important goods were clothing, foodstuff and household or drugstore goods. Men's and women's clothing from shoes to hats figured among the more expensive goods, with trousers ranging from eight shilling to over a pound, shirts from two to eleven and shoes from fifteen to twenty shillings in 1941. Different qualities of dressing material were sold as well, together with needles, buttons, twine and safety pins. Brilliantine, shoe polish, combs, mirrors and finger rings served to complement the modern clothing, while washing powder, caustic soda and washing blue could be used to keep it clean and shining, and sad irons (coal-heated washing irons) to get creases out after washing. Rice and mealie meal bought in the shops could be served on the enamel plates sold alongside them, and enamel cups would take the different brands of tea and coffee sold in the shop.

---

[39] NAN NAO 63 17/1, Report on Hawking Trip, May 1948. Profits after costs were judged by OTC at eight per cent, as compared to around twenty-five per cent at the store.
[40] NAN NAO 62 17/1, Manager Ondonga Store to NC, 3 November 1952.
[41] NAN NAO 20 11/1 Vol. 16, Annual Report 1943.
[42] Mandate for German South West Africa, Article 3 (HMSO 1921 Miscellaneous No.8 (1921).)
[43] For the history of cuca shops see Eirola/ Bradley/ Laitinen 1990, van Wolputte 2010.

Candles, hurricane lanterns, lamp wicks and paraffin spent light for those who could afford them, and mouth harps, concertinas and guitar strings are witnesses of new musical forms brought back from working in the South.

All these goods were associated with 'modern' life. European clothing was not yet worn by the majority of the population in the 1940s, and only few people drank tea or coffee and ate rice or corn meal instead of the locally grown pearl millet (*omahangu*). The adoption of a European clothing or eating style changed more than just the textiles worn on the body. From face powder to shoelaces, it made many different goods necessary, or at least meaningful. The 'conversion' to a European-style dress thus almost inevitably brought a conversion to trading stores and to the monetary economy.

Lebzelter, who visited the area in 1927, gives a paternalistic, but accurate account of shopping for modern clothing in Ondjodjo. It shows how, at least in theory, the decision to adopt a new clothing style entailed the acquisition of an entire ensemble of different items:

> Everything the native's heart desires can be had there, and many a demure Ovambo maid sends her suitor to the sandy desert of the South to earn money to buy all the nice things her heart desires. Among these are gloves, varnished half-boots and a colorful parasol. The ideal of all men, however, is the frock coat. In the store, we find large piles of old frocks. I have bought some for 22 shilling. Saddles and high yellow boots are equally appreciated.

> A common European men's outfit consists of shirt (echema), vest (okasore) and loin cloth (elapi jo kusula). The shirt costs 7 to 8, the vest 4 to 6, the loin cloth 2 to 4 shilling, so that 14–16 shilling can be found sufficient. In the cold season, an undershirt or bodice is added, which can be had for 4 shilling. For the full European adjustment, we have to add: shoes (15–18 shilling), coat (used, 18–20 shilling), jacket (ombaikisa, 12 shilling), trousers (omburukuea, 10–15 shilling), underpants (ondoromburuku, 5–7 shillings), woolen vest (omhindja, 8–10 shilling) and stockings (ikausino, 2–3 shillings). Altogether, this makes 75 shilling or £4 to 5 to fit a person out.[44]

But not only people who adopted new lifestyle elements made use of the shops. Some of the goods integrated well into the local subsistence economy. Industrially produced hoes, knives and hatches served the same purpose as locally forged ones. Just as most other articles, they were not only bought by people who actually had cash at their disposal, but bartered on to those who had not.

By all reports, people buying at one of the shops were quite conscious of their money's worth. When Beersmann was accused by SWANLA of charging too high prices and the Assistant Native Commissioner in Oukwanyama, Holdt, was sent to compare the prices

---

[44] Lebzelter 1934, 219. The price is high compared to yearly wages of around 14–18 pound, but it roughly corresponds to the price of an ostrich egg necklace of average (60 shilling) or high length (80 shilling) worn by women from wealthier households (Lebzelter 1934, 219).

of Omafo and Endola stores, he found differences in quality and price. The Endola store had a better and more varied stock of clothing at higher prices, while the Omafo store carried a larger assortment of groceries and tins, for which demand in Endola was hardly existent. The differences in price and quality were well-known to everybody and did not mean that Beersmann was exploiting his position. "Natives are quite shrewd business people and do not part easily with their money."[45] Far from feeling exploited, local people generally saw shops as services that gave them more convenient access to new goods. All four stores were welcomed by the respective chiefs or headmen and given new ground if they needed it. But the headmen also looked closely at the administration's trade policy. When Beersmann's licence was given to SWANLA, the Ovakwanyama senior headmen complained in unusually clear words. In Holdt's words, "Headman Nehemia then asked why, if Mr. Beersmann must go, was Endola given to SWANLA when they already have stores at Ondangwa and Omafo. When a person has a sixpence to buy paraffin he will receive the same quantity for it at all places. The store will all be one. If he is not satisfied at one place it will not help him to go to the other place. The Oukwanyama, he said, acknowledge that the Government has the right to act as it likes, but they wish the Administration to know 'that the hearts of the Oukwanyama are not happy about this'."[46] The headmen's statement is further witness that the stores had become an important element in the economic, social and political landscape of Ovamboland during the 1930s and 1940s, and local people became increasingly interested in both the stores and their goods.

Turnover

This is also reflected in the stores' turnover. The following table shows the available figures for OTC/ SWANLA stores and the recruitment figures from Ovamboland. As the aim of this graph is to capture the amount of goods bought in Ovamboland, I have adjusted the turnover figures to represent prices in 1938, using the consumer price index for Windhoek calculated by the Odendaal Commission.[47] The years 1948 to 1951 include the Endola store.[48] The recruitment figures given in different sources rarely match each other.

---

45 NAN NAO 63 17/1, Letter ANC Holdt to NC Eedes, 14 October 1947.
46 NAN NAO 63 17/1, Letter ANC Holdt to NC Ovamboland, 13 November 1947.
47 Odendaal Commission 1964, 317. I use the price index for Windhoek faute de mieux. Changing transport costs, monopolistic gains and rural-urban differences in supply and demand almost certainly led to divergences between price development in Ovamboland and Windhoek, but this error will be small compared to the uncertainties of both price indices and recruitment figures.
48 There is very little known about Beersmann's turnover. His store seems to have been of approximately the same size as Omafo; in 1945, he calculated the value of his stock-in-hand at £4000, a figure that in OTC's books corresponded with a yearly turnover of around £8000 or 9000. (NAN SWAA 1057 135/22 ii, Undated Letter Beersmann to NC, 1945). In any case, turnover at Ondjodjo was substantially

To have one consistent set of figures, I have used the numbers given by Notkola and Si-iskonen for Ovamboland.[49] Workers from Angola were excluded from the number, even if many of them probably bought at Ovamboland stores.

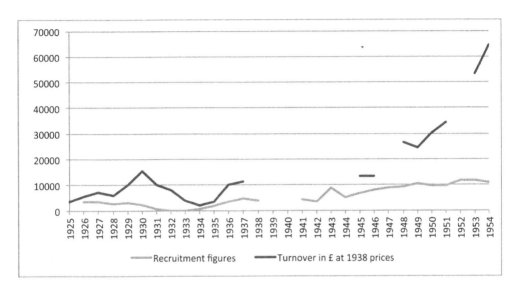

Image 9: Recruitment figures and shop turnover.

For the years before World War II, the most astonishing feature in this graph is per-haps the peak in 1930. It does not correspond to any rise in income; recruitment figures had been more or less stable between 1926 and 1929 and started to decline sharply in 1930. But one of the worst droughts of the last century hit Ovamboland in 1929 and resulted in widespread famine. Government reacted by a huge food-for-work program in which people were employed to build dams as a ward against further droughts. They were not paid in cash, but received millet or corn rations as daily payment.[50]

As the public works program neither gave payments in cash nor bought at local stores, the only explanation for the peak in turnover is that a part of the population of Ovambo-land had resources that could be converted to cash and spent on food during this crisis. Cattle herds which could not be sustained on the meager pasturage were sold, and what

higher. – The turnover figures for the stores are taken from the following sources: NAN SWAA 1057 135-22/1, Trading in Ovamboland: Ondonga Trading Company, Limited (23 September 1938) for 1925-1936; NAN SWAA KNL 1, SWANLA Balance Sheet and Annual Reports 1945 and 1946; NAN NAO 61 12/2, Annual Reports Ovamboland for 1948 to 1951; NAN BAC 88 HN3/16/2/1, SWANLA Annual report 1955 as cited by Cooper 2001, 250 for 1953–54. The two last figures are for the financial year from July to June 1953/54 and 1954/55.

49 Notkola and Siiskonen 2000, 157.
50 See Hayes 1998.

cash savings migrant workers had were used on food. In addition to such efforts within individual households, both headmen and missions bought supplies for their clients.

Rough expenditure figures Viktor Lebzelter gives for 1927 sustain the notion that a surprising part of the wages was in fact saved. Lebzelter judges a contract worker's yearly wages at a very high £30. Of this, a contract worker spent £5 for his own needs at work, £4 for his own clothes, £4 for gifts and taxation, while £10 and £5 financed purchases at shops in the Police Zone and Ondangwa respectively.[51] Lebzelter only looks at the immediate expenditure, but to calculate the likely turnover of stores, we have to add the indirect cash expenditures resulting from 'gifts' to the headmen and the resale of items bought in the Police Zone. Taken together, this would probably represent a sum of at least £8 available for purchases at the monopoly stores. The turnover in a normal year, however, only represents about £2 per returning worker. Even if one adds purchases made in Angola and allows for substantially lower wages, the figures suggest that most workers had at least some room for saving money for a time of crisis.

After the 1929/30 famine, depleted resources in combination with the recruitment slump caused by the world economic crisis led to a sharp decline in shops' turnover and indeed to the temporary closing of Omafo store. Sales picked up again with a time lag of more than a year on recruiting – witness to the fact that most of the money was spent by the workers on their return after a twelve- or eighteen-month contract.[52]

By 1938, the economy had recovered, and the part of workers' wages spent in the shops had markedly increased. A class A worker on the diamond fields earned 14 pounds and 4 shillings for his first year of work in 1938, a class C farm worker earned 5 pounds 4 shillings.[53] As eighty percent of the workers worked on farms, the total income of the 7.000 workers recruited in this year amounted to approximately fifty thousand pounds. The turnover of the OTC stores in Ovamboland was more than a fifth of this.[54] This might not seem much at the first glance, given that the stores had the monopoly of trade in Ovamboland, but under the circumstances, it is indeed a very high percentage. The wage level on mines and farms was not calculated to sustain entire families, and a sub-

---

[51] Lebzelter 1934, Vol. 2, 219. In 1938, Hahn reported that due to the high prices at Ondjodjo and Omafo, "the returning labourers spend by far the larger portion of their earnings in Tsumeb, Outjo, Luderitz, Grootfontein and elsewhere" (NAN NAO 25/17/1, Letter NC to CNC, 23 December 1938).

[52] A part of the income was, however, remitted by the workers: "The turnover has improved since the diamond fields recommenced operations and are employing from 2.000 to 3.000 Ovambos who are now remitting money to their dependents to enable them to fit themselves out with clothing etc. at the stores mentioned. Up to about February of the year under report business was practically at a standstill. The turnover now approximates £200 per month." NAN A450 7 2/18, Annual Report 1935.

[53] NAN NAO 20 11/1 Vol. 11, Annual Report 1938.

[54] The Europeans living in Ovamboland did of course buy some supplies in the local stores, but ordered most of their goods from Wecke & Voigts and other shops in Grootfontein.

stantial part of it had to be spent by the workers during their contract time. A further part went for goods bought in the South and brought back to Ovamboland, and a small percentage trickled to shops in Angola. If twenty percent of the wages were still spent in the local stores, it highlights the importance the stores had as a source of supply and as economic link to the police zone.

Almost all cash that was brought back to Ovamboland in the 1940s was finally filtered through the stores, even if some of it circulated among the local population for some time. Workers bought cattle from neighbors (although the majority of cattle were bought in Angola, where high taxes periodically forced people to sell their cattle cheaply), they paid taxes to traditional leaders and to the Trust Funds, and they made gifts to family members, friends and clients. But just as migrant labor was the main conduit for cash to flow into the reserve, the stores were the main gateway through which people living in Ovamboland could exchange cash for economic goods from the outside world.

Between 1937 and 1954, most importantly after the supply shortages linked to the war were over, turnover at constant price levels increased more than sixfold, while recruitment figures only doubled. The increase is caused by the combination of several factors. While real term wages remained stable or declined in South West Africa,[55] more and more young men went to South Africa, where wages on the Rand gold mines were much higher. They brought more cash with them to Ovamboland, and many of them do not figure in the official recruitment figures. At the same time, price differences between the Ovamboland stores and shops in the South lowered, so that it became less attractive to buy goods in Tsumeb or Windhoek and to transport them home. Thirdly, and perhaps most importantly, the increase is a sign for the ongoing transformation towards a monetary economy after World War II. From the small outposts of a monetary economy they had been in 1925, the monopoly stores had transformed into the center of an emerging, but already vibrant modern economy.

Getting supplies to Ovamboland

The storeowners profited enormously from the protectionism of the South African mandate government, but it was not always easy for them to bridge the gap to the southern towns and to bring the merchandise into Ovamboland. The main problem was transport infrastructure. Walking was always possible if you knew the way and the waterholes, but

---

[55]   Moorsom (1997, 53) argues that real-term wages fell between the 1920s and 1949 and only started to rise over the 1920 level in the mid-1950s for farm workers and the early 1970s for mine workers. As he freely admits, the data basis for his calculation is rather shallow.

track animals frequently died of thirst during the dry season and got stuck in the rainy season. Cars and lorries regularly broke down due to overheating or axle problems, and the seasonal floods often made the passage impossible. The gradual establishment of a reliable transport system from and to Ovamboland thus was an important precondition of all major developments in 20th century northern Namibian history. It is part and parcel of the closer integration of the reserve into the mandatory territory, of the increasing institutionalisation of colonial administration and not least of the institutionalisation of the contract labour system. This is not the place to give a full history of transport to Ovambland, but some indications are necessary in order to understand the organisation and the role of the monopoly stores in Ovamboland.

With the establishment of a government post in Ondangwa in 1915 and the Anglican Mission in Odibo in 1924, motorcars became a more usual sight in Ovamboland than they had before. Prior to World War I, almost all travelling was done on foot, on a horse or a riding ox, or with ox or donkey carts. Still in the 1920s, travelling by car from Tsumeb to Ondangwa was a chancy endeavour. So few cars drove on the sand track that the spoor of one car was obliterated by the time the next car looked for it. Especially on the first ten miles from Namutoni, a stretch of deep sand was very difficult to negotiate. During the rainy season, stretches further north were often flooded, while dry grass caught under the motor frequently started to burn during the dry season. In order to have a reliable means of transport, the Odibo Mission bought an old tractor, which was as slow as an ox wagon and used quite a lot of water and petrol, but could negotiate the roads more reliably than either ox wagons or normal motor cars. The administration often used camels for the post and for personal travelling through Ovamboland.

These means of transport, however, were not suited to bring migrant labourers to Tsumeb. Up to 1924, when recruiting was done in Tsumeb, they had to walk to the railhead there. When the recruiting office was shifted to Ondangwa, this no longer seemed the best solution. Quite apart from the hardships it caused to the workers, decentralised travelling made the flow of migrant labourers more difficult to control. The new store in Ondjodjo also needed a more stable source of supply. The Chamber of Mines contracted Karl Hartmann, a German farmer from the Grootfontein area, to transport persons and goods to Ovamboland in his lorry on a regular basis.[56] A few years later, Hermann Tietz,

---

[56] NAN SWA 1057 135-22, Letter Hartmann to Administrator, 17 January 1927. – Schutztruppe soldier Karl Hartmann (*1881) settled at Nagusib, close to Namutoni, in 1903. In 1904, after fleeing to Namutoni from his own farm, he helped to defend the fort against Kind Nehale's soldiers – his name is still commemorated today on the brass plaque in Namutoni. Ute Dieckmann mentions that he had illegitimate children with a Hai||om woman (Dieckmann 2007, 96). He started to transport laborers in June 1924.

Image 10: Major Pritchard's expeditionary force, 1915. Three cars were brought to Tsumeb by rail.

another German farmer, got a second transport contract. He bought two new Chevrolet lorries in the early 1930s and made transport his full-time business. The two companies transported both freight and people, but goods for the OTC stores had "absolute priority" over people.[57] In spite of this, goods for the stores, for the missions and even for the Native Commisisoner were frequently left behind for lack of space. The lorries used were not specially built to transport people; workers had to squeeze into the back of the closed lorries together with any merchandise transported.

In 1939, shortly before the opening of Endola store, the state railways inaugurated a regular bus service between Tsumeb and Ondangwa. It started as a weekly service; in the late 1940s, the railway bus made three return voyages per week. The more frequent use improved the roads, especially in the more sandy areas. The first systematic attempt at road-improvement with state money was made in 1942. Since then, the roads were regularly scraped and freed of encroaching bush.[58] All this made it much easier to transport goods from the Police Zone to Ovamboland. It did not solve all the problems: If a bus was delayed or rain poured too hard, merchandise still frequently arrived spoiled. In high

---

[57] It is not quite clear to me when Tietz took up the transporting business. His written contract is from 1930, but it replaced a verbal agreement. – The trucks' brand appears in reminiscences by Vic Leibrandt, later native commissioner in Bizana (Transkei), who passed several months in Ovamboland in 1929 (Leibrandt 1976, 144).

[58] NAN NAO 25 16/1.

season, especially before Christmas, goods sometimes took months to arrive, since the administration now gave precedence to returning workers whom it wanted to keep from 'loitering' at Tsumeb in wait for a bus.[59] But for the first time, a reliable system of public transport linked Ovamboland to the police zone.

Image 11: Harold Eedes on a camel during his time as Assistant Resident Commissioner in Oshi-kango, ca. 1924.

Image 12: Migrant workers on their way back home. The white man in the background might be Tietz. Probably Otavi, ca. 1929.

---

[59] See e.g. NAN NAO 17/ 3, Letter Hansa Bottler Store, Tsumeb, to Beersmann, 11 January 1940.

Image 13: Migrant workers travelling on foot, ca. 1929.

In the early 1940s, a regular bus service from Ondonga to Efulululu near Endola was established, which brought mail and merchandise during the dry season, but could not operate five or six months every year due to the seasonal floods and the resulting bad shape of the roads.[60] In the 1960s, the bus system was expanded to Ombalantu and Oshikango.

So by the mid-1940s, a relatively reliable transport system was in place. Over the years, lorries were replaced by real buses for the transport of people and heavy lorries for the transport of freight, and new routes were added to the schedule. But those improvements only upgraded the system designed in 1939. It cemented Ondangwa's role as the new economic and administrative centre of Ovamboland and defined the nature of the reserve's link to the Police Zone. For the traders, it offered the possibility to order supplies quickly and in smaller amounts, making it possible to change the assortment faster in relation to demand, and to profit from supply price differences more easily.

Apart from some groceries – "cattle, goats, fowls, eggs, pigs and sometimes a piece of meat"[61] – traded in from local producers, all supplies of the stores came from the Police Zone or from South Africa. The SWANLA store managers did not keep wholesale

[60]   NAN SWAA 1057 135/22 ii, Ernst Beersmann: Endola Store, Ovamboland 1945
[61]   NAN SWAA 1057 135/22 ii: Ernst Beersmann: Endola Store, Ovamboland 1945

Image 14: Railway Buses in the 1960s.

Image 15: Railway Buses in the 1960s.

accounts themselves; all goods for the stores in Ovamboland and the Okavango were ordered through SWANLA's headquarters in Grootfontein. Beersmann travelled to the Police Zone twice a year to sample new goods and pass orders.[62] Fresh supplies for Beersmann came from Wecke & Voigts in Grootfontein or from similar shops in Tsumeb, butter from the Rietfontein creamery, alcohol for European customers from Hansa Bottle Store in Tsumeb.[63] Textiles and hardware seem to have been mostly ordered from South African firms.

Trade and the administration

The European monopoly in trade in Ovamboland began and ended almost simultaneously with British-style indirect rule through Native Commissioners. The first shops arrived five years after the mandate regime replaced military rule, and their monopoly ended in the early 1950s, when the National Party government began looking on South West Africa as an integral part of South Africa and reformed political rule in Ovamboland towards a nominally self-governed apartheid homeland.[64] As we have seen, trade was directly linked to recruiting, and both the SLO and SWANLA were looked upon as close allies by the administration. This did not induce them to give a free hand to the stores, however. The native commissioners jealously guarded their turfs and frequently interfered with the stores when they saw other political interests threatened. In the remaining part of this chapter, I will try to disentangle these different interests and show how they came together in a trade policy that was made up from ad-hoc decisions rather than shaped by long-term planning.

When the Administration and the Chamber of Mines took up the old plan to establish a trading store in Ovamboland in 1924, their aim was certainly not the modernization of society. On the contrary: as far as the planners gave any thought at all to the local society, they wanted to avoid change and the 'disturbances' it could possible bring. Change should only go so far as to bring young men south to work on the mines. In retrospect, this seems rather naïve; it is clear that the consequences of labor migration could never

---

[62] NAN NAO 25 17/1, Letter NC Hahn to Deputy Chief Control Office, Windhoek, 14 February 1945.

[63] NAN SWAA 1057 135/22 ii: Ernst Beersmann: Endola Store, Ovamboland 1945; NAN NAO 17/ 3, Letter Hansa Bottler Store, Tsumeb, to Beersmann, 11 January 1940. Wecke & Voigts had opened their Grootfontein branch before 1909 (NAN HRA 16).

[64] The first step into this direction was the South West Africa Affairs Amendment Act (Act 23/1949), which transferred the power of legislation in many domains, including native affairs, to the South African Parliament. With the South West Africa Native Affairs Administration Act (56/1954), the Native Affairs Branch of the South West African Administration was abolished and Native Affairs in South West Africa came under direct control of the South African Minister of Bantu Affairs and Development. Native Commissioners were renamed Bantu Affairs Commissioners.

have been contained into the economic domain alone. But without taking this double interest seriously, it is impossible to understand the Administration's policy towards trade. The native commissioners in particular were seriously torn between their overarching departmental interest to have as many men as possible recruited – and their own fascination with a conservative local society characterized, in their eyes, by subsistence economy, patriarchal rule and a general pre-modern non-Europeanness. In 1945, towards the end of his career, Hahn summed up his uneasiness in a private letter to Cope. He criticizes the South African Minister of Native Affairs and goes on:

> No wonder the native policy in the Union is what it is and no wonder that the native territories, one after the other, have been exploited for labour, all to the detriment of the natives, so much so that they are to-day nothing else but heterogeneous or compound-like communities.

> The same process will, to my mind, happen here. Anyway, I am [glad] that I will be out of it all by the time Ovamboland follows the fate of the Transkei, etc., whose native tribesmen and their cousins are roaming the streets and the most select residential areas of our foremost cities, interfering with our women folk, robbing, plundering and murdering more or less to their heart's content, instead of living in and developing their own tribal areas. Gemmil [a WNLA manager] would do South Africa a wonderful turn if he could and would recruit these loafers instead of following his policy of depleting healthy tribal areas of all its men folk, areas where the natives live contented and happy and where they show the utmost respect for Europeans.[65]

These sentences show all the schizophrenia at work in the mandate time's native administration, a schizophrenia perhaps most visible in Hahn's regiment in Ovamboland. Detribalization, modernization and urbanization are seen as detrimental to 'the native'; he can only lose his roots and the bucolic village environment in which he happily lives under the rule of patriarchic headmen. White man's modernity has to be kept as far from the reserves as possible – just as the natives have to be kept from his towns. This goes well together with a feudal and patriarchic view on power that many interwar colonial officers share, from Robert Delavignette in French Sudan to Cocky Hahn in Ovamboland.[66]

This attitude towards native life is, of course, deeply political in itself. Mahmood Mamdani (1996) has shown how the doctrine behind it, the idea of an insurmountable principle difference between native and European social and political organization, has shaped colonial policy from British indirect rule to South African homelands, and how

---

[65]   NAN A 450, Letter Hahn to Cope, 13 October 1945.
[66]   Delavignette's anti-modernistic description of the colonial officer's personal rule in "Les vrais chefs de l'Empire" (1939) reads like an exposition of Hahn's principles of government, perhaps in a slightly more aristocratic, old-world form. He surely shares his holistic view of government and his contempt for bureaucrats no longer connected to the realities on the ground.

its legacy continues to haunt African politics today. But coupled with a practical policy that puts most of its energy into the promotion of migrant work in the modern sector, the attitude behind Hahn's letter becomes outright schizophrenic. He was part and parcel of the colonial government's attempt to harvest native labor, while trying to prevent social change in the areas the workers lived in. This impossible undertaking became the curse of Southern African politics in the twentieth century. It lay at the heart of segregation and of apartheid, and its inevitable demise finally led to the end of white rule in Southern Africa.

Hahn's letter to Cope was written at a time when the contradictions of this policy had become clearly visible. The years after 1948 formed the junction between an older policy of indirect rule that tried to close its eyes against the changes brought by the integration into the colonial economy, and the newer apartheid regime, which acknowledged these changes and tried to control them through a modernistic, bureaucratic administration. In Ovamboland, the transition came in steps marked by the appointment of new Native Commissioners. Hahn, and to a lesser degree Eedes, were of the old colonial school, steeped in the intricacies of local politics and 'custom', and suspicious of too much bureaucratic control of their fiefs. Bruwer Blignaut, Eedes' successor, was assigned to the post in July 1954 due to his political connections and without prior experience in the area. He seems to have seen it as a step to higher office in the capital, a transitional phase in his bureaucratic life rather than the possibility to carve out his own realm. After not even a year, he succeeded H. J. Allen as Chief Native Commissioner in Windhoek.[67] He was succeeded by a number of short-term Commissioners: M.C. Crossman (eighteen months, 1955–1956), J.F. Strydom (two years, 1956–1958), C.B. Richter (two years, 1958–1960), M.S.C. Backer from 1960 to 1965 and F.A. du Preez from 1965 to 1968, when the post was abolished with the proclamation of 'self-governing' Ovamboland.

The regulation of trading stores, in itself only a tiny facet of the administrative history of northern Namibia, is a prism through which the contradictory interests blended into colonial domination become clearly visible. In 1924, the diamond industry was so important for the territory that the administration's skepticism towards European trade could be swept aside by the mere assumption that a store would help recruiting. When the Chamber of Commerce complained in 1930 that the trade concession had not been

---

[67]   Bruwer Blignaut had come to South West Africa in 1948 as organizer of the South West African contribution to the celebrations of the tercentenary of van Riebeeck's arrival at the Cape. In that capacity, he worked closely with the Administrator and had contacts to the Governor General and Prime Minister Malan. Afterwards, he became regional labor commissioner in Pietersburg in Transvaal (Bruwer 1965). His labor and public works background was one of the major reasons he was given the post in Ovamboland – although one informant claimed his broederbond membership was even more important.

advertised, "the Chairman replied that the grant of trading rights in Ovamboland was a matter of policy, and that the interests of the Consolidated Diamond Mines were also the interests of the Administration."[68] This had changed by the mid-1930s, when the great depression had taken away the material basis of CDM's arrogance and Karakul farming and the northern mines had become the new mainstays of the territory's economy. Freed from economic pressure, the administration once more focused on preventing exploitation, injustices and possible unrest. It would be unfair to see this as merely instrumental or strategic. In the departmental balance of power, the Native Affairs Department had to represent the interests of 'the Natives', and the people involved often took this seriously. In 1938, for example, both Hahn and the Additional Native Commissioner charged with reporting on the trading stores were very critical towards OTC. It is sometimes difficult to decide whether they were concerned with the injustice, or simply disliked businesspeople interfering with their authority by sidestepping regulations, but instead of siding with their white colleagues and neighbors, they defended what they saw as native interest.

After 1943, when SWANLA represented the entirety of white employers, its leeway became again much wider. SWANLA's aims were not always synonymous with the administration's interests, but the concern was much more detached from the particularistic interests SLO had represented, and its lobbying at least had an inclusive agenda of white interest.

In addition to these institutional attitudes, personal ties played an important role, as well. While the brothers-in-law Hahn and Cope did not always see eye to eye (local gossip has it that the discord was caused by the wives, the two sisters nées Fogarty, rather than the men), they still were close to each other, and when Cope represented SWANLA instead of the SLO, they got along rather well. The same cannot be said for Eedes and Cope, who did not get along with each other at all and certainly resented each decision the other made. On a higher level, NLO chairman (and later SWANLA manager) Charles Gordon Courtney-Clarke was the nephew of Francis Priestley Courtney-Clarke, who had served as Secretary for South West Africa (and ex officio Chief Native Commissioner) in the 1920s and 1930s and was one of the most influential figures in the administration in Windhoek. Many other personal ties and animosities played together to influence local politics, but most of them are lost between the lines of archival paperwork.

Two ideological friction lines emerge more clearly from the surviving documents. One is the conflict between the doctrine of free trade and the imperatives of the reserve policy, the second the clash between the advocacy for local interests and for interests of whites in the Police Zone.

---

[68] SWAA 1056 135/22, Minutes of Executive Committee Meeting 6 May 1930.

In the 1930s and 1940s, the central government in Windhoek stood by and large in favor of a liberal policy of free trade, but this policy rarely extended to trade between black and white. The South African example had shown the dangers of free trade between systematically unequal partners, and various actors in the Department of Native Affairs had come to see traders as their professional enemies. Traders, as a class, were regarded as interested in quick profits rather than in stability or justice, and the natives had to be protected against their lack of scruples. The Native Commissioners in Ovamboland, Hahn in particular, were often adamant in their rejection of free trade in favor of state control over traders. In 1929, Hahn did not want to grant Portuguese traders permission to buy supplies at the OTC stores. He feared that, once in the country, they would trade with natives and drain the country of cash. The Secretary for South West Africa politely rejected Hahn's misgivings, hoped that more frequent visits of Portuguese traders would "open up trade" and stated that "we don't want to do anything in restraint of trade unless it is absolutely necessary."[69]

Similar declarations frequently occur in the official correspondence. They were never really put into practice in Ovamboland, but the rhetoric of free trade has to be taken into account for assessing the administration's attitude towards the monopoly stores and, later, towards native traders. Free trade was indeed the norm, and OTC's and SWANLA's trade monopoly always remained an anomaly linked to special circumstances which made free trade between Europeans and Africans undesirable in the eyes of the administration – mostly the imperatives of recruiting and of colonial control. The monopoly granted to certain traders was necessary, but it resulted in dangers. Where price policies could not be regulated through the free market, as the administration had abolished it, administrative control had to step in.[70]

When the first Africans started to open stores in Ovamboland, they were not protected against competition by any monopoly. Consequently, rules of free trade applied to them, and they were barely supervised by the state. This explains the apparent paradox that, as will be seen in the next chapter, a colonial government representing white interests was much more tolerant towards African than towards European traders in Ovamboland.

As the administration wished to control traders, it saw SWANLA as the lesser evil when compared to a purely private enterprise. OTC had been granted a licence in 1924 as

---

[69]   SWAA 1057 135/22, Letter Secretary to NC Ovamboland, 17 October 1929.
[70]   This was clearly seen by the Additional Native Commissioner who reported on OTC in 1938. He stated that the administration only had the right to inquire into the company's pricing policy under the special licence conditions applicable in Ovamboland; in the Police Zone, government would not have any justification to interfere with a trading store's books. NAN SWAA 1057 135-22/1, Trading in Ovamboland: Ondonga Trading Company, Limited (23 September 1938).

part of the recruiting scheme. When the firm turned out to be more and more connected to the private agenda of a single company, CDM, the administration's attitude towards it changed, and Beersmann was granted a licence in an attempt to soften the monopoly. But free competition did not last long when SWANLA promised better control and enough neutrality. Hahn even claimed that free competition would inevitably lead to the exploitation of the natives – a remark favored with a marginal question mark by the Chief Native Commissioner. Hahn felt that "SWANLA, being a recruiting organisation closely associated with the general policy of the Administration and firmly established in Ovamboland, could be controlled much more effectively by the Administration than could a private concern." This argument was again and again repeated by Hahn and Eedes and prevailed over the free trade concerns of his superiors.

But Hahn's ideal was not the monopoly store run by a recruiting agency. He would have preferred a co-operative store run by the Tribal Trust Funds, and advertised this idea at every occasion since the mid-1930s. "To my mind the ideal system of trading in Ovamboland would be the establishment of two or three co-operative stores conducted in the interests of the native tribal Trust Funds."[71] This idea sounds surprisingly progressive, but it fits in well with Hahn's ideas about native self-administration under European supervision, and with his scepticism towards industrial modernisation.

In 1938, the suggestion was simply ignored by his superiors, but when Beersmann's licence had to be reassigned in 1947, it had already taken root with the Chief Native Commissioner. When Eedes suggested granting the licence to SWANLA, the Chief Native Commissioner Allen commented in the margin: "W[oul]d prefer that Trust Fund take over provided a suitable person can be found to install as manager. Another reason why I do not favour SWANLA is that I do not think we should let them get too big a hold in the Northern Territories in case we want to terminate them recruiting [..] at any time."[72] At the same time, the Oukwanyama councillor headmen argued against a further SWANLA store. Instead, they wanted to open stores run by a European manager for the Trust Funds in Okalongo and Osandi or in the Oshivanda area.[73]

Eedes did not like the idea of private trading in his area, be it by Africans or Europeans. He told the headmen off rather curtly. His reply to the Chief Native Commissioner was more courteous, but no less categorical: "There is no Native in Ovamboland who is capable at present of conducting a Trading Strore on his own behalf, or on behalf of the Trust Funds. The recommendation that the existing South West Africa Native Labour

[71]   NAN SWAA 135/22, Letter NC Hahn to CNC, 27 August 1945.
[72]   NAN SWAA 135/22, Letter NC Eedes an CNC 23 May 1947, marginal comments by CNC.
[73]   NAN NAO 63 17/1, Letters ANC Holdt to NC, 14 October 1947 and 13 November 1947. See also Chapter 3.

Association's stores should be taken over, and conducted by Natives on behalf of the Trust Funds is an excellent one, and will receive the full support of all Native Commissioners, when they are satisfied that the Natives have reached the stage when they will be capable of conducting business concerns. It is not recommended that the present position, under which the South West Africa Native Labour Association conducts trading operations under the supervision of this office, be disturbed in the meantime."[74]

This line was adopted as a compromise when SWANLA was granted the new licence. In a meeting with high Native Affairs officials, SWANLA managers were told that "trading rights in Native areas are ultimately the "perks" of the Natives". "When Natives with the necessary capital and experience" would eventually emerge, these trading rights would be passed on to them.[75]

At the time of this meeting, the first African-owned store in Ovamboland had already opened and closed down, and a number of men and women were thinking hard about establishing their own stores. SWANLA, however, continued to operate its fours stores in Ovamboland until the company was dismantled after the strikes in 1972. The stores were then taken over by the parastatal Bantu Investment Corporation. In the 25 years between the two dates, an unprecedented boom in local trade transformed Ovamboland's economic, social and political landscape.

---

[74] NAN NAO 63 17/1, Letter NC to ANC Holdt, 15.November 1947; NAN NAO 89 35/21, Letter NC to CNC, 23 August 1948.

[75] NAN SWAA 135/22, Handwritten memo of a meeting between the CNC, Add.NC, NC Okavango and NC Ovamboland and Mssrs. Vlok and Courtney-Clarke of SWANLA, 5/6 June 1947. The Administration's line of thinking did not change with the implementation of apartheid. In 1955, for example, Chief Native Commissioner Bruwer Blignaut wrote that "die handelsperseel egter later wél in die hande van nie-blankes oorgaan", but that "nog baie jare deur Blankes beheer sal moet word aangesien die besigheid sin en vernuf van die Ovambo nog lank op 'n baie lae peil sal bly" (NAN BAC 112 HN 5/2/3/7, Letter CNC to NC Ovamboland, 29 May 1955).

3 The first locally owned stores, 1937–1955

The pioneer: Simon Galoua in Ombalantu

Major Lyall French W. Trollope, who served as Acting Chief Native Commissioner in 1937/38, was not a timid man. Native Commissioner in Caprivi from 1939 to 1953, he was equally well known for his collection of butterflies as for arbitrary decisions – so much so that he had to take a precipitate leave in 1953 and spent his last years tending bar in Kasane Hotel in Chobe.[1] But when Simon Galoua from Uukwaluudhi applied for a trading licence in 1937, Trollope was reluctant to act while Native Commissioner Hahn was on leave: "The present application", he wrote to Hahn's replacement, "is so novel insofar as Ovamboland is concerned that I hesitate to make any recommendation and shall be glad if the matter can await Major Hahn's return."[2] It was indeed the first time that a 'native' had applied for a trading licence in the reserve, whose only two shops were operated by the Lüderitz Chamber of Mines and served labor migration – the exact opposite of local business development. The choice to grant or withhold the licence was a watershed decision about local development and the region's integration into the national – and, by extension, global – economy.

In the next forty years, basic attitudes of the administration towards development, modernization and self-reliance in the reserves and homelands find their expression in its changing policy towards 'native' traders. But while it is clear that trade was relevant, it is not always easy to predict how the lines in trade policy were drawn. One could suspect, for example, that the proponents of migrant labor would be skeptical against trade, which offered a local business alternative; but many found the stimulus shops gave to consumption more important than the loss of the few workers who could establish themselves at home. On the other hand, developmentalists in the reserve administration did not automatically promote trade. Some of them saw shops as unproductive and wanted to strengthen industrial development instead.

Major Hahn, when he returned from his leave a few months later, had a very clear opinion about the matter. For him, trade by 'natives' could only strengthen Ovamboland society and make it less dependent of industrial capitalism, which he saw as responsible for the major part of modernity's bad sides. He granted the licence, reported about the

---

[1] See Gewald forthcoming.
[2] SWAA 1056 135/22, Letter Acting CNC to Acting NC, 10 January 1938.

new shop a number of times in very positive terms and tried to protect it from the central bureaucracy.

Simon Galoua opened his store in Ovamboland in 1939 or 1940.[3] The shop did not survive the war, but it was the first forerunner of the astonishing business boom in the 1950s. Simon[4] came from Uukwaluudhi in Western Ovamboland. He seems to have worked on the diamond mines before being employed as local Police Constable in the staff of the Station Commander at Orange River Mouth (Oranjemund) in the 1930s.[5] In the late 1930s, he wanted to return to Ovamboland and establish a store with his savings. He had saved more than £100 in cash, which represents the total wages for about five years' work on the diamond mines, or three and a half years for a native constable in Ovamboland. So Simon was definitely well off. He probably spoke English and had been in close contact with representatives of the administration over a number of years. Neither the archives nor living memory tell much about him, but he seems to have been an early representative of the new elite whose members would, in later years, become typical candidates for establishing pioneer stores: literate and educated, used to wage labor and the money economy, deriving their status more from their success in the modern sector than from traditional legitimacy.

When Simon Galoua returned to Ovamboland to establish his shop, he, according to Hahn, "fell foul of chief Mulua" of Uukwaluudhi and was not able to open the store in his area of choice. (According to Chief Oswin Mukulu from Ombalantu, born in the 1920s and himself an important trader since the 1950s, Simon had been accused of witchcraft.[6]) In late 1938, Hahn reported that he "has for the time being disappeared and has not been

---

[3]   The first approval for opening a shop in Uukwaluudhi was given by the Chief Native Commissioner on 31 December 1937; just like the permission to open a shop in Ombalantu (by telegram on 3 August 1939), this was rather the authorisation for Hahn to allow his trading than an official licence necessary according to the Licence Consolidation Ordinance (No. 13 of 1935) and the Licence Regulations for Ovamboland (No. 148 of 1936). Simon Galous officially applied for a licence on 7 December 1940, and the licence Nr. 124884 dated 3/1/41 was issued to him by the Magistrate, Grootfontein. It is not quite clear when his shop really opened. In mid 1941, Hahn claimed that Simon Galoua only really opened his shop in early 1941 "due to the non-arrival of goods ordered by him". This seems to be in discord with other sources, and it might have been a cover-up for Simon's lateness in applying for a licence. All NAN NAO 25 17/2, Letter NC to CNC, 28 August 1941.

[4]   The sporadic use of the Christian name alone does not show any disrespect on my part, but conforms to the standard Oshiwambo use of the time. People were usually designated with their own and their father's name. Family names denoting patrilinear families only came into current use in the 1950s; usually, a senior male family member chose a family name, often the name of a respected forefather. Brothers thus often had different names.

[5]   NAN SWAA 1056 135/22, Letter Acting CNC to NC, 20 January 1938.

[6]   Interview Oswin Mukulu, Ombalantu, 17 October 2006.

heard of again."[7] Half a year later, he had moved to Ombalantu and requested permission from the Native Commissioner to open a store there.[8] Mrs. Jakobina Sheehama remembers that he sold pearl necklaces and other local jewellery in his shop. (After her moved away, she and her friends searched for remaining glass beads in the sand and indeed found some.)[9] But business was not very good and deteriorated with the outbreak of the war.[10] According to Mukulu, Roman Catholic missionaries at Anamulenge kept their parishioners from buying at his shop as he was not baptized.[11] In addition, Simon had severe supply problems. In the war economy, even the SWANLA stores had difficulties finding enough supplies, and transport to Ombalantu was difficult to organize. In December 1942, Hahn reported: "The small native store in the Ombalantu area […] has closed down. He found it impossible to obtain sufficient stock for sale."[12] Hahn's report for 1943 was laconic: "There are no native trading stores in this territory."[13] It seems that Simon Galoua later moved to Ukwandonga in Ongandjera, but I was not able to establish this with certainty. Today, a millet field covers the area where his shop and homestead used to be.

Simon Galoua opened the first store, but he was of course not the first 'native' to trade. In the first half of the twentieth century, trading goods no longer was the prerogative of chiefs. Everybody who had anything to offer engaged in trade from time to time. Returning migrant workers bought things they expected to barter on; cattle and small livestock were exchanged for all kinds of local and imported goods. Cattle trade between Oukwanyama and Angola was especially lively. Wealthy Oukwanyama cattle owners had long sporadically sold cattle to Portuguese traders in exchange for goods. But in the 1930s, the reverse cattle trade became even more important. Colonial taxes in Angola were high and relatively strictly enforced.[14] As cash was scarce, returning migrant laborers often found Angolans who were willing to sell cattle cheaply in order to pay their taxes. This, as Hahn reported, was much resented by the traditional cattle owning class in Oukwanyama, "especially Headmen and other natives who do not go South as labourers, as they are losing opportunities of acquiring the much sought after cattle."[15]

---

[7]   NAN NAO 20 11/1 Vol. 11 Annual Report 1938.

[8]   SWAA 1057 135/22 Telegram NC to CNC, 26 July 1939.

[9]   Interview with Mrs Jakobina Sheehama, 2 September 2012.

[10]   "In Ombalantu, native Simon Galoua carries on trade under licence but his is a very small concern. He informed me recently that he is not very satisfied with the business as the Ovambos seem to have very little ready cash. He is a quiet and respectable native." NAN A450 7 2/18 Annual Report 1941.

[11]   Interview Oswin Mukulu, Ombalantu, 17 October 2006.

[12]   NAN NAO 20 11/1 Vol. 15 Annual Report 1942.

[13]   NAN NAO 20 11/1 Vol. 15 Annual Report 1943.

[14]   Kreike 2004, 62 ff.

[15]   NAN NAO 20 11/1 Vol. 11 Annual Report 1938.

The resentment is a sign of a momentous shift in 20th century social history of Ovamboland. In late 19th century, headmen had used their privileged access to the colonial economy's new resources to increase their power. Colonial pacification and the chiefs' integration into the system of indirect rule had normalized and stabilized this power. The Chiefs had even managed to establish legitimate claims on a part of the wages of the migrant workers under their authority. But they did not go south to work themselves. Some sent their sons – who, in matrilinear Ovamboland, were not their heirs – to work, but in the 1940s, it would have been an inconceivable loss of dignity for a headman to work on the mines himself.

Headmen did not lose their status, but migrant labor and integration into a colonial society created a parallel system of elite formation. Its most important media were cash income and access to the new knowledge systems missions and colonial administration had brought, and the means to acquire those were migrant work, schooling and conversion. This helps explaining the continuing attraction migrant work had for young men. Their wages were low in real terms, but as cash was scarce at home, the marginal utility for returning workers was very high. Wages could be multiplied through bartering in goods one could obtain more cheaply with cash, and migrant labor offered a parallel way of obtaining status in one's own society. It was not a smooth way; working conditions were harsh, and the social environment in the mines and on the farms was characterized by demeaning racism and often by brutality. But between the 1930s and 1950s, young men willingly opted for migrant work in order to better their own situation.

Headmen soon felt the loss of their elite status' exclusivity, all the more so since the emerging new elites successfully competed with them for resources, and used their authority to hamper the upstarts' progress. They tried to extract 'taxes' or 'gifts' from returning migrant workers and attempted to cash in on their income in other ways. In 1948, for example, Uukanyama Senior Headmen decided to hold an *efundula*, a puberty ceremony that was only held sporadically in years of good harvests. Migrant workers wrote to Eedes asking him to interfere, as the bad crops that year made it impossible to hold the feast on the land's resources alone. They feared that a large part of their income would be needed if the ceremony were to be held in this year.[16]

The Native Commissione was torn between two alliances. In such small matters, Hahn usually chose to intervene on the workers' behalf, as long as they showed that "utmost respect to the white man" he took for his due. He did not mind to recall his authority to the headmen, and he liked to appease any workers' unrest as early as possible. But in

---

[16] NAN NAO 26 19/3, Letters Thomas Fulanita and Helumani Ndafita to NC Eedes, 5 May and 4 May 1948.

general, the administration had decided early on to put their weight behind the chiefs, and strengthened their position by an unquestioning acceptance of 'customary payments' by the workers. This had the further advantage that the administration could call on the chiefs to intervene with letters or emissaries when strikes or labor unrest broke out on the mines, which they frequently did quite successfully.[17] In the 1940s, the administration introduced wages to Chiefs and principal Headmen payable out of the Tribal Trust Funds in order to allow "our Chiefs" "to become men of standing".[18]

So Simon Galoua's shop was opened in a situation where the emergence of a new elite had begun to change local society, and the trouble he ran into both in Uukwaluudhi and Ombalantu are probably linked to his status as a member of that new social group. His real innovation was not to use his wages to start trading, but to do so professionally and officially: to become a trader. The concept of distinct professions had barely existed in pre-colonial Ovamboland. Some artisans – mainly smiths, woodcarvers and potters – had specialized on a craft, but they had usually done so as part of a social group defined by birth and upbringing, and mostly only as a sideline to agriculture.

In the colonial economy into which young men were integrated through migrant labor, work was seen as a specialized tasked integrated in a system of division of labor. In the Police Zone, working in that sense meant to be dependent of a master and employed to do work one could not choose. When Simon Galous decided to become a trader in Ovamboland, he established the fourth 'modern' profession there – after the catechist, the teacher and the administrative clerk. We will later see that these four professions were very close to each other, and that many traders had worked in one or the other for some time. But among them, only the trader had an independent, self-employed profession in the modern sector.

Of course we do not know whether Simon planned, let alone succeeded, to specialize in trade alone. He probably had fields and cattle and might have worked in other professions, as well. But the fact that he left his police employment, used his considerable savings to establish himself and even applied for an official licence are strong indicators that he took trade very seriously. There might, of course, have been others like him who opened trading stores in the same era, but I could not find any traces of them in the archives or oral sources.

---

[17] Some instances are found in NAN SWAA 2083 and 2084, file A 460/20, Chiefs & Headmen.

[18] See NAN SWAA 2083, A460/20, Letter NC Runtu to NC Eedes, 15 October 1948. Seethe entire file for the discussions, and Government Notice 86 of 1948 for the result. Individual wages for headmen had experimentally been introduced some years earlier, the earliest being the monthly £2 paid to Andreas Shindjoba, Secretary of the Oukwanyama Council, from March 1939.

Population growth and settlement expansion after 1927

Economic changes and the competition between different elites were not the only background we have to be aware of in order to understand the emergence of new shops in the area. Settlement patterns in South West African Ovamboland changed dramatically between 1925, when the first store opened in Ovamboland, and 1952, when the first wave of successful store openings by locals started. Migration and population growth led to the cultivation of formerly barren lands and to the settlement of the formerly open spaces between the Oshiwambo speaking groups.

In the 19th century, settlement areas in Ovamboland were separated by large stretches of uninhabited wilderness in which only seasonal cattle posts existed.[19] When, after World War I, colonial administration started to matter in everyday life, the differences in taxation, forced labor and indirect rule made life harder in Angola than in South West Africa. Headmen, who had most contacts with the administration and were often used by the Angolan administration as a lever to guarantee tax payments, felt these changes most keenly.

An ambiguity in the 1886 border demarcation treaty between Portugal and Germany had left room for dispute as to the exact location of the border between Angola and South West Africa. A disagreement about the exact waterfall on the Kunene from which the boundary line should run due east until it reached the Zambesi resulted in two different lines, the Portuguese line being about eleven kilometers south of the German (and later English) one. The stretch of land between the lines, eleven kilometers wide and several hundred kilometers long, was declared a co-administered neutral zone in 1915. Long negotiations about the boundary finally resulted in an agreement in 1920, which was ratified in 1926 and declared the neutral zone to be Angolan territory. The new boundary was demarcated in 1927 and the office of the Assistant Native Commissioner for Oukwanyama moved from Namakunde (now in Angola) to Oshikango.

In an attempt to escape from Portuguese rule, many individuals and entire villages had relocated to the neutral zone between 1915 and 1926. After 1927, many moved on into South West Africa, together with new arrivals from Angola. Loeb (1962, 36ff.) speaks of more than 40.000 Oukwanyama who moved to South West Africa between the wars. Hahn and his administration welcomed the new arrivals, even if they officially denied any attempts to induce people to move.

Population density and water scarcity made it impossible for most of the new arrivals to settle in existing villages. Instead, the settlement areas were extended into the wilderness. Settlers invested a large amount of hard labor to create the necessary water infra-

---

[19] For a more detailed discussion of the following points with abundant references see Kreike 2004 and Dobler 2008.

structure in the wilderness and break up new areas for cultivation. By the late 1940s, the formerly separated populated cores had grown into a continuous settlement area covering the entire central Ovamboland.

In this process, social structures were remoulded. New settlements at the margins of the local polities gave room for individual advancement, and the need to start a new life made new ideas more interesting. Both Christianity and migrant labor profited from the new settlements, in which the search for spiritual security played as important a role as the search for outside resources to invest in agriculture. But the new settlements were integrated into the old system of political domination. As land had to be granted by local headmen, new arrivals were integrated into the old power hierarchy, and their presence crucially expanded the resources of patronage for the headmen. Border disputes evolving around the formerly uninhabited areas led to a clear demarcation of the tribal boundaries and a geographical stabilization of the chiefs' and headmen's rule. This played into the hands of the colonial administration, which could act as an arbitrator and fortify its system of indirect rule by stabilizing the chiefs' powers.

All in all, the break-up and rearrangement of Ovamboland society induced by the massive migration from Angola recast it into an evenly and densely populated, more homogenous and more easily governable entity. The divisions between the single polities transformed from natural borders into political boundaries, and the frontier zones between them were closed down. Gradually, the whole area grew into a social and political unit with a shared identity formed by the realities of reserve life. The chiefs and headmen who formerly had been confined to their territories by ritual sanctions now started to visit each other and to travel south to the Police Zone.[20] This might seem a minor change, but it shows the increasing integration of Ovamboland and was the first step towards the joint administration of Ovamboland by tribal representatives that would become reality with the administrative reforms in 1968. Ovamboland in 1950 already was a much more homogenous social space than it had been in 1920. Without this transformation, the social and political changes in the 1950s would have been much less rapid, and probably less radical as well.

---

[20]   The first such visit was probably the voyage of Ondonga Chief Kambonde to the Police Zone. Accompanied by Eedes and his wife, Kambonde visited Swakopmund, Walvis Bay, Lüderitz, Keetmanshoop and Usakos in 1948. Visits to the Oukwanyama area in 1953 and again to Windhoek in 1954 followed. The visit to Oukwanyama, where he met with headman Nehemia Shoovaleka, was only reported because Kambonde illegally purchased wine and brandy from Angola for his daughter's wedding. In his statement, Nehemia writes about "one thing more I want to metion: I reminded Kambonde about the old Ondonga custom according to which the Chief does not visit other tribes and asked him if he was breaking the custom. Kambonde replied that he was not concerned with the old customs – they are merely superstitions." (All NAN NAO 105 51/2)

The first wave of new traders, 1951–55

Locally owned village stores were one indicator, and simultaneously one of the most important media, of the social change that followed the consolidation after the massive population movements of the interwar years. They formed the material basis of a new elite, became the cores of new village clusters and brought global goods into the most remote villages. But their development seems to have been disrupted by World War II. After Simon Galoua closed down his shop in 1942, no further attempts to open private stores have left traces in the archives until 1951. The only application to open a store was made in 1947 by the Oukwanyama Council of Headmen. As already described in the last chapter, the headmen's "hearts were not happy" that SWANLA was allowed to take over Beersmann's store. They looked for alternatives to SWANLA's monopoly and applied for permission to open their own store for the Tribal Trust Fund. This idea (which might or might not have been brought up by the Assistant Native Commissioner Holdt, who was strongly in favor of the idea) looked like the ideal solution to them. It would have made cheaper goods available to themselves and to their subjects, and it would have allowed them to regain a part of their old control over trade goods from the new elite of migrant workers.

The Chief Native Commissioner liked the idea that had often been suggested to his office by Hahn, but, as already mentioned above, Harold Eedes put his foot down without consulting his superiors. He let the headmen be told "that I am unable to consider their application at present, as the type of store they ask for would merely be a replica of Swanla, except that the profits, if any, would go to the Trust Fund, which is not in need of funds." Trade by the Trust Fund would, in his opinion, blur the line between government and a commercial undertaking, and he did not consider the headmen competent enough to oversee a business. He tried to attenuate his letter by adding: "The Oukwanyama headmen could be told that the Trust Funds will conduct Trading Stores in Ovamboland when the right time arrives, and that individual Natives will be given the right to trade on their own behalf when they are competent to do so. The whole subject will be discussed with the Chiefs and Headmen of Ovamboland later."[21]

This time came when, in 1951, a number of individuals applied for the authorization to open stores. The first application was made by Teofilus Mafita Tueumuna. He asked the Native Commissioner to allow his wife, Helena Tueumuna, to open a store in Ondobe, and his brother, Moses Tueumuna, to open a kafee (a small eating place) in Oshikango.[22] Teofilus Tueumuna was a teacher at Olukonda Finnish mission school in Ondonga, only

---

21   NAN NAO 63 17/1, Letter NC to ANC Holdt, 15.November 1947.
22   NAN NAO 64 17/7, Letter Teofilus Tueumuna to NC Eedes, 3 February 1951.

a few kilometers from the Native Commissioner's residence. He probably knew Eedes and acted as middleman for his brother and wife.

As both Ondobe and Oshikango are in Oukwanyama, Eedes asked the Assistant Native Commissioner W.H. Olivier to discuss the matter with the Oukwanyama Council of Headmen. Olivier brought the matter before the meeting on 10 April 1951. I will cite his minutes in full:

> Headmen Johannes and Nehemia expressed themselves not in favour of granting trading privileges to any natives, stating that if the time was not ripe for the Tribal Trust Fund to trade, with a European manager in charge, then the time was also not ripe for individual natives to trade. The other headmen agree with this point of view.
>
> ANC draws attention of meeting to the fact that the Tribal Trust Fund is not a business undertaking and that much thought will have to be given to the advisability of allowing the Tribal Trust Fund to engage in trading activities. Trading by individuals is however quite a different proposition. Suggests that thought be given to the consideration of such application on its merits with special reference to the following:
>
> 1. Suitability: Has the applicant the confidence of the people and will he receive the necessary support?
>
> 2. Ability: Is the applicant sufficiently educated to run a business, to order merchandise and keep the necessary books of account.
>
> 3. Financial Stability: Has the applicant sufficient cash to purchase the necessary stock and conduct the business on proper lines.
>
> 4. Building and Locality: is the proposed building suitable for trading purposes and what is proximity to nearest existing stores. Will the needs of the people be better served by the opening of such a business.
>
> 5. Is applicant fully aware of the transport difficulties in Ovamboland. Does he realize that, as a small trader, his nett profit may be negligible when selling at competitive prices in order to keep his custom.
>
> Matter postponed to give members opportunity for discussion among themselves during the luncheon adjournment.
>
> On resumption, Headman Johannes expressed Council's acceptance of the suggestions put forward by A.N.C. All members unanimously agree with Headman Vilho's suggestion that all applications be first investigated by A.N.C. and then brought before Council.[23]

The minutes are a good illustration of the role government representatives played in 'tribal self government' in Ovamboland. Officially, all decisions were taken by headmen as representatives of their people, but the outcome of their decisions was heavily influenced by

---

[23] NAN NAO 64 17/7, Minutes of Oukwanyama Council of Headmen, 10 April 1951.

the Native Commissioner.[24] Unsurprisingly, the headmen did not like the idea of shops run by members of the emerging new elite, and used the opportunity to remind the administration of their own claims on controlling trade. After having given them the opportunity to voice their opposition, the Assistant Native Commissioner proceeded to tell them what they should decide, and the council adopted his opinion. The criteria he had developed in order to judge licence applications were officially endorsed by the headmen and became the guiding principles for further decisions.

The second criterion is perhaps the most important. It was merely meant to prevent business failure, but in practice, it restricted access to independent trade to literate applicants – which almost invariably meant Christian alumni of mission schools. If one adds the third and fifth criterion, financial resources and awareness of transport difficulties, licences are virtually confined to applicants of the new elite: to Christians sufficiently educated to keep books and endowed with a start capital and a knowledge of the transport system that could only come from migrant work.

This local regulation defined the outlines of the application process, but Eedes still needed the authorization of his superiors. He wrote to the Chief Native Commissioner in June 1951, arguing that "as the Natives are not required to pay wheels tax, arms licences etc., there is no reason why they should be called upon to pay trading licences". His recommendation was that "I be authorized to allow certain approved Natives to start small concerns such as butcheries, cafes and small stores, etc., etc., without having to pay any fee or establish any substantial building."[25]

The central administration took its time answering. Only in August 1952, The Chief Native Commissioner submitted a memorandum to the Administrator. "It is our policy to encourage Natives to trade in their own areas and I therefore recommend the Native Commissioner's proposal for favorable consideration. The Natives whom he has in mind will not be in a financial position to pay a licence fee of £8 or to build substantial buildings. I think the matter could be left to the Native Commissioner to regulate in consultation with the tribal leaders, i.e. the Chiefs and Councils of Headmen." The Executive Committee agreed to the proposition.[26] Trading was now officially allowed to 'natives' in

---

[24] In 1947, Eedes had unwittingly summed up the principle in a confidential letter to the Secretary about Ondonga King Kambonde: "It seems to me that if the standard of the Ondonga Natives is to be raised, and if the country is to be developed, it will be necessary for the Chief to agree to eliminate all ancient unnecessary customs which retard the progress of his subjects. If the Chief fails to do this, or is incapable of doing so, it will be necessary to depose him, and all Headmen who obstruct progress and development." (NAN NAO 71, 31/7, Letter NC to Secretary, 21 April 1947).

[25] NAN NAO 64 17/7, Letter NC to CNC, 9 June 1951.

[26] NAN NAO 64 17/7, Letter CNC to NC, 8 August 1952. The resolution passed by the Executive Committee laconically took up the CNC's words in the new official language Afrikaans: "Besluit: dat die saak

Ovamboland, subject only to authorization by the Native Commissioner after consultation of the local Chief or Council of Headmen.

In the meantime, the Native Commissioner had received three further applications. Petrus Ekandjo from Ondjodjo asked Chief Kambonde for authorization to make bread and sell it in the Ondjodjo area in May 1951, who referred the query to Eedes. Taimi Abraham from Oshitayi applied for authorization to import £20 worth of mealie meal from southern Namibia in order to sell it during a period of drought in April 1952; and one month later, Salom Zakeus asked to be allowed to open a kafee in Ondjodjo "for the men who come back from the South. They don't have anything to eat when they come here, and I will gladly supply them."[27] To all three applications, Eedes had to answer that the question was still being considered by the Administration. Only in July 1952 could he finally sent for them by special messenger and inform them that they could open their stores or eating-places.

All further applications had to pass to the respective Chief first, who then forwarded them to the Native Commissioner, who granted the official approval.[28] The following list gives the information I could find about the shops that opened before 1955 and their owners:

Helena Tueumuna, Oshitayi, wife of Teofilus Mafita (or Petrus) Tueumuna, a teacher at Olukonda mission school. She first applied for authorization in February 1951 and opened a small shop in October 1952 at her house in Oshitayi, in one of the three rooms of a modern-style brick building. The Oukwanyama Council of Headmen estimated she would start with around 80 clients there. Her husband planned to help her with book-keeping and with ordering goods from Metje & Ziegler in Lüderitz, and she wanted to bring the goods from the bus stop in Ondangwa to Oshitayi by donkey cart. She had a capital of £55 in mid-1951, which was continuously increased by savings from her husband's salary. She planned to buy a counter, a balance and a shelf as soon as her application was granted.

Moses Tueumuna, Oshikango. He asked to be allowed to open a kafee near Oshikango in February 1951 and sold meals, bread and meat obtained from slaughtering his own stock from 1952. He had a capital of £63 and wanted to erect a new building for his

an die Naturelle Kommissaris oorgelaat word om dit te reguleer, in oorleg met die stamleiers."
27 NAN NAO 64 17/7, Letter Chief Kambonde to NC, 12 May 1951; Letter Taimi Abraham to NC, 12 April 1952; Letter Salomon Zakeus, 3 June 1952 (Original in Afrikaans).
28 The NC forwarded the first applications to the CNC for approval, but in 1955, the latter remarked that no further approvals were necessary, as the authority lay with the NC (NAN SWAA 1057 135/22, Letter NC to CNC 31 January 1955, handwritten marginal note by the CNC).

kafee, which he felt would meet a great demand in Oshikango. He had almost no schooling but felt that he did not need education for this line of business.[29]

Petrus Ekandjo, Ondjodjo. Applied for a baker's licence in May 1951, but had left Ovamboland to work in South Africa by the time the application was granted in mid-1952.[30]

Taimi Abraham, Oshitayi. She was the wife of Pastor Johannes Iitope from Oshitayi Finnish Mission station. When Eedes informed the applicants in July 1952, she was in the Police Zone on a visiting pass – in itself a rare thing for a woman at the time. On her return in October 1952, she opened a store "for selling the following articles: Ovambo cloths, mealie meal, sugar, sweets, soaps, cottons, bread and other articles" in Oshitayi.[31] She became a rather successful trader and was mentioned in the Native Commissioner's 1957 annual report as making an annual profit of £100. Her son Cleophas Johannes started an important religious revival movement as a young man in 1952.[32]

Salom Zakeus (also called Mbundu Salom or Simon Zacheus), Ondjodjo. Applied in May 1952 and probably opened in early 1953. The kafee was run by his wife and situated near the SWANLA compound and the railway bus stop. Sold bread for 1 shilling per loaf, cakes for 6d, coffee for 6d, hot meals for 1 shilling in 1953. Sold lemonade which he ordered in the police zone from October 1954.[33]

Absalom Nathanael, Ondangwa. He wanted to establish a rest house at Ondjodjo and sell bread and coffee. Kambonde was in favor of the application, but Eedes turned it down as Nathanael was employed by his own office and "cannot undertake business while in the employ of the Administration".[34]

Ndjau Mandel, Mashaka (Ondonga). Baker. In business in 1953. 1/- per loaf, 6 d per cake.

---

[29] NAN NAO 64 17/7, Letter ANC to NC, 16 May 1951 (original in Afrikaans). Olivier relates the information he supplied to the Council of Headmen. The council "felt that applicants should be given a chance" and recommended approval. – "Donkey cart" is my interpretation of skotskar, which might also be drawn by oxen.

[30] NAN NAO 64 17/7, Notice [Absalom?] Nathanael (office employee) to NC, 5 July 1952.

[31] NAN NAO 64 17/7, Letter Tribal Secretary Uandonga to NC, 29.10.1952.

[32] NAN OVE (2) 9/4/4/369, Storage Box 46: Licence Taimi Abraham, mother of Kleopas Johannes; Olivier 1961, 384 for the annual report. Johannes Iitope was ordained as a pastor in 1937, in the second group of ordinations of local Lutheran pastors after the first in 1925 (Löytty 1971, 152). McKittrick 2002, 245–264 extensively covers the revival movement Epapudhuko, which quickly spread all over Ovamboland after the young Cleophas Johannes had started it on his return from a mission school in South Africa. – One Kleopas Johannes, teacher, was held in detention in 1985 as a SWAPO activist. I suspect it was the same man, but could not establish this with certainty. (Dateline Namibia 1, 1986).

[33] NAN NAO 64 17/7, Letter Salomon Zakeus, 3 June 1952; Undated business register (probably late 1953); Business certificate by Office NC, 22 October 1954.

[34] NAN NAO 64 17/7, Letter Chief Kambonde to NC, 11 November 1952; Letter Absalom Nathaniel to NC, 15 November 1952, and marginal notes by Eedes.

Andjelino Dumbaka, Mashaka (Ondonga). Baker and Meals. In business in 1953. 1/- per loaf, 6d per cake, 1/- meat pie.

Temus Abet, Ondangwa. Baker. In business in 1953. Bread 1/-.[35]

Festus Muashindanga (also called Emuasi Ndanga). No further information about any business, other than that he had an account with Wecke & Voigts in Grootfontein and ordered two bags of sugar in October 1954.[36]

Kalolina Mbekele, Onamunama (Oukwanyama). Unspecified business, opened in 1954. Had a capital of £250.[37]

Joel David, Odibo (Oukwanyama). General store, applied for licence in November 1954 with a capital of £200 – see detailed biography in Chapter 5.

Alfeus Hamukoto, Ohangwena (Oukwanyama). Applied for licence in January 1955. Kafee, sold bread and meat. The business was close to the new tribal office which was visited by many people from all of Oukwanyama. See detailed biography in Chapter 5.[38]

This short enumeration probably does not appeal much to most readers outside Ovamboland. I include it for two reasons. First, every person on the list has started an innovation from scratch, seeking for a new way to earn a living in a changed and changing social environment. Some of them were successful, others had to close down after a few years, but each and every one was responsible for establishing a new social and economic reality. We know much less about their shops then we know about the closely watched SWANLA stores, but they certainly were the greater innovators.

Secondly, even from the few facts we can gather from the archives and the memory of people who knew these traders, some general patterns emerge. The pattern that meets the eye first is not surprising: almost all traders had links to mission education, to the colonial government or the Churches and to migrant work. Shops were an innovation that depended on the colonial cash economy, both in the underlying concepts and in the practical necessities. The idea to open a store came from practical knowledge of stores, be it SWANLA stores in Ovamboland or shops in the police zone. The cash necessary to start a business invariably was earned by migrant work, or, for some successful few, by paid work for European institutions in Ovamboland. The skills necessary to order goods

---

35   All three NAN NAO 64 17/7, Undated business register (probably late 1953). Bakeries usually did not own ovens even in the 1970s. Fire was made in a two feet deep hole in the sand; when the heat was sufficient, the wood was replaced by the loaves of bread and a metal cover placed over the hole; the bread baked in around 30 minutes (Interview Mano Haindungo, Outapi, 6 October 2006).

36   NAN NAO 64 17/7, Letter Wecke & Voigts Grootfontein to NC, 5 October 1954, and answer, 23 October 1954.

37   NAN NAO 64 17/7, Letter ANC to NC, 9 July 1954.

38   For both NAN NAO 64 17/7, Letters ANC to NC 17 December 1954 and 14 January 1955.

in the Police Zone had been acquired at mission schools and while working in the south; the contacts and social skills to ask the Native Commissioner for authorization had often come from close contact with the administration. No chief or headman applied for a licence to open a private store in the 1950s; the headmen were still powerful and wealthy enough not to need a trade of their own.[39] Three of the twelve early store owners were women, and at least one further store was run by the owner's wife.

All new stores were opened either in Ondonga or in Oukwanyama – not only the largest polities, but also homes to most mission stations, government posts and migrant workers. Almost all shops in fact clustered around the new centers of power, places people had reason to travel to. This is most obvious for Ondjodjo, where all migrant workers and a good number of others passed through, but it equally holds for Oshikango (seat of the Assistant Native Commissioner), Ohangwena (seat of the Traditional Authority for Oukwanyama since 1949), Odibo, Onamunama and Oshitayi (Anglican and Finnish Mission).

Why Stores?

These commonalities describe the social milieu from which the new store owners came, but they offer no answer to what is perhaps the most important question: why did all these dynamic members of an emerging new elite open stores – and not workshops, small manufactures or commercial farms? The trend had far-reaching consequences, as it put Ovamboland on a distinct development path which still shapes today's economy: not production, but a combination of dependent labor and distribution became the paramount mode of integration into the world economy.

The creativity, energy and material resources invested by the new elite could indeed have created a sustainable manufacturing sector from the grassroots level, if structural circumstances and political regulation had not pushed their initiative into trade. The early traders' choices established a pattern others followed, and they influenced structural conditions so that following the pattern became the logical choice for their successors.

Migrant labor and its consequences for structural underdevelopment in Southern Africa have often been analyzed, but the links between migrant labor income to entrepreneurship in the modern sector have rarely found interest. The most notable exception is the discussion on a 'black bourgeoisie' in Southern Africa since the 1970s (see Introduction). In Ovamboland, migrant labor provided the starting capital for traders and made

---

[39]   The only notable exception was Oswin Mukulu from Ombalantu, but by the time he opened his store, he was not yet the senior headman he later became.

trade lucrative, as wages earned in the industrial sector fostered demand. Trade, on the other hand, gave incentives for young men to look for work in the industrial sector. Far from providing *an alternative way of development*, trade provided *an alternative income within the same development path*. Its strong growth, as a consequence, reinforced the division of labour between the reserve and the industrial cores.

A number of political, social and economic factors combined to influence the new entrepreneurs' choice. First of all, no alternative model of economic success in the modern sector offered itself in the 'Native reserve' of Ovamboland. There was, of course, a tradition of crafts in the area, mainly iron- and woodworks, pottery and basket weaving. But instead of becoming part of a monetary economy, these crafts were slowly dying out.[40] Industrially manufactured imports had increasingly replaced local products since the late 19th century, and the remaining local production became more and more detached from the modern colonial economy. Locally used products – pots, hoes, knives, baskets, but also smoking pipes or walking sticks – were usually bartered for grain, not sold for cash. In the conceptual divide that separated chiefly kraals from missionary schools, barter from cash income and millet fields from office work, they stood on the side of "tradition", while shops were perceived as distinctly "modern". If you remained on the traditional side, you had no need of becoming an entrepreneur. If you defined yourself as part of the new, you would not use the old crafts to establish yourself in the monetary economy.

Since the early 20th century, missionaries tried to revive and develop local crafts. All mission stations taught at least basket weaving and sewing, and the Finnish Mission established industrial schools in Engela and Oshigambo in the 1920s. The missions looked for means to create an independent income for their flock, especially for the converts who settled around the mission stations, and wanted to foster local development that would lessen dependence on migrant work. Paradoxically, their attempts did not serve to lead local crafts into the industrial age, but rather confined them into traditional patterns. Only curios and items connected to the rural world of Christian converts were produced in the Engela school. It taught the manufacturing of hoes, buckets and shirts, which were sold locally, and of baskets, which were mainly exported to South African curio shops. The sale of the school's products and of all exported basketware was controlled by the mission, which paid fix prices to the producers.[41] Additional basketware was bought and exported

---

[40] "Wood and metal work is only done by a few individuals and fast disappearing," Rodent Inspector Kurt Schettler wrote in a report on native crafts in 1948. Many women practiced pottery, but only women in the Uukwambi area, where clay was good and plentiful enough, specialized on market pottery (NAN NAO 78 32/9, Letter Rodent Inspector to NC, 12 July 1948).

[41] NAN SWAA 135/22, Memo Missionary Petäjä to NC Hahn, 24 July 1930; NAN NAO 64/17/7 for the export of basketware. The Rodent Inspector found in 1948 that "there is a great improvement in the design of basketware. Under the influence of missionaries (especially the Finnish Mission), women

by the SWANLA stores. The school was successful to a degree; some of its alumni established themselves as part-time tailors, and basket weaving brought a welcome additional income for women. But few innovations had their roots in the school, and I could not find any sources about full-time craftsmen, let alone mechanics or builders, influenced by the school before the 1960s.[42]

Migrant labor, too, provided only limited training for proto-industrial skills which could have been used by entrepreneurs. Even though workers had to operate modern machines, they were not usually trained to service, repair or even fundamentally understand them. They acquired a practical knowledge that was not easily transferable to other domains. Formal training and qualifications were – in practice, if not in law – reserved for white mineworkers only, and the short duration of contracts helped to keep qualifications to the necessary minimum.[43]

Perhaps most importantly, though, there was no market which could have sustained small scale manufacturing development in Ovamboland. This, again, was mainly due to migrant labor. The regional partition of the dual economy – wage labor in the modern sector in the South, agriculture and barter at home – was no longer all pervasive in the early 1950s. Monetary exchange had become important in Ovamboland, and the two sectors of production were linked through subsidies in both directions. The subsistence sector provided reproduction costs of wage labor, and savings from migrant work were re-invested into agriculture. But the new cash economy had not gradually emerged from a partition of labor in the agricultural sector, as it had in European proto-industrialization.

---

and girls have learnt to make baskets of many different shapes and designs" (NAN NAO 78 32/9, Letter Rodent Inspector to NC, 12 July 1948).

[42] Harold Eedes, admittedly a biased observer, writes in 1948 that "the industrial training of Natives in the Northern Native Territories by Missionaries is entirely unsatisfactory. Missions have been undertaking this work for some years, and have recently been subsidized by the Administration, but the Missionaries have never yet passed out a sufficient number of qualified Native artisans, who could be usefully employed on public and other works. When the Administration has had to undertake building and other operations in the Northern Native Territories, European and Native workmen have to be imported from the Police Zone." (NAN NAO 89 35/21, Letter NC to CNC, 23 August 1948.) Three years later, in a plea to expropriate the Finnish Mission and move Native Affairs headquarters to Oshigambo, he writes: "Up to date this part-industrial school has not produced a single Native motor driver, carpenter, mason or blacksmith. Baskets have certainly been produced there, but basketmaking is a purely Native industry of Ovamboland." (NAN SWAA 485 50/222, Letter NC to CNC, 9 October 1951.) The Roman Catholic Mission station in Oshikuku took over building contracts for the administration and for SWANLA in the early 1950s (see NAN NAO 63 17/1 Letter SWANLA manager Vlok to Missionary Bücking, 22 September 1950), but I could not find any sources about the organization of these activities or their consequences for local development. – The first full-scale technical school in Ovamboland, Valombola Technical Centre in Ongwediwa, was established in 1980, financed by CDM and training plumbers, carpenters, welders and motor mechanics (Cowley 1980).

[43] Gordon 1977, 151ff., Tötemeyer 1978, 156.

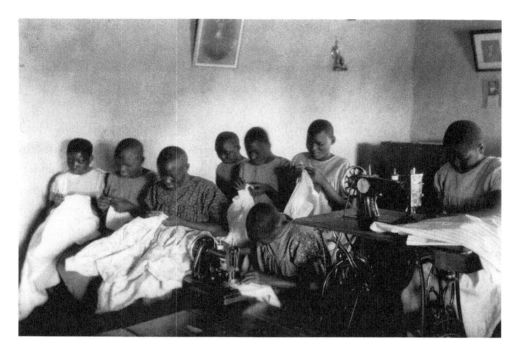

Image 16: Engela Mission Industrial School, ca. 1929.

Instead, it had become relevant as a parallel, full-fledged economic system which existed independently and remained largely detached from the village economy. Locally produced goods did not usually find their way into the distribution cycles of the cash economy.

Cash was, on the other hand, readily available for imported goods. Wages for migrant workers were of course low, but so were cash needs in everyday life on a homestead. As the monetary economy was still new and, in normal years, subsistence-oriented agriculture could generate all essentials, a relatively high percentage of the wages was available for consumption. Returning workers could easily bring money into Ovamboland. They usually spent a large part of the wages in the South before returning, and another part left the country for Angola. The remaining cash often circulated for some time in the area; then, it found its outlet in the stores of Ovamboland. The inhumane pass laws and travel restrictions in force since the early 20th century may never have been perfectly enforced, but they created a relatively effective market protection for the traders in Ovamboland.

The four European-owned stores in Ovamboland, as well as similar companies in the south or in Angola, offered well-known and visible examples that trade was lucrative. What is more, they were the *only* colonial economic enterprises in the reserve. Not a single manufacturing venture or market-oriented farm was available to serve as a role model for prospective entrepreneurs. This, as well, is due to the restrictive residence regime which made it impossible for people from outside Ovamboland to establish a business there.

Under the circumstances of the reserve economy, trade was indeed the ideal solution for members of the new elite who looked for ways to invest their capital at home. Their customers, confined to the reserve area, could not escape. If traders managed to bridge the cultural and spatial gap to their suppliers in the Police Zone and had some business sense, their shops were bound to be profitable. Profits were not very high, but compared to the alternative (underpaid migrant work), they were very interesting, all the more so since owning a shop allowed one to live at home and be one's own master. The capital and the skills necessary for obtaining supplies (mostly literacy and numeracy, but also a certain ease in dealing with white traders and the authorities) were not very specialized, but they required an access to the colonial world which set the new elite apart and made them exclusive. The low degree of initial specialization enabled the traders to continue farming and to choose how much time and capital they wanted to invest in trade. As most traders started their shops at home, relatively low initial investment was necessary.

Finally, not many other options were available in Ovamboland for an emerging elite who preferred white collar work to manual labor. In the early 1950s, fewer than two dozen office jobs in Ovamboland were open to 'natives'. Earlier, in the 1920s and 1930s, many alumni of mission schools had set themselves up as independent village teachers, living on payment by the parents. Hahn saw these teachers as destabilizing element threatening the rule of headmen: In "quite a short time innumerable large shady trees and other suitable places were pre-empted by natives who called themselves "teachers". The missions lost control and many of these teachers proceeded to develop the prestige thus attained to enter into competition for power with the headmen of their Omukunda."[44] He achieved that the Control of Sites Proclamation (No. 31 of 1932) was passed, ruling that no school could be established without prior authorization by the Administrator. Under the new regulation, teaching no longer was an alternative for most school alumni. Trade, then, was the most obvious, easiest and most lucrative choice for an educated person who was looking for a way to establish him- or herself with an independent business in Ovamboland. As a consequence, almost all entrepreneurial energy was channeled into trade. This not only led to an enormous boom of small shops in the area; it had long-term structural consequences for the Namibian economy. Ovamboland was integrated into

---

[44]   NAN NAO 20 11/1 vol. 10, Annual Report 1937.

the global economy through migrant labor and through trade – a combination which mirrored the international division of labor and prevented a more sustainable development of a local manufacturing sector. Parallel to this, the only way people who stayed in Ovamboland could participate in the modern economy was through the consumption of imported goods. Consumption became the foremost mode of integration into the wider world. Both the economic and the social concentration on consumption have consequences until today. The establishment of trade as *the* modern business model for northern Namibia thus became a watershed moment between two phases in the longue durée – a choice that could be made, but not unmade.

Image 17: Teaching under a tree: a teacher and schoolchildren at Odibo mission, ca. 1929.

4   From indirect rule to liberation war: Ovamboland 1948–1978

The rapid development of locally owned stores in Ovamboland really started in the second half of the 1950s and lasted well into the 1970s, before the beginning liberation war brought stagnation during the late 1970s and generated a new boom in the 1980s. In order to understand trade development (Chapter 5), the development of new forms of spatial and social organization around the shops (Chapter 6) and the political role of traders (Chapter 7), it is necessary to have a closer look at the overwhelming political changes which shaped the everyday life of 'black' people in South West Africa: the way from segregation to apartheid and the beginning of the fight for political liberation.

Modernizing the administration, 1948–1978

In retrospect, 1948 is a watershed year in Southern African history. The National Party (NP) came to power in South Africa and started to reweave the fabric of South African society, gradually supplanting the old policy of segregation by apartheid. But it is always easier to interpret history after the fact. Revolutionary as this change in the mandatory's government might have been, it passed almost unnoticed in Ovamboland. While Pretoria was far away, the Native Commissioner was the ruler one had to reckon with, and the departure of Hahn and the arrival of Eedes in the same year sent far greater ripples through the region. As the highest colonial authority anybody was likely to meet, Hahn and Eedes embodied the Administration. Their orders could often be dodged, but they could not be effectively opposed. A different personality as Native Commissioner therefore meant a different political regime, while a new government's decisions were always filtered through its local representative.

This in itself is a characteristic of the old style of Native Administration as personal rule, whose days were counted under the new government in Pretoria. Eedes was the last representative of the old system. His departure coincided with the first thorough reorganization of Native Affairs in South and South West Africa and of the way Ovamboland was governed. Many more reforms were to follow, reforms that implemented Apartheid principles and made South West Africa more and more integrated with, and dependent on, South Africa. Trade policy and trade realities were heavily influenced by this ongoing administrative reform. To put this in context, I have to widen the scope and outline some trends in South African politics.

Changing South African Policies

Having attained power with a minority of votes, the National Party Government's first aim after the 1948 elections was to consolidate its electoral domination in South Africa. One of the means to ensure this was to give franchise for South African Parliamentary elections to the mostly anti-liberal white South West Africans. They were given six seats in parliament; not one of these seats was ever won by an opposition party.[1] This contentious extension of voting rights was only possible in the context of another, even more contentious policy change: the new government tried to annex South West Africa as an integral part of its territory. With the founding of the United Nations, South Africa argued, the League of Nations mandate over South West Africa had ceased to exist as a legally enforceable instrument, as the United Nations were not the successor, but only a substitute for the League of Nations. South Africa was therefore under no obligation to honor the 'sacred trust' of the mandate. The UN General Assembly challenged this argument before the International Court of Justice, which largely refuted the South African position in 1950.[2] South Africa nevertheless continued to ignore its obligations under the mandate and intensified the area's integration into the South African administrative system – a policy that over the next decades led to increasing conflict between South Africa and the United Nations.

All regulations concerned with Native Affairs in South West Africa had been under the authority of the South West African Administrator from 1921 to 1951. In 1951, this authority was transferred to the South African Parliament, but for all practical purposes exercised by the Governor General. With the South West Africa Native Affairs Act of 1954, finally, the administration of Native Affairs in South West Africa was transferred to the South African Minister of Native Affairs (or, from 1958, Bantu Affairs and Development).[3] The administration of Ovamboland came under direct control of the South African government, whose policy of 'separate development' set the course for the South West African reserves, as well.

---

[1]   In addition to the 6 seats in the Assembly, five members represented South West Africa in the Senate, two being elected, three nominated by the Governor General.

[2]   For the South African position, see the "Statement submitted by the Government of the Union of South Africa", nrs. 12 and 13, in International Court of Justice 1950, 74f. The ICJ advisory opinion is found in the same volume, 128–219.

[3]   In the same Act, 'Coloureds' and 'Baster' were for the first time excluded from the category of 'Native'. They remained under the authority of the South West African Administration, while the Ministry in Pretoria was responsible for governing Bantu speakers and Nama (Lau/ Reiner 1993, 11). In 1958, the Native Affairs Department was renamed and split into the Department of Bantu Administration and Development and the Department of Bantu Administration, with the Minister of Bantu Administration as the head of reserve administration (Evans 1997, xiii).

In the early 1950s, it was not clear yet if and how this policy would be put into practice in South Africa. A decisive moment was defined by the debates around the "Report on the Socio-Economic development of the Native Areas in the Republic of South Africa" (usually called Tomlinson Report after the Commission's chairman). This massive 19-volume document was based on perhaps the most extensive social research program ever conducted in South Africa. The commission's work started from the assumption that South Africa had to make a clear choice between integration and separation. It strongly favored separation, but argued that this large-scale project of social engineering could not be successful without sustainable development of the native areas. This would make large sacrifices by the white population of South Africa necessary. The scattered homeland areas would have to be consolidated and huge amounts invested into their economic development – £104.000.000 over ten years.

Prime Minister Verwoerd welcomed the idea of separate development, but rejected all concrete recommendations of the report. Reluctant to spend the massive amounts the report's vision would have required, the NP government instead opted for a policy of muddling through. Over the next ten years, it tried to separate black and white living spheres without bearing the social and economic cost involved.[4]

The 1950s and 1960s saw the gradual development of apartheid's legal framework. On the macro level of regional spatial organization, the reserves were transformed into 'homelands' on their way to a nominative independence under South African supervision, and large-scale relocation programs served the attempt to sort people's living places according to their newly defined tribal affiliation. On the level of everyday life, petty apartheid legislation tried to press all social interactions into the categories of race.

It is clear today that, for a variety of reasons, this seemingly all-encompassing program was condemned to failure. It violated the dignity and corrupted the life chances of the majority of South Africans. It was built on sand as long as separation was not accompanied by homeland development, and as long as the country's industries needed migratory labor. The ideology of separation clashed with the real world, and even government policies furthered economic integration. Pretoria's policies thus remained fraught with unavoidable contradictions. The short-term price for pursuing apartheid in an integrated

---

[4]   Much on the newer literature on South African history in the twentieth century, especially in the orbit of the History Workshop, has stresses this lack of a coherent master-plan shaping NP policies, and insists on the situational, pragmatic and conflictual character of decision-making within the apartheid governments. As Phil Bonner, Peter Delius and Deborah Posel have expressed it, "the state compounded, rather than resolved, the contradictions it confronted." (Bonner/ Delius/ Posel 1993, 3). Excellent examples for such a perspectives can be found in their edited volume, just as in Posel 1991, Beinart/ Dubow 1995.

country was a consolidation of black residency in urban areas. As most of the homelands lacked sufficient resources for the people already living there and white industries continued to rely on a black labor force, large-scale relocation of urban blacks into the homelands was not an option. The long-term consequences were the entrenchment of structural inequality, the country's separation into developed and underdeveloped areas, increasing repression – and the long liberation struggle, ending in the National Party's final demise in 1994.

Black urbanization in 'white' areas and the systematic underdevelopment of homelands also brought a constant struggle for state control over both urban and rural areas. The state apparatus was massively enlarged and nominative administrative control expanded to all areas of everyday life. This totalitarian extension of state control was a necessary component of apartheid social engineering, but it was a losing battle from the start: the consequences of a failed policy could not be contained by policing.

But the repressive use of superior force prevailed for an astonishingly long time. One reason was that contradictions within the apartheid system opened up possibilities of economic and political participation to a part of the black population. In the face of internal struggles and external pressure, South Africa tried to strengthen this participation while restricting it to the less dangerous areas of public life – mostly homeland self-administration and petty commerce. The attitude of South Africa's administration towards native traders was shaped by these conflicting tendencies: the search for separate development without high costs, the need for political appeasement and a general modernist outlook on society.

Ovamboland administration under apartheid

Homeland policy was not put into practice in Ovamboland until the mid-1960s, but even in the absence of structural reforms, the new regime brought important changes in Ovamboland's administration. From 1951, Afrikaans gradually replaced English as everyday language in the Native Commissioners' office. Eedes still used his English mother tongue wherever he could, but official letters from Native Affairs administrators in Windhoek were more frequently written in Afrikaans, and newly printed forms were bilingual from the early 1950s. Eedes' successor Bruwer Blignaut was Afrikaans-speaking and routinely used that language in his correspondence.

This was not the only change. Hahn and Eedes had been staunch colonialists, but they had seen Ovamboland as their fiefdom. Their career was not in an office in Windhoek, not even really in the Native Affairs Department: it was 'in the field' where they could reign as supreme lords. They knew the area, understood the language to some degree (Hahn apparently better than Eedes) and had a deep interest in their subjects' culture (again Hahn more strongly than Eedes). While they could and would deal with the necessities of bureaucratic government, they saw the essence of power in the personal realm, not in bureaucratic control. Their relations to their superiors were mostly shaped by colonial camaraderie, and they essentially governed a foreign, if well-known country.

Their successors were of a new generation and had a different outlook on life. They were younger, born between the wars and farther removed from the first establishment of colonial rule; but most of all, the department employing them changed profoundly after the National Party came to power.[5] This is clearly visible in the reform of the Native Affairs Department coming into effect in 1955.

The Minister of Native Affairs in Pretoria now gained direct control over native administration in South West Africa, and the South African Prime Minister, not the Commissioner General, was now regarded as the "Supreme Chief" of South West African natives. Until the reform, the Secretary for South West Africa had been Chief Native Commissioner ex officio, and while he signed letters with the departmental title, it was just one of his functions.[6] Lord Hailey in his "Survey of native affairs in South West Africa" writes about the old regime that "it is undoubtedly the fact that the Secretary to the Administration is the busiest officer in the Territory, liable to be burdened with business which has its origin elsewhere than in Native affairs. He has little or no opportunity of touring."[7] This, in practice, had given a lot of leeway to the Native Commissioners, as their superior was mostly happy not to be bothered; and it gave their decisions official backing, as one of the most influential persons in the administration was interested in and could lobby for Native Affairs concerns.

Under the new regime, the office of the Chief Native (later 'Bantu') Commissioner in Windhoek became a separate post under the authority of the South African Minister of Native Affairs. This brought a new weight to the central post and cropped the Native Commissioners' autonomy. The Chief Native Commissioners were chosen by their political loyalties, and most of them were staunch National Party supporters. They made it their job to govern Native Affairs according to Party opinion and to streamline the different reserve administrations. Through the new regulation, the internal logic of Native

---

[5]   Shaun Johnson's novel "The Native Commissioner" (Johnson 2006, e.g. 69f.) offers a very informed literary perspective on how the changes in the Native Affairs Department were seen by longer serving officials. It is based on the papers of Johnson's father, who was the model for the novel's protagonist.

[6]   Olivier 1961, 168.

[7]   Hailey, A Survey of native affairs in South West Africa. Typescript, 1946. Bodleian Library at Rhodes House, Oxford, MSS Afr.s.744.

Affairs was turned on its head: the highly personal local despotism of the old Native Commissioners was replaced by central bureaucratic control.

Internally, Native Affairs officials in South West Africa learned to think in a wider departmental logic. South West Africa was no longer an occupied country to them, no longer a colony. Ovamboland remained a remote outpost, and most officials sent there still appreciated the more adventurous sides of the post, but ultimately they saw the area as just a part of South Africa inhabited by black people. While Native Affairs officials still rarely transferred into other government branches, Ovamboland's Native Commissioners could and would no longer rely on closing their career in the area. They instead aspired for posts in Windhoek, Pretoria or one of the larger South African homelands. Through this conduit, as well, personal rule became less important, and intimate knowledge of their more powerful subjects (second only to the potential of military force as a source of domination for Hahn and Eedes) was replaced by bureaucratic domination. The white administration in Ovamboland became more predictable, more closely integrated with government policies and less anchored in local experiences.

Not surprisingly for the 1950s, it became more modernist and developmentalist, as well. Hahn's ideal had been the largely untouched native society governed by benign patriarchs, which delegated contacts to a modern industrial world to the migrant workers. He was certainly in favor of overall economic development and did not try to keep the area backwards and poor. But he saw stability and traditional life as more important, and looked upon any development that could have affected the means of subsistence of rural households (which at the same time were the backbone of the mining economy) as dysfunctional. By contrast, administrators of the early 1960s sought to integrate Ovamboland into modernity and favored tertiary sector development over small-scale agriculture.[8] Their long-term aim, utopian under the regime they served and embodied, was a homeland in which living conditions were similar enough to the white areas that a black majority would no longer threaten white minority rule.

In the 1960s, the gradual changes in the Administration's interests were formalized into legislation. The crucial step towards the establishment of homelands in South West Africa was once again a voluminous report. The "Commission of Inquiry into the Affairs of South West Africa" (commonly called Odendaal Commission) was charged in 1962 with developing a five-year plan "for the accelerated development of the various non-White groups of South West Africa [...] and for the further development and building

---

[8] On agricultural development policy during the apartheid era, see Moorsom 1982, 52f.; Lau/ Reiner 1993.

up of such Native territories in South West Africa."[9] Just as the Tomlinson Report, the Odendaal Report was based on social research and was equally in favor of development and of segregation. But the report was written after the South African government had defined its approach to separate development, at a time when the nominal self-governance of the Transkei was already prepared. Its recommendations therefore match apartheid policies. The commission's economic analysis is much weaker than the Tomlinson Commission's was, especially in regard to the southern homelands and the police zone. The task of proving to the world that "all the homelands will provide a proper livelihood in the future for their respective population groups"[10] seemed much easier in Ovamboland than in the more fragmented southern and central Namibian homelands, while the positive effects on world opinion promised to be greater. From many recommendations, one gets the sense that the commission envisaged a model homeland Ovamboland – the South West African region least affected by colonialism and the political, economic and social changes it had brought.[11]

The Commission's recommendations combined limited self-administration in ethnically homogeneous homelands with an equally limited modernist development policy.[12]

---

[9]   Report of the Commission of Enquiry into South West Africa Affairs 1962–1963, 3.

[10] Report of the Commission of Enquiry into South West Africa Affairs 1962–1963, 81.

[11] On the Commission's neglect of economic analysis, see Thomas 1986, 50f.

[12] The Commission stated that "primarily the individual belongs to the ethnic group into which he is born. Within the setting of his own group he develops to maturity, and accepts as axiomatic the comprehensive whole or totality of the group thinking and group behavior as built up, adhered to and upheld by his own people in their own characteristic way. The individual cannot therefore be separated from his own ethnic relationship." But culture was not the only feature differentiating one group from the other, and 'axiomatic group thinking' did not entail equality: "It is a known fact that different groups do not necessarily attain and maintain the same standards of development." Culture contact leads to acculturation, "a process of inevitable one-sided imitation of the [White] by the [non-White]." (1964, 425) The ensuing "fundamental differences in socio-cultural orientation, stages of general development and ethnic classification" render "the differences between the groups concerned [...] so profound in nature that they cannot be wiped out: a policy of integration is unrealistic, unsound, and undesirable." (1964, 427) – These passages show a close familiarity with anthropological theory and terminology. They were probably written by Johannes Petrus van Schalwyk Bruwer, one of the six members of the Commission. Bruwer (1914–1967) had been a mission worker, school principal and educational administrator in Northern Rhodesia from 1935. He turned anthropologist, passing his BA at the University of South Africa in 1945 and his MA and PhD at the University of Pretoria in 1948 and 1955. In 1951 he became senior lecturer and in 1956 professor and head of department in Stellenbosch, with a stint as visting professor at Johns Hopkins University in 1959. After his time with the Odendaal Commission, he was appointed as the first Commissioner General for the Indigenous Peoples of South West Africa in 1964 (an office suggested by the Odendaal Commission), but left the job on 1 January 1965 to become founding professor in anthropology at Port Elizabeth University. He was active in the South African Bureau of Racial Affairs (SABRA) and a high-ranking member of the Broederbond. In 1959, he spent 6 months in Omhedi in Oukwanyama, trying to assess the reasons for the opposition's beginning success. (Bruwer 1961, van Tonder 1967, de Jongh 1987, Gordon 2005; NAN Acc 744).

Politically, the Commission recommended enlarging and consolidating native reserves into ten "homelands" with limited self-government by executive councils made up of chiefs and of elected members. The black homelands would be under the authority of the Department of Native Affairs, with a Commissioner General as the main link between Pretoria and South West Africa. On an economic plan, the Odendaal Commission recommended two five-year development plans, concentrating on infrastructure (mostly water and electricity), livestock farming and education (see below).[13]

Both the political and the economic recommendations of the Odendaal report for Ovamboland were largely put into legislation after 1964. In an official Memorandum which could not differ more from the White Paper on the Tomlinson Report, the South African Government endorsed the majority of recommendations, most importantly the Kunene hydro-power scheme and other infrastructure projects. As long as the case against South Africa was pending in the International Court of Justice, however, the government hesitated to immediately implement the homeland policy; but the memorandum made it very clear that there should be no "unnecessary delay" in putting it into practice.[14] In 1964, the new office of a Commissioner General for the Indigenous Peoples of South West Africa (Kommissaris-Generaal van die Naturellebevolke in Suidwes-Afrika, called KG by his subjects) was established to serve as a link between the Kaoko, Ovamboland and Okavango reserves and the South African Government.[15] The post of the Assistant Native Commissioner in Oshikango was upgraded to Native Commissioner. Four years later, in 1968, the *Development of Self-Government for Native Nations in South West Africa*

---

[13] For the recommendation, see du Pisani 1985, 161ff.

[14] Republic of South Africa 1964, 24.

[15] The first Commissioner was Johannes van Schalwyk Bruwer, the anthropological member of the Odendaal commission (see footnote 12). It is possible that the idea for the post actually came from Werner Eiselen, his pre-predecessor as anthropology professor at Stellenbosch, who had become Commissioner-General for the Northern Sotho in 1960 after working as Secretary of Native Affairs for ten years. Bruwer was succeeded by Martie J. Olivier, who had worked in Native Affairs in Okavango and Windhoek before writing a PhD on Native Administration in South West Africa in Stellenbosch (Olivier 1961) – with Nic J.J. Olivier as supervisor and J. P. van Schalwyk Bruwer and Werner Eiselen as co-examiners. All three were broederbond activists and members of the South African Bureau of Racial Affairs SABRA (N.J.J. Olivier, member of the Tomlinson Commission, vice-president of SABRA and on the 'visionary' side within the Bureau, later joined the opposition liberal party (Olivier 1959, 25, Dubow 1992, 232, Gordon 1988, 574, Gilliomee 2003, 523f; see also Posel 1987, Lazar 1993, Norval 1996, 162 on SABRA's internal conflicts)). Thus both qualified and well connected, M.J. Olivier became Native Commissioner in Ovamboland in 1962 and was promoted as Bruwer's successor. After Olivier, Johannes Marthinus ('Jannie') de Wet (1927–2011), a SWA member of the South African Parliament from 1965 to 1970, held the office from 1970 to 1977, when it was abolished and its powers transferred to the Administrator-General. – From 1972, the KG was authorized to take part and speak in the sessions of the Owambo and Kavango parliaments (SAB URU 6128, Magiting van J.M. de Wet, Kommissaris-Generaal vir die Naturellebevolke in Suidwes-Afrika om sitting van die Ovambolandse en Kavango Wetgewende Rade by te woon en toe te spreek).

Act (No. 54 of 1968) was passed. It confirmed the allocation of "nations" to certain areas and made provisions for the self-government of each "nation" by a Legislative Council and an Executive Council.[16] "Ovamboland" (renamed "Owambo" in 1972) was one of the six homelands to be established. In October 1968, the first Legislative Council for Ovamboland was instituted. It consisted of 42 members, 6 named (not elected) by each tribal unit. Each group of tribal representatives elected one LC member into the Executive Council, the homeland government.[17] The system was consolidated by the introduction of formal self-government (including flag, national anthem, limited legislative power and taxation) in 1973.[18] Owambo was declared a self-governing territory in April 1973 and ruled by a partly elected Legislative Council and a cabinet of seven ministers from August 1973. (40 percent of the parliament's members were elected; due to an election boycott by Swapo and Demcop, only 5 percent of registered voters actually cast their votes.[19])

The everyday work in government departments was only very slowly taken over by local personnel. Even the central South West African administration in Windhoek, which was dominated by white experts born in the territory, was by-passed, and administrative personnel was directly dispatched and supervised from Pretoria instead. Each department of the new homeland government was led by a white Director under the coordination of a Chief Director, who was the real power in the land.[20]

Not long after the homeland system was fully established, the slow progress towards Namibian independence questioned its validity and made all its institutions look like temporary makeshifts. Under severe internal and external pressure and after long negotiations in the Turnhalle Conference – a national constituent assembly composed of representatives of South West Africa's various 'tribal groups' –, the South African Government partly revised its policies in 1977–79. South Africa accepted that Namibia would become independent, but blocked the process by negotiating on specific points while increasing its military presence.

A number of petty apartheid regulations, like the Pass Laws, the Mixed Marriages Act and the Immorality Act were abolished, and a common National Assembly for South

---

[16] See du Pisani 1985, 184f.
[17] Simultaneously, the South West Africa Affairs Act (No. 25 of 1969) accelerated the integration of the South West Africa into the South African administrative system, a further step towards centralization and bureaucratization of South West Africa.
[18] Development of Self-Government for Native Nations in South West Africa Amendment Act, No. 20 of 1973.
[19] Tötemeyer 1977, 124.
[20] In theory, the white personnel were there to work on their own replacement by local administrators. In practice, Dennis Nandi, the Deputy Director of Education, was still the only non-white senior administrator in 1986 (Pütz/ von Egidy/ Caplan 1986, 259).

West Africa composed partly of a fixed number of elected representatives of the homeland areas was established. This was the end to the utopia of independent homelands, but not the end of ethnic government. Instead of the ethnic administrations responsible for areas, eleven administrations for the different population groups were established as second tier of administration. The Owambo government was renamed Owambo administration, but it remained in place largely unchanged.[21] The real power lay neither with the ethnic administrations nor even with the National Assembly, which was dissolved in 1983, but with the Administrator General installed by Pretoria. In the 1980s, the Legislative Assembly of Owambo became more and more critical towards the South African government, especially after the long-time Chairman of the Owambo Executive Committee, Peter Kalangula, left DTA, founded the Christian Democratic Action (CDA) and took over the majority in the Owambo Legislative Assembly. In the mid-1980s, the parliament was a venue for lively and controversial debates and partly for harsh criticism against the South African defense forces, but it did not have any real political power.[22]

In protest against Pretoria's unsatisfying reforms, the liberation movement Swapo (South West African People's Organisation) intensified its guerilla activities from exile. Without ever being officially ended, the national independence process stopped for more than a decade. During the drawn-out negotiations that finally led to Namibia's independence in 1990, the homeland administration remained in place, but emergency regulations, military rule and Pretoria's strong hand often curtailed the official government's relevance in Ovamboland.

These administrative reforms stood against the background of social and political upheaval. The peaceful and monolithic patriarchal society which the Native Commissioners had dreamed of was, by the mid-1970s, no longer even thinkable as a utopian aim. With new infrastructure and higher incomes, everyday consumption in the growing towns changed rapidly. Cars, electric light, European-style fashion and furniture became omnipresent in households with monetary income, whereas they only slowly trickled into rural households without wage earners. As William Beinart observed for South Africa, "with ever greater finality, the bulk of the population was sucked into modes of living that demanded new forms of consumption, [and] the social and class divisions within both their communities and the society as a whole were further recast."[23] Migrant workers experi-

---

[21]   Forrest 1998, 35ff. provides more information on these second tier administrations, unfortunately with a number of errors in details.

[22]   See for example Owambo Legislative Assembly 1985 or Bryan O'Linn's speech at the opening of the 17th Session (O'Linn 1985). On Kalangula, see Pütz/ von Egidy/ Kaplan 1989, 103. He was Chairman of the Executive Committee from 1980 to 1989.

[23]   Beinart 2001, 144.

enced apartheid more acutely and as more degrading than their relatives at home, where virtually no whites lived. On the mines and farms, migrant workers lived along their white 'masters' and experienced racial discrimination as an everyday occurence. On the basis of these experiences, they developed a clearer consciousness of the system's oppressive character. The old establishment of tribal leaders mostly sided with the administration, while many young people found their political home with the more and more politicized modernist elites. With the foundation of opposition parties, in the first place Swapo, the social rifts between old and new elites started to overlap with political fights. From 1966, Swapo's military wing, organized from exile, led a guerilla war against the South African occupation, and South Africa retaliated with a gradual militarization of Ovamboland, that took a massive weight in the 1970s. Societal and political identifications left the framework of Ovamboland, into which they had largely been confined in the 1930s and 1940s, and became connected to the national and increasingly the global level.

Apartheid development policy

Apartheid policy from the 1950s to the early 1970s closed its eyes to many of the pressing political questions, but it thoroughly engaged with the economic dimension of modernization. "The Nationalists", again in Beinart's words, "liked to think of the country in these terms: a conservative but modern industrial, capitalist, Western-oriented nation".[24] In South West Africa with its smaller population, the developmentalist dimension of apartheid had better chances of being implemented than in South Africa. Ovamboland in particular looked a promising ground for economic development: it was relatively prosperous, structurally and spatially homogenous and barely affected by resettlement programs and other destructive elements of apartheid social engineering.

If we look at Namibia as a whole, apartheid's development efforts failed to bring sustainable development, in a large part because they did not address the political framework of systematic inequality and selective protectionism. This was not only the "anti-politics machine" of developmentalism at work.[25] Most white officials indeed principally agreed with the political agenda of apartheid and saw their actions as a contribution to a better political future by building up a successful homeland economy.

South African development policies thus increased inequality between the Police Zone and the homelands. Production and employment opportunities remained concentrated in the white areas. The large-scale infrastructure projects were led by white-owned con-

---

[24]   Beinart 2001, 145.
[25]   Ferguson 1990.

tractors who made high profits on the state contracts and could establish a lasting domination over the market. The ties between white businesses interests and government officials in the police zone became even stronger, making it difficult for new actors to enter the market. The logic of political patronage was extended to the homeland areas, where the state sector covered an even higher share of economy activities. Businesspeople with good connections to the administration could make unjustified profits on state tenders or licences; this encouraged inefficiency and squandering of public funds.[26] In stark contrast to the rhetorics of 'self-government', the entire economy was functionally integrated with South Africa's in a more and more dependent position, leaving little regulatory power on the local or national level and often sacrificing South West African economic interests to South African ones.[27]

In spite of these systematic failures, apartheid development efforts had some positive effects in Ovamboland and increased overall prosperity, at least as long as the homeland system was in place and markets remained protected. Due to the relatively favorable preconditions, development projects could bring real benefits to the population. Unlike in the South African homelands, projects did not have to patch apartheid's most blatant social and economic deficits. They could build on a sound subsistence sector to generate some growth in manufacturing and service industries. South African and South West African development planners did this with all the enthusiasm of modernist experts who believed in change by engineering. They had a free hand in the closed territory, and for many white representatives of the administration, working in Ovamboland became an adventure and a fascination. They saw themselves as the advanced experts living an adventurous life, and they did their best to find solutions to the technical problems of development in the region, ignoring the political issues that became more and more visible.

The first field of action for development planning was water infrastructure. The great famines of 1915 and 1929 had sensitized the Administration for the effects of a drought. Ovamboland only has high rainfalls from January to March, but almost no rain in the rest of the year. Seasonal watercourses bring floods during the rainy season, but the water quickly evaporates; the remaining ground water is mostly brackish and salty. Small dams and other water harvesting systems sufficed for human consumption and agricultural demand in normal years, but only larger water reservoirs could solve the problem of droughts and simultaneously provide enough water for industrial development or larger settlements.

---

[26]   See Wood 1983 and Thomas 1978, 55ff. with further references.
[27]   See e.g. Lau/ Reiner 1993 for the agricultural sector.

Already during the "famine of the dams" in 1928/1930 had Hahn started to improve the water infrastructure in his large work-for-food program. Other dams were constructed over the years, but systematic planning only started after 1948. The SWA Water Department was brought in and designed a first five-year plan for 1954 to 1958 jointly with the new Native Commissioner Bruwer Bilgnaut, who had a public works background himself. Mostly German speaking engineers planned and oversaw the building of around forty dams all over Ovamboland, and constructed three large reservoirs in Ondangua, Okatana and Oshikuku. Further, new roads were built on dams to withstand the seasonal floods, which were equipped with water pipes and could simultaneously serve as water banks.[28]

In the second five-year plan, an old idea was taken up: instead of merely damming locally available water, a canal which would bring water from the Kunene River to central Ovamboland was designed. This possibility had already played a major role in the boundary negotiations between South Africa and Portugal in the 1920s, but it had never been realized. Now a large reservoir was built in Okatana (today's Oshakati) and a 65 miles canal constructed that fed water from different seasonal watercourses into the reservoir. This project was completed in 1964.[29]

The new water infrastructure had from the start been conceived as a first step towards economic development in the reserve. When the Odendaal Commission took up its work in 1962, it incorporated the existing projects and ideas into a large master plan that combined infrastructure measures, economic development and political reform. For the sake of clarity, I have dealt with the political side above, but political and economic measures were inseparable from each other. Economic development was seen as a means to sustainably achieve apartheid. It should provide the 'welfare of the indigenous population' that even the proponents of apartheid saw as a necessary precondition for a stable white rule. In South Africa, the massive expenditure on South Africa's homelands recommended by the Tomlinson report had never seen the light. Much smaller and blatantly insufficient sums were indeed invested into homeland development, but these dubious efforts did not succeed in fostering development in the fragmented and impoverished South African Bantustans.

In South West Africa, the sums needed were less substantial, and they promised a large political dividend in a situation in which South West Africa's status was fiercely contested

---

[28]   See Bertelsmann 1959, Lempp 1963 and Stengel 1963 for a more detailed overview. After their principal engineer Hans Stengel, the system of large dams, some of which are still functional, is known as "Stengel dams" even today.

[29]   Davis 1964, 65

internationally. As a consequence (and because many recommendations built on existing plans anyway), the economic recommendations of the Odendaal Commission were largely realized.

In continuation of the five-year plans by Water Affairs – and quite typical for African modernist regimes of the 1960s – the centerpiece of the economic measures was a hydro-power scheme which had first been developed shortly after World War I. The Okatana canal was extended to a dam in Ruacana on the Kunene, where a 240 MW power plant was inaugurated in 1978 after five years of construction. The electricity produced by the plant was mostly meant for the mines in central Namibia, but the new power grid which linked Ruacana to the South African network also served to bring electricity into new parts of Ovamboland.[30]

A second canal linked to the first was also constructed and brought Kunene water to Western Ovamboland. From different reservoirs, the water was processed and distributed through pipelines to public water outlets. The fast urbanization of central Ovamboland in the 1970s and 1980s (see Chapter 6) rested on this combined water and electricity infrastructure development. Today's water infrastructure is still largely based on this system, which was gradually expanded to include new villages and towns.

The new canals helped agricultural development to some degree, but this had not been a priority of the Odendaal Commission. The Commission had found that central Ovamboland already was at the brink of its agricultural capacity, and that its soils did not allow intensive agriculture using mechanical ploughs: the top soil in the floodplains is very sandy and permeable, while a deeper layer is almost impermeable to water. The evaporation of seasonal floods thus leads to high concentrations of salts in the deeper soil layers, which in the Commission's view would make intensive irrigation agriculture uneconomical. The only recommendation the Commission gave for Ovamboland's agriculture was to try the cultivation of groundnuts.[31] Agricultural development was still often used as a justification for water infrastructure development, but few efforts towards it were undertaken. The new state Hospital in Oshakati opened in 1966 had a large vegetable garden, and some peasants close to the new dams started to irrigate their fields. The agricultural college opened in 1969 in Ongongo had only produced six graduates by 1975, and the only other sizeable agricultural development project of the 1960s and

---

[30]   The first diesel power station in Ovamboland had been built in Oshikango in 1959 with a power output of 5 KW. A second and third station with 400 KW and 35 KW respectively were opened in Oshakati in 1963 and Ondangwa in 1967. They were replaced with new plants with an output of 4.900 KW (Oshakati, 1972), 750 KW (Ondangwa, 1972) and 250 KW (Oshikango, 1974). A further 500 KW station in Ongongo was built in 1970 for the new agricultural college (Louw 1976, 70).

[31]   Report of the Commission of Enquiry into South West Africa Affairs 1962–1963, 307f.

1970s was the opening up of the Mangetti area in South-Western Kavango for white cattle farmers in 1973.[32]

Even if agriculture could have been developed further, 'development' for the Odendaal Commission and its initiators meant the establishment of modern urban institutions much rather than the intensification of a peasant agriculture. More and more 'modern' infrastructure institutions were founded in Ovamboland. In 1962, post offices existed in Ondangua and Oshikango, and post boxes in the seven tribal areas. According to the Commission's recommendations, a further post office was opened in Okatana (today's Oshakati) and nine postal agencies and twenty post boxes established all over Ovamboland. In addition, a mobile postal service drove through a large number of villages along the major roads on a regular basis.[33] The telephone service was extended to Ovamboland in the mid-1960s, at first linking up to the radio network, and "Radio Owambo" took up broadcasting from Oshakati in 1968.[34] Airfields in Ondangua, Oshivelo and Ruacana were opened between 1969 and 1971. The road from Ondangwa to Tsumeb was tarred and new all-weather gravel roads from Ondangwa to Oshikango and Ruacana were completed in 1969.[35] The first private bus companies were licenced in the same year, and in 1976, eight buses owned by five local companies operated in Ovamboland.[36] The first banks in Ovamboland were BBK's (see below) bank in Ondangwa opened in March 1966[37] and the Barclays Bank branches in Oshakati and Ondangwa opened in 1969, which became very important for local businesspeople. They greatly facilitated financial transactions, increased the savings rate and gradually supplanted the old credit networks.[38]

All these projects were both conceived and regarded by the local population as signs of the region's way into the separated modernity of an apartheid homeland. The infrastructure projects also provided the necessary precondition for a wide array of further development measures. The centerpiece of these measures was a new development agency, the Bantu Investment Corporation (BIC) or Bantu Beleggings Korporasie (BBK). Originally, this agency had been the outcome of the Tomlinson Report, which had proposed

---

[32] Moorsom 1982, Louw 1979; Louw 1976, 72 for Ongongo. For the history and sociology of Mangetti farms, see Thomas Widlok's seminal "Living on Mangetti" (1999).

[33] Report of the Commission of Enquiry into South West Africa Affairs 1962–1963, 393. Hangula 1993, 20 puts the opening of Oshakati's post office at 1964. The first post agency had been opened in Ondangwa in 1929, a second one in Oshikango probably in the late 1940s.

[34] Hangula 1993, 20.

[35] Republic of South Africa, Department of Foreign Affairs 1971, 22. The road to Oshikango was tarred in 1985.

[36] Louw 1976, 67.

[37] NAN BAD 2 B1: Bantoe-Administrasie en –ontwikkeling: Bankfasiliteite Owambo – Postjekdiens.

[38] Post offices had provided savings books and postal cheque services since at least 1965; see NAN BAD 2 B1.

a £25.000.000 Development Corporation. The government White Paper responding to the Report slashed this notion and instead announced the funding of a 'Bantu Areas Investment Corporation' to mobilize Bantu capital, with an initial investment of a mere £500.000.[39] The BIC was installed with the Bantu Investment Corporation Act (No. 34 of 1959), and its capital was increased to £1.000.000 by 1962. It came to be the main vehicle of apartheid's small- and medium-scale business development policy in the homelands. Financed by subsidies from the central government and the homeland authorities, it invested in middle sized factories and shop or workshop premises, held training courses and gave credits to local entrepreneurs.[40]

The Odendaal report recommended an extension of BIC's activities to the South West African native areas. BIC started its activities in Ovamboland and four other Namibian reserves in 1964. Twelve years later, in a move to increase a sense of ownership and better adapt policies to local conditions, independent South West African development institutions for different homelands were formed. The new Owambo Development Corporation took over BIC's operations in Owambo. In 1978, finally, these institutions were merged by proclamation No. AG 61 to form the First National Development Corporation of South West Africa (FNDC), better known under its Afrikaans name ENOK (Eerste Nasionale Ontwikkelings Korporasie). ENOK's activities continued after independence; in 1993, the organization was transformed into the National Development Corporation (NDC).[41]

In their 25 years of pre-independence existence, the development institutions followed more or less the same policy. They lived mainly on state subsidies, which they spent on different development measures in the homelands.[42] They set up their own factories, built business facilities that they rented out to local businesses, organized training courses and gave credit to entrepreneurs. In 1973, BIC expanded its activities to agriculture, with a focus on mechanized and often irrigated commercial farming in Okavango and Caprivi.[43]

In Ovamboland, the company's most important investments were concentrated in the newly founded town of Oshakati, and they profited from the market closure in the home-

---

[39] Lazar 1993, 374f.

[40] On the South African BIC see the critical evaluations by Kuper 1965, 276ff. and Best 1971.

[41] In 1992, its butcheries and meat factories were taken over by the new parastatal Meat Corporation of Namibia (Meatco). The remaining assets were transferred to the newly founded Namibia Development Corporation (NDC) by Act No. 18 of 1993 (Namibia Development Corporation Act). All assets and liabilities were either taken over by NDC or transferred to the parastatal Amalgamated Commercial Holdings Ltd. (Amcom); all FNDC staff was taken over by NDC.

[42] By including repayments of loans to customers, which had been financed by the state in the first place, into the company's operational income, the share of subsidies could be decreased to 23% in 1987. FNDC 1987, xii.

[43] Girvan 1995.

land system. The first industrial venture was a furniture factory established in Oshakati in 1965. A building company followed in 1967 and soon became the largest field of business, employing 500 people in 1976.[44] Two workshops in Oshakati (1969) and Ruacana (1974), a petrol station (1965) and a garage (1970) were equally established by BIC. In early 1971, the company obtained a franchise for Coca Cola products and opened a soft drink factory (today operated by NamBrew). In the same year, the company established a bakery, whose capacity was finally expanded to 17.000 loaves of bread a day.[45] (Prior to the opening of the bakery, bread had either been home-baked in earth pits or fish tins or brought from Tsumeb on a weekly basis.[46]) A butchery and a meat processing factory built in 1973 were conceived to provide a market for the Mangetti Farming scheme and – to a lesser degree – for Ovamboland's cattle herds.[47] The veterinary restrictions on cattle exports to central Namibia held cattle prices low and created a niche for a local meat factory.

BIC had become the largest employer in Ovamboland by 1972, giving work, in the official categorization, to 199 white and 1530 Ovambo employees.[48] A number of further large projects were linked to BIC or its successors, among them Oshakati's open market built in 1968 jointly with the Homeland Government.[49]

In 1969, BIC took over the wholesale stores in Ondjodjo, Omafo, Endola and Ombalantu from SWANLA in a move that foreshadowed the recruiting agency's dismantling after the general strike of 1972.[50] This finally ended the era of the early monopoly stores in Ovamboland, and trade was for the first time completely separated from recruiting. The original justification of having stores owned by a recruiting agency had been to educate people in the use of money in order to push them towards migrant labor, and to prevent disturbances by white private traders. When both were no longer necessary, the opposition against a trading concern which used profits made off migrant workers to lower recruiting costs for the workers' employers became more pronounced in the 1960s. The considerable profits of the wholesaler, even government agencies argued, should better be reinvested in economic development in the homeland. (In the mid-1970s,

---

[44]   Louw 1976, 77.
[45]   Hangula 1993, 22; FNDC 1987, ix.
[46]   Hangula 1993, 22.
[47]   Louw 1979, 44.
[48]   Tötemeyer 1978, 151. Louw (1976, 77) counts 975 employees in ODC's industrial ventures in 1975 – among them 500 in the building division, 150 in the meat factory, 118 in the furniture factory and 55 in the Oshakati workshop.
[49]   FNDC 1987, ix.
[50]   Louw 1976, 75; NAN OVE 12 9/2/8/1/1, Minutes Handelsvereiniging Ovamboland, 16 October 1970.

Ondjodjo wholesale bought goods for an average of R200.000 per month and sold them for R255.000. As its 42 employees only earned an aggregated R5.800 per month, this added up to a rather comfortable profit rate for a wholesale company.)[51]

At the same time, wholesale trade was seen as a means to promote private enterprise. BIC opened a further wholesale store in Oshakati in 1969. The wholesales gave short-term credits to resellers and BIC offered training courses, preferential credit facilities and consultancies for traders. This was in line with BIC's overall policies, in which support for entrepreneurs played an important role. Creditors were offered after-sale assistance to increase the likelihood of success, and prospective traders could start their business in the protected environment of BIC-owned store buildings.

In all these measures, the apartheid development companies pursued policies comparable to those of similar companies in other African countries, and they even did a creditable job in promoting market-based economic development in the protected Ovamboland homeland. They have indeed founded most of the few industrial companies operating in the region today.

But BIC's and ENOK's activities did not really lead to sustainable development, least of all to the industrial development the companies had envisaged. This is partly due to the economic and political framework in which their policies were placed[52] and partly to the internal division of labor cemented by their actions. Even in the 1980s, most prospective entrepreneurs started trading ventures, and only a minority went into manufacturing. This was not merely a matter of choice by businesspeople. As one of BIC's aims was to provide employment opportunities, it established large companies in all promising areas. These companies were state-subsidized, mostly exempt from taxes and favored by official procurement agreements. The furniture company in Oshakati, for example, provided school benches and office desks for the homeland administration; the meat factory delivered food to school kitchens; the construction company was almost exclusively employed for government projects. Even the real advantages given to private companies did not allow them to compete with state firms nourished on state contracts.

Apartheid homelands with their closed markets and bureaucratic central planning mechanisms were perhaps the ideal places to promote infant industries in a protected environment. But due to the political imperatives, the protection was never lifted until

---

51 NAN OVE 44 9/4/4, Application for licence for new shop premises, 29 January 1975.

52 The economic designs and consequences of apartheid are fiercely disputed in the literature. One school sees apartheid as a plan to increase the profits of capital as compared to labor, and blames inefficiencies and incompetence for the system's economic decline; the other faction argues that apartheid had never been an economic undertaking, but an ideological framework insufficiently explained by economic argumentation.

independence, and the infant industries never developed into competitive companies – they only barred the way for small-scale private enterprises in the manufacturing sector. As private traders had been successful in Ovamboland prior to BIC's arrival, trade had always been seen as a profitable sector in which development measures should help local agency without replacing it.[53] In consequence, there was no competition from large subsidized retail sellers. Some of the BIC wholesale businesses were indeed even taken over by local businessmen: Johannes Hamutumwa took over Omafo wholesale after working as a manager for BIC for three years; Endola and Ombalantu wholesalers were equally transferred into local ownership between 1970 and 1974.[54] Frans Indongo took over Cuvelai Bottle Store in Oshakati, and the important Okatana Service Station was converted into a limited liability company, with forty percent shares sold to local businesspeople.[55] All these transfers are surprisingly similar to today's Black Economic Empowerment deals – including the importance of political connections on the side of the transferees.

Economic life in Ovamboland changed profoundly between 1950 and 1970. Especially in the new towns, new forms of social life, of communication and of consumption developed (see Chapter 6) which were more closely integrated with the world outside of the reserve boundaries and often took its models from life in central Namibian and South African towns. The Odendaal Commission's report did not start these changes, but it incorporated earlier plans and developments into a single framework of political and economic reconstitution and thus provided a blueprint for turning the native reserve into a native homeland. The Commission conceived of economic development as a precondition to the successful establishment of an apartheid homeland, and the South African government in consequence took real efforts to develop Ovamboland's economy. But economic and political development finally appeared linked in a rather different way: the new elites did not only look for economic success, but also for political freedom and equality. With all its efforts to develop the economy, South Africa partly succeeded to forestall the liberation movement in the short run. In the long run, economic emancipation and integration made liberation inevitable.

---

[53] As Walter Louw, anthropologist and at the time of writing public relations officer of the Owambo Development Corporation, described BIC's decision to go the easy way: "The BIC soon realized that it was advisable to begin with situations familiar to the Black man and to build from that base." (Louw 1976, 74).

[54] SWA Yearbook 1976, 45, corroborated by George Namundjebo in October 2006. Hamutumwa later went into exile and the Omafo store was taken over by Eliakim Namundjebo. – Ombalantu Wholesale was taken over by David Sheehama (NAN OVE 9/1/3).

[55] Hangula 1993, 22.

Liberation movement and guerilla war

The history of South West African protest movements against colonial rule is less well documented than the history of the ANC and similar groups in South Africa, and organized civil society pressure against colonialism has a much shorter history than in South Africa's urban centers. Nationalist history writing in the 1980s and 1990s tended to integrate earlier conflicts between colonizers and colonized with the liberation movement into a long history of popular struggle against foreign oppression. But the fights of Ondonga King Nande or Uukwambi King Iipumbu ya Shilongo against colonial powers were very different from, for example, the labor unrest of the 1970s.[56] The earlier 'acts of resistance' were often committed by despotic rulers who disliked power sharing, be it with their own subjects or with a rivaling military power, and they are better interpreted as fights for domination over the masses than as acts of liberation.

The political movement that led to the founding of Swapo, SWANU (South West African National Union) and other groups has different roots and was borne by a different social stratum. By a combination of force, conviction and cooptation, the headmen in Ovamboland were integrated into the system of indirect rule between 1915 and 1945. When Ovamboland was transformed into a nominally self-governed apartheid homeland, headmen's cooperation with the government solidified. Resistance could not be expected of the rulers, who would have had to protest against themselves: Instead of opposing colonial rule, they were its most important instruments.

A new political movement instead formed among migrant laborers on the one hand and church activists on the other. Members of both groups started to lose their patience with being treated as second-class human beings in the early 1950s.[57] The first complaints

---

[56] The tendency of a nationalist history to integrate different moments of protest and defiance into a long history of anti-colonial struggle is most visible in Peter Katjavivi's pioneer 'History of Resistance in Namibia'. For him, every act by a Namibian against a colonizer can be seen as "general opposition conducted by Namibian communities to foreign rule". "Resisting in culture and religion in some epochs, through strike action and boycotts in others, Africans have united across clan boundaries to demand an end to apartheid and to struggle for complete independence."(Katjavivi 1988, xiii, xi). Writing in 1988, Katjavivi had clear political aims, but his fascination with resistance and struggle and a tendency to tolerate despotism if it was linked to anti-colonial sentiments are shared by many of his younger colleagues (see e.g. //Gowaseb 2007). It often finds its expression in the political domain, as well. Its most remarkable monument is Heroes' Acre in Windhoek, where Swapo liberation heroes are commemorated alongside numerous representatives of the pre-colonial elites.

[57] The prehistory of the liberation movements is obviously much more complicated than I can present it here. The Mandume movement of the 1930s, for example, linked old feudal elites of Oukwanyama and urban migrant workers in Windhoek, and many of the important "first generation" activists of the 1950s and 1960s came out of it. For central Namibia, Chiefs and traditional leaders like Hosea Kutako, Hendrik Witbooi, Hans Beukes or Clemens Kapuuo played an important role in the beginning liberation movement from World War II; before the War, the Herero 'Truppenspieler' movement had been a

concentrated on concrete experiences of injustice, exclusion and disrespect. On the mines, where many workers were concentrated in compounds and could develop joint agency on common complaints, strikes and workers' unrest had started in the early 20th century.[58] They were usually confined to workers themselves and centered on industrial relations. For most people in Ovamboland, domination by headmen was much more concrete than colonial oppression well into the 1940s.

In the early 1950s, migrant workers brought political issues into public life in Ovamboland. At the same time, the region's integration into a centralized colonial system began to be more acutely felt. Where Native Commissioners' decisions had been the decisive source of domination before, more and more rules were now set by authorities in Windhoek and Pretoria. Under the National Party government, colonialism and apartheid became more easily discernible as *systematic* discrimination. Whether it was the closure of Etosha game reserve for cattle grazing, the obligation to take off glasses before entering the SWANLA store in Ondjodjo,[59] or the low quality of food served by mining companies: all these concrete experiences could now be interpreted as caused by the system of colonial oppression.

I will use two examples from the early 1950s to illustrate the increasing discomfort with colonial rule in central northern Namibia. The first began when the Administration in Windhoek and Chief Native Commissioner Johannes Neser introduced what they perceived as a measure to protect the weak and increase social justice. In 1952, shortly after Native Affairs in South West Africa came under South African authority, the central administration reformed marriage law in Ovamboland. It introduced civil

---

rather critical voice both towards the chiefs and towards colonial domination (see Werner 1990).

[58]   For an overview of the early history of strikes, see Gordon 1975.

[59]   In 1950, Annanias Stephanus Shipena complained to Native Commissioner Eedes that he had not been allowed to enter Ondjodjo Store wearing his eyeglasses. "I do not know why the Storekeepers do these sort of things. I do not wear glasses for nothing. I wear them because my eyes are bad. I do not wear the glasses because I wish to give the impression I am cheeky. I wear the glasses for my eyes." As Shinana was a member of Windhoek's Location Board and "often consulted in matters affecting Native interests in Windhoek and elsewhere in the Police Zone", Eedes took the complaint seriously. SWANLA's store manager Badenhorst replied that "for years past, it has been the practice, that all natives entering the store, are asked in 'OVAMBO' by the native store assistants to remove their glasses, this is entirely done for their own protection, because it was found that on occasions, while natives are making their purchases at the counter they suddenly swing round to speak to friends, and in doing so accidently smash the glasses of another native standing at the back of them, it has happened that the eye lids and eye brows of several natives were cut by the broken glass, and to obviate any serious eye damage this practice of having their glasses removed was resorted to. But if a native explained that he wears glasses for optical purposes, he is allowed to keep same on and is served by himself away from the crowd." (NAN NAO 95 42-6). Even if one could accept the explanation as the truth, the seemingly small incident is a frightening example of everyday discrimination. On Shipena's political activities in the Mandume Memorial Committee of 1937, see Shiweda 2005, 41.

marriage according to South African civil law as the only legal marriage form; only after the civil marriage could the union be blessed by a pastor. This galled the Churches; but what incensed local people most was that under the new regime, community of property between husband and wife and mutual inheritance automatically became the norm.[60] Under matrilineal traditional law, wife and husband had belonged to different lineages, and the homestead and most of the cattle and other goods belonged to the man's lineage. When a husband died, the wife and small children had to move back to the wife's relatives, who were supposed to care for them, and the offspring of the men's sisters inherited the homestead. Colonial authorities repeatedly tried to reform this system. According to the South African civil marriage law applied to Ovamboland in 1952, the homestead and its possessions should be owned in community of property by the couple; if the husband died, the wife should inherit it and continue living there with her children. To evade community of property, husband and wife could make written wills signed by the Native Commissioner, a Magistrate or an authorized marriage officer.

It is difficult to imagine a regulation that would have more tangible consequences for the distribution of status and power within the families. The new regulation indeed protected the weakest – widows and young children – and curtailed the power of men in general and lineage heads in particular. Its stipulations do not differ much from the new family law finally introduced in independent Namibia in 1996 and hailed by many activists as pro-poor and gender sensitive. But the weakest are rarely the first to organize against oppression, and the new law aimed into the heart of existing power relations. Opposition to the new regulation was fierce. In rare unity, all missions aligned with Native Commissioner Eedes in adamant resistance. When the new system was explained to the headmen, Anglican Mission Director in Odibo George Dymond wrote to his Bishop that the central administration's attitude had turned Ovamboland "from being an Earthly Paradise into a cauldron in which universal discontent and indignation are seething." Slightly later, a delegation of headmen protested against the new regulation. Answering his Bishop who had lauded the protest, "the more vocal the better", Dymond compared the South African administration's attitude towards local people with Nazi Germany and Stalinist Russia and wrote: "[The headmen] and I and the older members of our Mission staff know that vocal protest on the natives' part has no effect on the Native Affairs Department and on the Administration, at all. The uselessness of vocal protests is recognized by

---

[60] The reform had a curious origin: the Finnish Lutheran Church had inquired about the possibility of couples to make a will to mutually inherit their property. Eedes answered that this was not possible, as the Church marriage had no legal binding. The Church therefore applied for the introduction of a voluntary civil marriage status – and got rather more than it had bargained for in the introduction of an obligatory one. (See Tuupainen 1970, 119).

every intelligent native south of Angola and Rhodesia. Deeds not words are needed now. […] We have done with words now in Ovamboland; we have entered on resistance."[61]

This was slightly premature. Opposition to the colonial government continued with words alone for some more time (perhaps also because the Administration retracted the new marriage regulation in 1954). But words could be used to considerable effect, especially since locals had found ways to address a global forum. In 1946, Herero Chief Hosea Kutako had, with the help of Anglican Priest Michael Scott, written the first petition to the newly founded United Nations, protesting against South Africa's incorporation plans. South Africa regarded the petition as illegal, but the International Court of Justice in its opinion on the South African mandate affirmed the right of inhabitants of South West Africa to bring petitions before the United Nations.[62]

Image 18: Teophilus Hamutumbangela in front of the old store at Omafo, before 1944, posing with 'heathen' women for a mission photographer.

---

[61]   Letters George W. Dymond to Bishop, 8 December 1952 and 10 February 1953, Odibo Mission Archive (Originals in William Cullen Library, Johannesburg). For more material on local opinion on the marriage law, see NAN BOS, Views on the marriage law expressed by headmen and pastors, 13th January 1953.

[62]   International Court of Justice 1950, 137f. On Kutako, Scott and the petitions, see e.g. Gewald 2007, Saunders 2007.

My second example of 1950s opposition to South African rule used the UN as its forum. For some time, the luggage of returning contract workers had been searched by policemen at the control post in Namutoni, and policemen often confiscated goods under the pretext that they were stolen; very often, they then privately sold the goods. Most frequently seized were goods deemed "'inappropriate' within what [the policemen] conceived of as 'traditional' Owambo culture": "scented soaps, perfumes, small radios, and good-looking women's clothes."[63] Workers were particularly angered by this combination of theft and insult, and the confiscated goods often represented a considerable part of the workers' earnings. The young activist Eliaser Tuhadeleni (Kaxumba kaNdola) collected complaints by migrant workers and wrote a petition to the Assistant Native Commissioner Strydom in January 1954. When this petition was ignored, he invited Church leaders to a public meeting. Teophilus Hamutumbangela, an Anglican priest in Etale, collected further evidence and wrote a petition to the United Nations in April 1954. "The letter was given to the coloured woman from Onamakunde to post it in Angola."[64] After receiving an encouraging reply (which was intercepted by the police, but handed out to him), he started to hold political meetings in Onekwaya. When this brought him in conflict with traditional leaders, he was reassigned to Windhoek in 1956, where he was arrested several times. He returned to Ovamboland in 1958 and continued to organize resistance.[65]

---

[63]   Johannes Amwaalwa in Namhila 2007, 32.
[64]   Handwritten notes by Lazarus Haukongo, Odibo archives.
[65]   Lazarus Haukongo (*1928), at the time Rector of Onekwaya Parish and later Archdeacon of Ovamboland, wrote in retrospect: "The political meetings began to be held at Onekwaya in the same year of 1954 after replying the letter by United Nations. In those meetings, Fr Hamutumbangela explained to the people that South West Africa was a mandated territory which was given to South Africa by the League of Nations to supervise it but South Africa had no right to ill treat its people. So political meetings went on to be held until the Ovambo People Organization was formed which became to be South West Africa People Organization. According to my observation if I was not wrong, the Ovambo people at first were demanding to be given good treatment by South African Administration which was ruling the counry. But South Africa did not bother about their demanding until people decided to leave the country for exile." ("A brief history of Fr. Theofilus Hamutumbangela at Onekwaya", undated manuscript, Odibo Mission Archive.) – Hamutumbangela (1917–1990) was the son of a younger brother of Oukwanyama King Mandume. He went to school in Odibo from 1934. After spending a year as a contract worker, he became a qualified teacher in 1938 and studied Theology at St. Bede's in South Africa from 1944 to 1946. He was ordained as a deacon in 1946 and as a priest in 1947 and worked as a teacher in Odibo and Windhoek. (Biographical notes by Petrus Nandi, Odibo archives). He was a central member of the Mandume Movement (an important precursor of Swapo), and became a founding member of OPO and Swapo. He was Andimba Toivo ya Toivo's landlord in Odibo (personal communication Andimba Toivo ya Toivo, 20.8.2012), and during his time as a teacher in Windhoek, he taught English to Sam Nujoma. In March 1956, after his forced removal from Ovamboland to Windhoek, 300 workers in Walvis Bay went on strike when rumours said the authorities had arrested him (NAN BAC 6 HN 1/9/2/3, Disturbanes Walvis Bay). He was once more imprisoned in 1966 and, according to his widow, poisoned, leaving him physically and mentally impaired (Ondjokonona tai etwa komufi kadi meme ulalia yaHa-

These two incidents did not leave many traces in the administration's archives; the Native Commissioners at the time perceived them as minor disturbances. In retrospect, they mark the beginning of a serious liberation movement in Ovamboland. It was not born out of ideological concerns or political utopias, but from everyday grievances. People did not originally rebel against the system as such. They felt treated unfairly and oppressed by administrative measures that interfered with their everyday lives and neglected local rules of decent behavior. When justified complaints were not taken seriously by the authorities, the system was exposed as complicit to the infringements of one's rights, and formerly isolated instances of mistreatment could gain symptomatic value as intrinsic elements of the system. In that way, a new inheritance law which impaired senior men's rights and favored women instead could represent colonialism as effectively as petty apartheid on the workplace or theft by policemen.

The institutional history of the different liberation movements in Namibia has, at least in fragments, been written elsewhere.[66] Herman Adimba Toivo ya Toivo, Fanuel Kozunguizi, Solomon Mifima, Emil Apollus, Andreas Shipanga and others formed the Owambo People's Organisation in 1957 in Cape Town. It was launched in Windhoek in 1959 and reformed into Swapo, the South West Africa People's Organisation in 1960, with Samuel Shaafishuna Nujoma as its founding president. Other liberation movements, most importantly SWANU (South West African National Union) were founded at roughly the same time, but they did not play a significant role in Ovamboland. In the 1960s, Swapo developed into the most important liberation movement and gained a quasi-monopolistic status on the level of international diplomacy.[67]

This successful institutionalization is not the beginning of resistance; it is rather a symptom of the generalization of acts of defiance against colonial domination. It was only possible because people had previously mobilized around concrete issues, like the new inheritance law or policemen's thefts in Namutoni. Numerous similar issues existed throughout the country. Opposition to these experiences of injustice mostly clustered

---

mutumbangela, undated, probably written in 1990 by Petrus Nandi, Odibo archives). – On Tuhadeleni (or Kaxumba kaNdola, as he was mostly called locally) see the excellent collection of recollections by Namhila 2007. The accounts of his life by people who knew him personally show very well the status and respect accorded to him, and give excellent examples of the way hope and anger were invested into personal leadership in the early liberation movement. It might be mentioned in passing that when Toivo ya Toivo first met Kaxumba kaNdola in 1943, the latter sold guavas, sweets, soap and perfumes in Ondjodjo (Namhila 2007, 23).

[66] See, among others, Ngavirue 1997 [1972], Du Pisani 1985, Emmett 1999 [1987], Katjavivi 1988, Dobell 1998, Namhila 2007.

[67] In 1973, the UN General Assembly in its Resolution 3111 recognized "the national liberation movement of Namibia, the South West Africa People's Organisation", as "the authentic representative of the Namibian people". Swapo was then invited as an observer to OAU meetings, representing Namibia.

around respected community members who were close enough to the people concerned to be approached by them, but had enough public weight that their patronage could be seen as promising. Reverend Hamutumbangela, for example, had high status in several value systems. He was a nephew of King Mandume ya Ndemufayo and thus had a high place in the traditional status hierarchy; he was a well-spoken and well-known priest; and since his return from studying in Umtata from 1944 to 1946, where he had come into contact with ANC members, he was well connected to the leaders of the new political movements in South West Africa. Eliaser Tuhadeleni had started his political career as a music organizer, who gradually developed into a spokesperson for migrant workers.

All over Namibia, similar local political leaders emerged from grievances and small moments of opposition in the 1950s. With increasing economic and political interaction, more people experienced marginalization in the workplace, in everyday interaction with authorities and in society in general. The people complainants trusted to interfere on their behalf were often men and women who had been to European schools and knew their way through (or around) the colonial system. If these men and women rose to the situation and dared to voice the complaints, their reputation increased, and other people used them as spokespersons. Even before the liberation movement was institutionalized and found a political frame of reference, many of its protagonists were thus politicized, tested in concrete situations of conflict and well-known in their communities.

The founding of the Owambo People's Organisation in 1957 was of course influenced by the drive for independence all over Africa; it came in the year of Ghana's independence and two years after the Congress of the People had adopted the Freedom Charter in South Africa. But it was also anchored in grassroots activities in many places. More and more Namibians had learned to see local frictions not as isolated phenomena, but as symptoms of an unjust system. Anti-colonial movements elsewhere provided a framework of interpretation and a program for change, but the drive behind the movement was very concrete experiences of exclusion.

The rise of a nationalist movement went hand in hand with a decline in headmen's authority. In folk theory, headmen would have been the logical representatives of ordinary people whenever problems with the colonial power occurred. But for several reasons, chiefs and headmen could not fulfill the expectations set into them. They were closely integrated into the system of colonial administration. The new power had not only allowed them to reign on, but even had backed up their domination over their subjects; the price headmen had had to pay for this consolidation of power, however, had been their integration into the colonial hierarchy. In the 1950s, traditional authorities were no longer in a position to effectively question the Native Commissioners or the central government.

While the external stability of their rule had increased, they could no longer fulfill the social contract towards their subjects.

In consequence, their legitimacy started to crumble. It was weakest with migrant workers and the educated elite. Both groups lived in different worlds as the headmen, and traditional leaders could neither understand the problems they faced, nor sympathize with them. Instead, they perceived workers' protests to the administration as disrespect towards their own rule. Where migrant workers no longer felt represented by their headmen, the headmen saw the workers' spokespersons as usurpers threatening their own power and their personal dignity.[68]

Even though it was a slow process, headmen's authority degraded throughout the 1950s and 1960s. Confrontations between political groups and headmen became more frequent. The headmen reacted rather nervously and used their dominant position to apply pressure on critics. They imposed detentions, house arrests and floggings on political activists. The national government increased its pressure, as well. After both beatings and prison sentences had become more frequent, the first political leaders left for exile around 1960. They built up an efficient and diplomatically well connected external opposition. When South Africa ignored the UN General Assembly's termination of the mandate over South West Africa, Swapo's military arm PLAN (People's Liberation Army of Namibia) took up the armed struggle for independence in 1966.[69] Gradually, Ovamboland became a theatre of war, at first an intermittent low-intensity conflict characterized by sporadic guerilla actions, later a highly militarized, if still intermittent, counter-insurgence war by an occupational army against a guerilla opponent who used bases in MPLA-controlled Angola.

In December 1971, a general strike of contract workers broke out in Walvis Bay and quickly spread all over the country.[70] The strikers demanded to abolish the contract labor system and replace it by a free labor market with equal wages for white and black employees. After the protests extended to Ovamboland and led to local peasant revolts, the administration decreed draconian emergency regulations in early February 1972. Public meetings were forbidden and police and military troops resorted to force to dissolve anything they perceived as a public gathering.[71] This marked the beginning of tougher

---

[68] See, for example, the account by Ndemwoongela yaHashingola in Namhila 2007, 26 ff.

[69] For accounts of the first, still rather amateurish operations see Namakalu 2004.

[70] For an overview on the strike and its consequences, see Kooy 1973, Moorsom 1975, Bauer 1998, Jauch/ Sjipki 2003.

[71] In the most violent confrontation, eight people were killed at Epinga on January 30, 1972, even before the emergency measures were officially declared. According to local eyewitnesses, police surrounded an Anglican congregation gathered for a Sunday service. When a young man carrying a walking stick resisted to harassment by an officer, he was shot into the head. In the ensuing chaos, at least three other

confrontations between government and liberation movement and led to the militariza-tion of Ovamboland. The regulations were replaced by a new security regime in 1976 and again in 1978.[72] Following the Grootfontein agreement that ended the general strike, SWANLA was disbanded and recruiting transferred into the responsibility of the home-land government, without however changing the contract system as such. This further delegitimized the homeland administration.

The most emblematic sign for the estrangement and enmity between traditional au-thorities and liberation movement were the public floggings in 1972 and 1973. In the af-termath of the strike, 'troublemakers' were handed over by the police to the tribal courts, who often condemned them to be publicly flogged with palm branches on their bare buttocks. This form of punishment had occasionally been used by Chiefs in pre-colonial times, but suppressed by the colonial administration after World War I. In the face of growing opposition to chiefly rule, it was reintroduced in late 1952.[73] To have it applied by headmen on men and women whose only crime often was to oppose colonial rule and to express widely held opinions in public was a traumatic experience for many political activists in Ovamboland. For the new generation of political activists, it destroyed much of the remaining legitimacy of traditional leaders. It also triggered a move into exile and an intensification of political and military opposition to the South African government.

---

people were shot dead and several injured (see typed memorial by Lazarus Haukongo, Odibo Mission Archive). According to the official inquest, 30 policemen were trying to disarm and disperse a political meeting of 100 persons armed with pangas, axes and knobkerries. When the order to disarm the crowd was given by the commanding officer and somebody lifted an axe against a police officer, he fired his R1 automatic rifle into the crowd. (Windhoek Advertiser, June 26 1972). Ellen Ndeshi Namhila and Betty Hango-Rummukainen have collected oral history data on the massacre, which can be accessed at NAN AACRLS.105.

[72] On the regulation of May 1976, see Tötemeyer 1978, 127f.. Proclamation AG 26/1978 issued by the Administrator General – a former Supreme Court judge – authorized him to detain any person whom he considered a threat to the peaceful political process for an indeterminate time, without recourse to the courts.

[73] Eedes reported in that year that "Chiefs and headmen were informed that they could flog those young men who committed serious offences or showed disrespect to Chiefs and Headmen. They were quite content about it." NAN NAO 60 12/1 Quarterly Report 1/1953. The first reported case of a flogging I have come across is Ondonga Chief Kambonde's punishment of a woman with "four cuts with a palm stick" (NAN SWAA A 456 A50/93, 18.12.1953.) Two years earlier, in 1951, however, Elifas Kambuta complained in a letter to a friend about migrant workers who misbehaved: "Because once they get be-yond Namutoni, they throw off their ways of behavior, and change themselves as if they were animals, in order to spoil our names. They somehow behave the same here, but we have a palm stick (oshipokolo) and some fines." (NAN NAO 89 35/22(v1).) – After the 1973 floggings, the Churches applied to the Supreme Court in Windhoek for an interdiction. The Court ruled on 24 January 1975 that Ovambo tribal authorities were interdicted to arrest people on the grounds of being Swapo or Demcop members. Punishments would have to be carried out in private and could not exceed ten strokes; women were no longer subjected to it. Any corporal punishment would first have to be reported to a magistrate, who had to notify the registrar of the appeals court. (Tötemeyer 1977, 14).

The establishment of a homeland government and the emergence of an active liberation movement thus coincided and influenced each other. Between 1950 and 1975, what had been different social milieus consolidated and developed into political and military enemy camps. Headmen had been co-opted into the homeland government to such a degree that they had become indistinguishable from it and were seen by the liberation movement as their enemies. The trenches and high earth walls that protected many homesteads of headmen against attacks by their own subjects were symbols of the fission apartheid caused in Ovamboland society.

New social actors became political spokespersons for dissatisfied groups. But Swapo's political organization happened to a large part in exile. The leaders of the liberation movement became professional politicians who often had no way of earning a living and who believed in a revolutionary solution to Namibia's problems. Just as the homeland government and the South African occupation troops, the guerilla forced people to take sides and to prove their loyalty. In the widening gap between government and liberation movement, local people had to tread cautiously. Members of the political opposition who remained in the country and had to lead their everyday life there often were less radical in their opposition to the existing powers, and opted instead for a more pragmatic cooperation and reforms. The role of traders in Ovamboland provides ample material to come closer to the realities of political life in a divided society under military occupation, at a moment when personal life chances were inextricably linked to involvement with, or opposition to, government structures.

5 Traders in a modernizing society

All through the 1960s and 1970s, while the implementation of apartheid's homeland politics and the increasing strength of liberation movements transformed Southern Africa's political landscape, the number of locally owned shops in Ovamboland continued to grow. There were 28 licenced shops in Ovamboland in 1956 and 49 in 1959; ten years later, in 1969, the number had risen to 747.

The following figure shows the development of shops in the different polities. The figures for 1959 to 1968 were taken from a nominative list of licenced shops drawn up in early 1969 and seem rather reliable. Shops that went out of business before 1969 were only listed in that source for Oukwanyama and are not integrated into the total. Judging from the Oukwanyama data, however, only a surprisingly small percentage of licenced shops closed down during the 1960s – eleven out of 112.[1] Figures for the 1970s were collected in a more careless way and seem much less reliable.[2]

The overall trend is clear enough that minor inconsistencies in the figures can be neglected. After the pioneer phase in the 1950s, the number of shops grew by an average of 30 per cent each year during the 1960s. The 1970s were difficult years of stabilization during political crisis, while all informants described the 1980s – for which no figures have been accessible to me – as boom years.

---

[1] NAN OVE 11 9/2/5/2, Nominative list of traders. – Among the expired licences one finds Simon Sam Kaukungua's, which was last renewed in 1964 – the date when this co-founder of Swapo had to leave the country, only to return in 1989. Kaukungua was born in 1919 in Ohalushu in today's Ohangwena region as the son of a Lutheran priest. He took courses in building and carpentry in Ongwediva Training College in 1939/40 and served in the South African forces in Egypt and East and South Africa during World War II. After the war, he worked as contract laborer (1945/46), for the South African Railway Police in Port Elizabeth (1946–52) and for the Railway Police Criminal Investigation Department in Usakos (Central Namibia) from 1952 to 1958. In that year, aged 39, he opened a shop in Ohalushu. He became a founding member of OPO and of Swapo and was one of the party's most important organizers in Ovamboland. After organizing protests at a meeting with South African Minister of Bantu Affairs, M.C. de Wet Nel, in Ongwediva in 1964, he went into exile and became Political Commissar for Swapo's military wing SWA Liberation Army, later renamed People's Liberation Army of Namibia (PLAN) from 1964 to 1970. He went to China for military and political training and continued to play an important role in Swapo's exile organization, mostly in the Elders Council. (Hopwood 2006, 185f.; Thomas 2009.)

[2] They were probably compiled from lists drawn up by the different tribal authorities, and not all tribal secretaries took the task very seriously. I have left out the most wildly improbable data, but I am not too confident about the accuracy of the remaining figures.

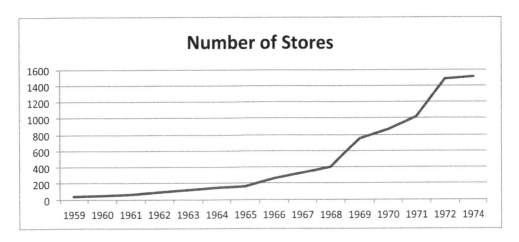

Image 19: The number of stores in Ovamboland according to official statistics.

The graph does not only include general dealers' licences, but all licenced trade businesses. If we break down the numbers according to the percentage of different trades, the following picture appears:

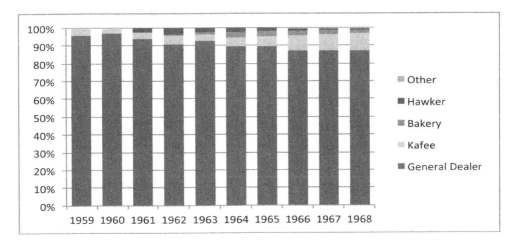

Image 20: Kinds of stores according to official statistics.

Chapter 3 has shown that among the first licenced businesses, there was a fair percentage of bakeries and restaurants. By the late 1950s, general trade was clearly more lucrative, and virtually all traders first established general stores. The percentage of eating-places grew again by the late 1960s, as successful businesspeople who already had a general dealer's licence opened bakeries, restaurants and cafés.

For the remaining part of this chapter, I concentrate on the establishment of trading patterns in the 1960s. In Chapter 6, I look more closely at urbanization and spatial changes connected to store development.[3] The dynamics of the 1970s and 1980s, which are intimately linked to the war economy, and the political role of traders are the subject of Chapter 7.

Three biographies of early traders

Who was behind the structural developments visible in the figures? What common experiences did traders share, and how did they find their ways into a new profession? The following three short biographies of successful traders will give first answers. They introduce themes that will become important in the following chapters and anchor them in the lives of individual people. None of the three traders, David Sheehama, Alfeus Hamukoto and Joel David, followed established career paths. They moved from place to place and from job to job before settling down as traders, and only in retrospect does a new pattern emerge from their decisions. In a moment of rapid social change, they made up new typical life-courses that others could follow later.

David Sheehama (Outapi)

David Sheehama was born in Outapi in July 1934. As a young man, he left as a contract worker in the South after a few years of primary school spent at Anamulenge. He found work as house servant with a family van Zyl in Windhoek and soon gained the trust of his employers, looking after the children and the house when they were on holidays. While in their service, he learned driving and sewing, and was later given a sewing machine by his employer.[4]

He took up tailoring bedding and clothing for his employers, but also began to sew bed sheets and dresses he sold to his acquaintances. Soon, he started to send clothes to Oranjemund and to Ombalantu with migrant workers, who sold them there on commission. When he was at home between contracts, he also collected eembe berries (*Berchemia discolor*), and made elder women from his village distill liquor from them, which he sold.

---

[3] One important trend in spatial organization is already visible in the figure above: until 1965, there is almost the same number of shops in Oukwanyama and in Ondonga. From 1966, business development in Ondonga leaps ahead of Oukwanyama, and Uukwambi does not lag much behind Oukwanyama in spite of much lower population numbers. This is due to the planned urban development in the Ondangwa – Oshakati axis on the one hand and the militarization of the Angolan border on the other.

[4] This short biography of David Sheehama mostly relies on coversations with his widow, Jakobina Sheehama, and his children Lucia Shikwambi, Rose-Mary Kashululu and Ras Sheehama in September 2012. Rose-Mary Kashululu was also so kind as to proof-read my text.

By the mid-1950s, he had saved enough money to think about establishing a home in Outapi. He moved back to the area around 1956 and continued tailoring and selling clothes. In addition, he put up a small mobile stall, selling different inexpensive goods after church service or at weddings. Shortly after his marriage to Jakobina, who came from a neighbouring homestead, in 1959, the couple established their home and a new shop about 800 metres from his parents' house, south of today's Outapi-Oshakati main road. They stocked sugar and other food items, paraffin, blankets and clothes, but also Cuca beer from Angola. His wife, to whom he had taught sewing, tailored dresses and baby carriers for sale and looked after the shop.

Image 21: David Sheehama.

When they established their own homestead, Sheehama had already earned enough money to buy one of the first cars in the area. He used it to buy goods for his shop, but more importantly, he started transporting migrant workers from Ruacana, Ombalantu, Tsandi or Okahao to the labour compound in Ondangwa. This was the first public transport in the area, and it proved very lucrative. Sheehama was soon able to buy more trucks and expand his service.

On their way to and from the South, migrant workers would congregate at his shop and stay in the yard for a few nights until the next truck left for Ondjodjo. If they bought their provisions at his shop on the return journey, he took them from the shop to their homes free of charge. Sheehama drove the first truck himself, but as his fleet expanded, he employed young men as drivers – among them Oswin Mukulu, today senior headman of Ombalantu and an important early trader himself.

Towards the end of the 1960s, after the railway bus had been extended to Ombalantu and Ruacana, the transport business declined, and Sheehama concentrated on trade instead. The money earned in transport and in his first shop allowed him to expand his activities. He opened a new store in Okalongo, 40 km west of Outapi, and in 1970 and 1973, he was able to take over the two BBK wholesales near Outapi;[5] one of them was managed for him by his sister Maria, the other (including the filling station) by his brother Peter. When Oshakati and Ongwediva grew as new towns, he opened shops there, as well. By the time of his death, he owned nine stores. When he applied for a wholesale licence after taking over Ombalantu wholesale in 1974, he listed the capital in his bank account as R273.559.-[6]

One bottle store outside Outapi, close to the Onakayale mission station where a school and a hospital brought customers, made good business – also from the Italian construction workers busy building Ruacana hydropower station. In 1972, he moved the family home and his largest store there. The new building was the most impressing private home and the largest locally owned store in Ovamboland. Planned by a Portuguese architect from Luanda, it was the first two-storey building in the area. A large shop and storage rooms were situated in the ground floor, the family apartment on the second floor. A peasant homestead behind the building housed guest rooms, kitchens and fireplaces and granaries. Sheehama inaugurated the house in November 1972 with a feast that drew large crowds.

The building was not only a proof of wealth. In the face of official racism and paternalism, it was a proud statement that black people could live in the same standards as whites. From the floor tiles to the furniture (which he had bought from Hotel Brumme in Otjiwarongo), the house was solidly modern. Lighting came from a generator that could be operated by a switch in his office wall, and around the house, he had orange, lemon, banana and fig trees brought from central Namibia for an orchard modelled on Anamulenge mission's.

---

5   NAN OVE (1) 9/4/4/97; NAN OVE (1) 9/4/4/110.
6   NAN OVE (1) 9/4/4/97.

Business at the new place was brisk, and stock for the shop came from many places. The SWANLA/ BBK wholesales in Ondjodjo and Oshakati were the most important suppliers of foodstuff and other items of daily consumption. Clothing or household goods, however, came from further away. Sheehama regularly flew to Cape Town in the 1970s to order finer clothes; the wholesalers in Tsumeb, Grootfontein and Windhoek were alternatives to BBK and means to widen the selection of goods. Among his most important customers were government employees, mostly nurses and teachers, many of whom became family friends. When they bought from his shop, Sheehama accepted their paycheques as payment, giving the change in cash and banking the cheques in Oshakati. Sheehama usually got up at 4am and started to work. He was frequently absent, buying new stock or looking after the other stores; while he was away, a large part of the work in the store was done by his family.

By the late 1970s, the business' rapid expansion came to an end. The shops suffered from the new security regulations and the increasing oppression. During this time, Sheehama became more active in politics. Even though he did not openly support the liberation movement, he had long had good contacts in Swapo and seems to have used his wide network and his mobility in order to support the movement. In 1979, the still new house was partly destroyed by a grenade; fortunately, nobody was killed in the attack. The family moved from the main house to a provisional hut in the homestead. There, in the night of March 14, 1980, a group of armed men raided the homestead, forced him to hand in the cash he had at hand, made him lay down on the floor and shot him dead with automatic rifles. The soldiers shooting him were black and used AK47s, but they were accompanied by white men who meanwhile raided the store, burned it down and destroyed the cars parked in the compound. In the official inquest, his death was marked as due to a terrorist attack.

After his murder, his businesses were taken over by his family. During the 1980s, they started to decline. Not only was the prime mover behind the business empire gone; his death left the family traumatized and much poorer for the destruction linked to it. In addition, the manner of his death singled the family out as politically suspicious to the authorities – a crucial point for businesses during the war situation of the 1980s.

Even though he died more than thirty years ago, David Sheehama's name is still very present in people's minds. When I asked about early businesspeople, everybody mentioned him, mostly together with Eliakim Namundjebo, Frans Indongo and Thomas Nakambonde from Oshakati. Even though he was a rich man and seemed rather strict to many, he managed to be well liked and very accepted in his community. He gave money to the churches (including ELCIN, although he himself was a Roman Catholic), donated a car to Ombalantu senior headman Kaimbi Mundjele and could be generous to poorer customers. Although he had little schooling himself, he had a great respect for learning and financed school fees for promising pupils. He had ten children with his wife Jakobina, the majority of whom went to exile in the 1970s, and quite a number of children out of wedlock. In addition, several foster children grew up in the household. As many traders of his generation, Sheehama was both proudly modern and firmly anchored in the rural world: he built the largest modern house in Ovamboland and simultaneously invested his wealth in a large herd of 5.000 heads of cattle; he wanted his children to become educated and work in government jobs, but kept good relations to the traditional authority; he knew Cape Town well, but he had no wish to live in a city.

Alfeus Hamukoto (Ohangwena)

Alfeus Hamukoto was born in Angola in 1920. Like many young Angolans, he looked for work in South West Africa and spent several years on contract in the Tsumeb copper mine. He saved some money and started to trade informally among his follow workers. He gradually moved to South West Africa, living with relatives in Ohangwena. In 1955, he decided to leave contract work and establish a business in Ohangwena, where the new traditional authority office had become a small centre of activity. People came there from all over Oukwanyama to consult senior headmen, apply for land grants or settle disputes in the tribal court. Hamukoto's shop was the first formal business in the area. He sold bread, meat and drinks, "little things for little money", as his son Mathias Hamukoto said.[7] A major part of his business was the sale of *tombo*, local beer from sorghum and sugar brewed by his wife. He bought the sugar needed for *tombo* and most other things at Omafo store, and sometimes in Ondjiva or Namacunde in Angola. Bottled Cuca beer and Gazosa lemonade regularly came from Angola, transported on bicycles by store hands. As

Image 22: Alfeus Hamukoto (ID photo).

---

[7] Interview Mathias Hamukoto, Ohangwena, 22 September 2006. Mathias Hamukoto lives as a teacher in Ohangwena.

most customers drank *tombo*, the four cases of beer transported on every bike could cover demand for several weeks in the early 1960s.

Hamukoto's first store was located at the place where Ponofi Secondary School was built in 1961, so he had to move his business to the other side of the traditional authority hall. The new school and the gradual expansion of Ohangwena village brought more demand, but the shop remained a small village store. Although Hamukoto never became rich, he could finance the education of his children, and gained considerable respect and status in the area. He often worked together with Joel David and Eliakim Namundjebo (see below); they gave each other credit, organized new supplies and regularly visited each other.

For him like for many businesspeople of his generation, especially in Oukwanyama, the war made things worse. He was often caught between his own Swapo sympathies and the necessities of doing business with customers from both sides. His eldest son went to exile to join Swapo in the early 1970s. When a brother of his was caught by SADF bringing food and clothes to PLAN soldiers in 1979, his shop was destroyed by SADF soldiers. He rebuilt the store and the boom of the 1980s restored his income, but he felt closer to retirement than to expansion and gradually abandoned trading. He died in 2001.

Joel David (Odibo) and Eliakim Namundjebo (Olunghono)

Joel David and Eliakim Namundjebo were two brothers[8] who independently opened successful trading stores. Their parents had come from Onghala, an Oukwanyama village west of Oshikango, to the Anglican Mission in Odibo. Both parents had been single children and only heirs and were rich in cattle.[9] They had seven children; three sons and one daughter opened their own trading stores.

Joel David was born in 1936.[10] He started to trade while he was still in school, driving around the villages on his bicycle and selling sweets. In November 1954, he opened a small store in a hut in his parents' homestead in Odibo. "It was a hut just like mine. You had to bow down to get in, and it was dark inside. Joel sold clothes, food and mahangu [pearl millet]. I bought mahangu from him", as Julia Mbida, who was born around 1918

---

[8]   Prior to the 1950s, people in Ovamboland were designated with their name and their father's name (e.g. Mandume ya Ndemufayo), not by European-style family names. When asked to define a family name by either the missions or the colonial administration, brothers often chose different family names. In this case, Joel kept his father's name David, while Eliakim opted for Namubdjebo. He still signed account books with 'Eliakim David' until at least 1969, however.

[9]   Interview Julia Mbida, Odibo, 29 September 2006.

[10] This, at least, is the official date given in the inquest into his death in 1976 (NAN LON 6/5-49/76). Some informants claimed he had been older, without being able to provide a clear date for his birth.

Image 23: Joel David (3rd from left). 5th from left is Petrus Kalungula, 2nd from right Petrus Ndongo.[11]

and spent most of her life in Odibo remembered. In his application to obtain a licence, Joel David states that he had a capital of £200, which he had earned as a migrant worker in Windhoek.

In the late 1950s, he moved his shop to a new building. The store and the adjacent cuca shop soon became one of the most important meeting places in Odibo. "There were other shops, too. Festus Kapapaleni had a small shop, in a hut; and Kaxukura had the nicest building. But he was so unfriendly that not many people went to buy there. The building was nice, but he did not have many things to sell. Joel's shop was the largest. And he was a good man. I knew his granny, his mother, his father. They were good people. Joel was a strong personality, he was very self-motivated. And he used to give to the people. He helped the community a lot. Later, when he had a car, he took the people to the hospital free of charge." Joel David became a respected member of the Anglican parish in Odibo. He was a church elder and part of the elite circle around the local catechists and teachers, who often met at his shop, and became so well known in the region that even the new

---

[11] Lukenge Archive, Odibo. The photo shows, left to right: Nikolas Shepelonia, Elifas Kanime, Joel David, Verisimus Pohamba, Peter Kalangula, Victory Samuel, Simon Shikangale, Petrus Ndonga, Philipusa Hamuntenga.

Ondonga Chief Paulus Elifas attended a cattle feast he held in Odibo in May 1968.[12] In addition to his Odibo store, he opened at least a second store at Onekwaya East in the mid-1960s.

In the night of May 1st, 1976, a group of around fifteen men speaking Oshiwambo came to his shop. They wore camouflage uniforms and automatic weapons and locked Joel and his customers into the shop, loading blankets, clothing and shoes onto Joel's pickup and taking 800 Rands from the office. Joel David was led into his office and executed by a rifle shot in the head. The official inquiry into his death only spoke of a "terrorist aanval" by unknown persons; in the village, most people think that he was killed by UNITA, while some blame Swapo. "I think it was Unita. They came on purpose to kill him, not as robbers. Joel was Swapo. Well, you could never tell who was Swapo. He may have been a Unita member before, when they were working together", Julia Mbida told me.

Image 24: Eliakim Namundjebo

Joel David's elder brother Eliakim Hinomenua Namundjebo was born on 16 December 1930. He grew up as a herd boy for his foster father Eliakim Haikonja from Okahandja, after whom he had been named, and received very little education until 1946. In 1947, he lived as a hunter in Angola and started to work on a farm near Omaruru in 1948. He was employed by a hotel in Mariental in southern Namibia from 1951 to 1953, a Windhoek hotel between 1954 and 1956 and the Windhoek Railway Club from 1956 to 1958. In 1959, he came back to Ovamboland, where he followed his brother's example and opened his first store at Olunghono, before marrying Teresa Shalimaxyena in late 1960.[13]

Namundjebo seems to have been an impressive and friendly personality who was well anchored in the community and used his wide network to expand his business very quickly. He was a churchwarden at the important Anglican parish of St. Mary's through

---

[12]   Diary Petrus Ndongo, Odibo Mission Archive, entry for 11 May 1968.

[13]   The biographical details were taken from a short obituary by his friend Petrus Ndongo, which can be found at the Anglican Mission archive in Odibo.

the late 1960s and early 1970s. He opened a second store at Ohandi (an outpost of Odibo Anglican Mission) in 1961 and ten other shops all over Ovamboland between 1966 and 1989. In 1987, he was the first trader from Ovamboland to open a business in Tsumeb.

When he travelled to Durban in 1965, he was very impressed with the economic life in the city, especially with the Indian traders there. On his return, he renamed his first shop "Durban Natal Store". From the mid-1960s, he also ordered clothing and textiles from Indian owned stores in Durban; other supplies came from Cape Town, Windhoek, Tsumeb or Otjiwarongo. Due to the number of stores he owned, he was able to buy large amounts of goods and to undercut most competitors; in Oukwanyama; only the BBK's Omafo store was cheaper.

Although he got rich rather fast, Namundjebo (just like the other two) managed to remain popular with a wide variety of people. When he died in a car accident in 1992, more than 3.000 people attended his funeral. Together with Frans Indongo and David Sheehama, Eliakim Namundjebo became one of the first 'black millionaires' of apartheid era Ovamboland. They were the richest and best known among the first generation of businessmen. The three embody different attitudes towards politics in the apartheid era. Sheehama was killed in 1980 probably for his Swapo support, Indongo became Minister of Economic Affairs in the homeland government, and Namundjebo mostly kept out of politics, even if he seems to have had Swapo sympathies.

After his death, his children took over Namundjebo's shops. Some of them still exist today, without really making money; the family invested the bulk of his fortune in real estate and tourism in Windhoek and the Coastal region in the 1990s (see Conclusion).

Types of stores

Alfeus Hamukoto, David Sheehama, Joel David and Eliakim Namundjebo are members of the first generation of traders. They were successful in business, became well-known and respected in their society and provided role models for younger people. Early in their lives, they experimented with different ways of earning a living. Earning money invariably meant leaving home and being employed by white bosses in a racist society. Opening a trading store was a new way to escape this imperative: a means of establishing oneself at home and gaining wealth and status without being subjected to the rules of a racialized workplace. By finding this alternative, living its advantages and becoming successful, the first generation of traders established a pattern which others followed.

An astonishing number of people managed to escape migrant labor and still earn a living by opening their own store. But not all shops were successful, and not every trader became rich. Towards the end of the 1960s, different types of shops were clearly distinguishable and influenced customers' choices.

Most traders started as informal itinerant traders. They sold sweets or other inexpensive items by walking or cycling through the villages around their living place, or by setting up a stall at church days. This trade did not require much capital and was not very risky. A new business could start with one bag of sweets, making a profit on the difference between bulk and retail price. If the trader managed to economize and reinvest the profits, investment and profits could gradually increase.

While many successful traders started as informal hawkers, far from all hawkers became successful traders. The three most important factors for success seem to have been business acumen, popularity and ability to reinvest. School children, who had few financial responsibilities and rather more time to spare than herdboys, were often very successful in hawking.

But hawking paid less well than migrant labor. After school, or when they turned sixteen, most young men started working in the South. Those who had traded before usually continued to buy and sell thing to colleagues on the mining compounds, and many others took up trading.[14] After some years of work, many men sought to settle down and found a household at home. Only very few people – usually the most educated – found formal employment in Ovamboland. For almost all returning migrants, establishing a homestead automatically meant becoming a farmer, as well. Without the capital to build a proper shop, trading in one of the homestead's huts offered a viable diversification strategy. It was also interesting for teachers or catechists who did not have the time or energy to engage in trading as a career, but who wanted to earn some extra money. These small stores catered for a village public who knew the store, its offer and its prices. They had no external signs, no special furniture (apart from a shelf or a table on which the goods were presented) and often no trading licence. People went there to buy specific items – sugar, sorghum, matches, tobacco or sweets, sometimes inexpensive household goods or textiles. There were no regular opening hours. People from the village usually knew when the owner or a family member would be at home, and outsiders rarely visited such stores. For the owner, trading in a hut did not involve many risks. It was necessary to have some capital which was not urgently needed otherwise and thus could be invested in the current stock, but if business was not good, it was relatively easy to dispose of the stock without high losses.

The really significant step towards becoming a professional trader was to construct a special building as a trading store and to formalize one's business. In 1959 – the year of

---

14   On trade in mines, see Gordon 1978, 178ff.

the Old Location Uprising –, the administration reformed the old licence arrangement which had left licences more or less to the Native Commissioner's discretion and harmonized it with the rest of the territory. The new regulation introduced an annual licence fee and made the granting of a licence subject to specific conditions.[15] All licences had to be approved by the Administrator of South West Africa, no less.[16] The highest administrative authority in the territory thus had to countersign every licence application, even every yearly application for renewal.

Seen from Ovamboland, this sounds rather excessive, but the main goal of the new regulation was not a formalization of trade in the northern reserves, but the control of shops in the native locations of central Namibia. Just as in South Africa, the number of Africans permanently living in the urban areas was constantly growing. They were needed as workers and increasingly as consumers, but their presence went counter to the idea of separate development and could only be allowed as a 'temporary' makeshift. To avoid the institutionalization of capital-intensive businesses whose presence would indicate permanence and make expulsions difficult, tight control of African trade in the urban locations was seen as necessary by the apartheid authorities. Under the new regulations, shops in urban areas were only allowed to sell "the Natives' daily household requirements", and that only if the necessities could not be obtained "without undue inconvenience" from shops in the white areas. Businesses could not be owned by a company or partnership of Natives, and no financial institutions, industry or wholesale concerns were allowed to be licenced. To avoid any appearance of continuity, all store buildings had to be "erected by the relative urban local authority and hired to the dealer".[17] In practice, however, controls were often less rigid than the regulations implied, especially in the reserves themselves.

Shop buildings officially had to meet certain criteria. The shop had to have a floor area of at least 180 square feet (16.7 square meters), of which at least 40% had to be

---

[15]   Counter-Memorial V, 108. Licence fees were paid into the Tribal Trust Funds. While some regulations in place in the police zone were introduced in Ovamboland, the licensing process was still much easier in the reserve. – The new regulation was presented to a gathering of headmen in Ondangua by the Chief Native Commissioner Bruwer Blignaut in May 1959: "Alle winkels in Ovamboland sal vanaf hierdie jaar behoorlik gelisensier moet word. Die kapteins en hoofmanne moet toesien dat die winkeliers die mense nit te veel laat betaal nie." (Olivier 1961, 383).

[16]   In legal terms, the authority to issue licences had been delegated by the South African Minister of Bantu Administration and Development to the Bantu Affairs Commission, of which the Administrator was an ex officio member; in practice, the approval of licences was left to his discretion alone (NAN OVE 11 9/2/1, Memo on Trading Licences, unsigned, undated (1963 or later)).

[17]   NAN OVE 11 9/2/1, Memo on Trading Licences, unsigned, undated (ca. 1963)). When Leo Kuper, in his excellent book on the "Black Bourgeoisie", states that "partnership does not attract Africans" (1965, 264f), he is obviously unaware of the legal impossibility to set up partnerships.

free from furniture; the floor had to be constructed of cement or a similar material, the ceiling dust proof and at least 10 feet high. Even the size of the counter was regulated: it had to be "not less than 6 feet long by 2 feet broad".[18] If a trader planned to erect a new building, plans had to be submitted in advance.[19] From the 1960s onwards, most traders used a simple standard design or rented their shops from BBK, who constructed the building according to one of several blueprints. Even today, these models are easily recognized in every town and village of the region. Other stores were built in more individualistic ways often modeled on the better-known stores; the corrugated metal walls of Namundjebo's Durban Natal Store, for example, became a blueprint for a number of other shops.

Inside, most stores were organized in a similar and easily recognizable fashion very close to what we have seen from Beersmann's Endola store. A rectangular central space, often furnished with benches or chairs, was reserved for the customers entering the store and separated from the goods and the salesperson by a large counter, often in horseshoe form. Shelves lined the walls behind the counter; on the counter, balance, cash register and display stands were placed.

These shops usually had names painted on the outside. If they served drinks, posters of breweries often decorated the outer walls. While they were known to everybody in the village and often had a reputation for specific kinds of goods, they also attracted customers who did not know the owner personally.

In the early 1980s, a last type of store made its appearance in Ovamboland: self-service chain stores. The most successful shop owners had started to expand by opening branches in different areas in the 1960s. Frans Indongo, Eliakim Namundjebo, David Sheehama, Israel Jona,[20] Thomas Nakambonde, later Jairus Shikale were some of the better-known businesspeople who owned several stores. This allowed them to get more favorable prices from suppliers and to economize on the high transportation costs to Ovamboland. In the early 1980s, the first of these branch stores were opened as or transformed into self-service stores modeled on similar stores in Windhoek and South Africa. On a much larger shop surface than most counter stores had, goods were placed in display shelves in the

---

[18] NAN LGR 7/1, Trading Licence Regulations.
[19] Applications had to be made to the Administrator by way of the Bantu Affairs Commissioner until 1968, when responsibility changed to the Department of Economic Affairs of the Ovamboland Executive Council.
[20] Israel Jona also was a member of the Owambo Legislative Assembly until he resigned in 1985 (Owambo Official Gazette 13, 6/85). At about the same time, he was one of the Oshivambo-speaking farmers allowed to farm in Ukwangali. After independence, he continued to combine farming and business, being for example on the Board of Directors of Meatco, the cooperative which handles 80% of Namibia's meat exports.

customer area and paid by the customers at central cash registers. These stores were more expensive to build and had higher fixed costs; they only made sense in busier areas, where quicker turnover compensated for the increased investment. Among Eliakim Namundjebo's stores, for example, the ones in Ondangwa, Eenhana and Oshakati were opened as self-service supermarkets.[21]

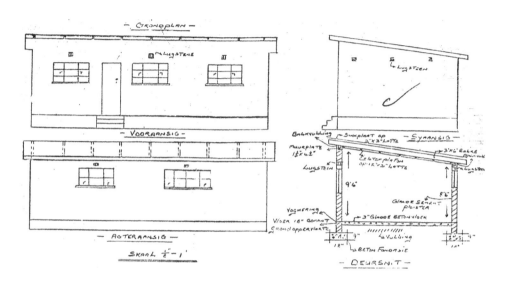

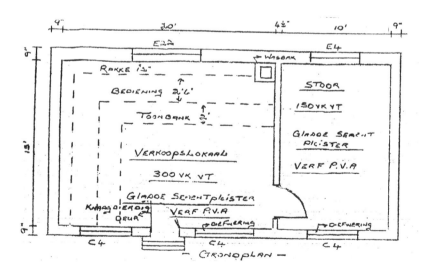

Image 25 and 26: Blueprints for BBK stores, late 1970s.

[21] Interview George Namundjebo, October 2006.

Image 27: A variation on BBK's blueprint: Evaristus Shipoh's store in Onhuno

Image 28: My translator, field assistant and friend Joesph Ndakalako inside Shipoh's store. Evaristus Shipoh's son, who is Permanent Secretary in the Ministry of Youth, National Services, Sport and Culture, has restored the shop's interior to its 1970s design.

Image 29: Shopping at a local shop, 1970.

Image 30: The interior of Namundjebo's Durban Natal Store is empty today, but still reflects the shop's spatial organization. The corrugated metal walls, too, are clearly visible.

Image 31: Oshakati Wholesale, 1970.

Image 32: A contemporary informal store.

Image 33 and 34: Two examples of small and large stores built in the 1970s: Oneshoko Store near Ondangwa and Sadeg Kristian's store south of Omafo.

Licenced and unlicenced trade

In 1974, the Department for Statistics in Windhoek wanted to find out the number of unlicenced shops in Ovamboland, and the Owambo Department of Economic Affairs asked the headmen to provide figures. It is not quite clear what businesses were included in this category, but the number is astonishing: In addition to 1.388 licenced shops, there were 6.075 unlicenced ones.[22]

---

[22] The total number of shops is impressive for a rural area with a low degree of division of labour, even if the

Most of these probably were 'Cuca Shops', as the local equivalent to a South African shebeen was called: small drinking places selling *tombo,* soft drinks, beer or wine. The administration had largely tolerated them in the 1960s. In 1973, a new regulation officially legalized the sale of beer in Ovamboland and brought a further boost to their number. The boundary between cuca shop and store was rather blurry: most cuca shops also sold a few goods as a sideline, and many shops also served drinks. It is thus understandable if the column mentioning 6.075 unlicenced businesses was labeled "Cuca shop sonder licensie" in one version of the statistics, "ongelisensieerde winkels" in another. In any case, at least four times more informal shops and/ or cuca shops than formally licenced stores existed by the mid-1970s. In Ondonga alone, 3001 unlicenced shops were counted, and in Uukolonkathi, 408 unlicenced shops stood against 39 licenced ones.

The administration seems to have taken the existence of a large number of unlicenced stores for granted. Even though unlicenced shops were officially illegal, no real effort was made to formalize informal businesses. In the eyes of the modernist administration, this petty trade seemed hardly worth bothering; real economic activity started with book-keeping, concrete floors and exclusive occupations.[23] As long as trade was a mere sideline for peasants or migrant workers, it almost escaped their notice: in spite of the scale of informal trade, there is virtually no mention of it in the archives apart from the reference cited.

So if they could escape official notice, why did traders bother to obtain a licence at all? They had a number of reasons to do so. If a trader was politically active, the administration or the police could use the lack of a licence as a pretext to close his or her business down, or to cause more trouble than taking a licence would. But the real advantages were economic, not political. First of all, a trading licence was necessary to buy wholesale. Wholesale stores in the Police Zone mostly asked for the licence number, the SWANLA/ BBK/ ENOK stores always did. Sure enough, licenced traders often passed their licences on to unlicenced traders or made purchases for them,[24] but this gave the patron a certain power over his unlicenced colleague and was punished by temporary licence suspensions if detected. Secondly, obtaining a pass to the police zone was much easier for licenced traders; for Tsumeb, yearly permits were issued without much ado. Finally, only licenced

---

percentage of traders does not reach the same level as, for example, in Ghana, one of the classic examples of market societies. One in thirty-nine people in Ovamboland owned a (cuca-)shop in 1974. In Ghana in 1960, one in twenty-two people traded goods, but the vast majority were part-time market traders. Even the capital Accra had less than 400 shops for 488.000 people in 1966 (Lawson 1971, 380ff.).

[23] The new government after 1990 inherited much of this attitude. When shebeens came to the legislators' attention, it was as a problem of public hygiene and security. A new liquor law requiring shebeens to take licences was finally enforced in 2006, but had to be retracted after popular protests (see Dobler 2010).

[24] Interview Mano Haindungo, Outapi, 6 October 2006.

traders qualified for most BBK support measures. Credits, training courses and rented facilities were only available to licenced traders.[25]

Licences had to be renewed every year, and while a trader might forget the renewal or be late for it, only very few slipped back to informal trade. If a businessman or -woman had made the necessary investments and taken the trouble to obtain a licence, it was seen as an asset rather than an obligation.

Image 35: A Cuca Shop in Odibo, 1972.

Turnover

Even though a licence marked that a business had reached a certain threshold, turnover differed widely between licenced shops. In 1975, traders were asked about their monthly purchases and sales, about the value of their stock, the number of people they employed and the total wages paid. Due to reorganization in the National Archives in Windhoek, I was only able to compare a small opportunistic sample of 27 shops. The average shop bought goods for 376 Rand a month and sold goods for 496 Rand – a profit rate of 31 per cent. The average stock was worth R 1.800, and 1.8 people were employed, earning

---

[25] The first credit program for informal businesses was started in 1986 only. ENOK 1987, ix.

an average of R 11.30 per person per month. This brought the average net profit to about R 100 per month – about as much as a well-paid underground mine worker earned, including overtime.[26]

A few large stores earned much more than most others. Only six of the 27 stores earned more than the average; taken together, their turnover was as high as that of the remaining 21 shops. The smallest shop sold goods for R 60 a month, while the largest store in the sample, Jacob Nangolo's Kontanto Store, bought goods for R 2.400 a month and sold them for R 4.000 (with six employees collectively earning the princely sum of R 56). The benchmark, however, was set by BBK, whose Ondjodjo wholesale had a monthly turnover of more than R 250.000. Even the smaller Oshakati branch sold goods for an average of R. 21.000.

So even among licenced shop owners, the disparities in income, status and wealth were huge. Most traders managed to live on their income, but only a few became rich, and the school kid selling sweets by cycling through the villages had little in common with the owner of a supermarket chain. But hawkers, small and big shops, jointly formed a distribution system that offered flexible choices to customers and introduced Ovamboland to consumerism. As transport was either expensive or time-consuming, small village stores charged slightly higher prices than the supermarkets, but were the obvious choice for everyday purchases by the rural population. For goods that were not available in one's village or for the more expensive acquisitions – clothing, shoes or other consumer goods – shops in the new towns offered better choice and lower prices, as the higher turnover made it possible to invest larger sums in stock.

Stock and supplies

In the 1960s and 1970s, virtually all shops in Ovamboland were general stores; only very few businesses specialized in clothing, hardware or bicycle spare parts. A core range of the most important products was available in almost every shop. The larger the shop, the more different goods it stocked and the wider the selection became. Among the core goods were brown sugar needed for brewing beer, salt, sweets, biscuits, paraffin, 'Lifebuoy' or 'Sunlight' soap, often mahangu or rice, sometimes tinned foods, tobacco, groundnuts or beans.

---

[26] NAN OVE (2) 9/4/4. For the difficult calculation of mine worker's wages in the mid-1970s, see Gordon 1977, 152ff. – The only earlier turnover figures I could find are from 1957, when Native Commissioner Bruwer Blignaut mentioned Silas Kuejo from Ondangua as the most successful native trader, selling goods for £600 and making a profit of £220 per year; Taimi Abraham from Oshitayi was second with a profit of £100 (Olivier 1961, 384).

The next step in the expansion of a shop was the inclusion of clothing and textiles and simple household goods. In the late 1950s, most people could obtain "lappies" (pieces of usually striped cotton cloth), shirts, skirts, trousers, blankets, dried fish, vaseline or paraffin lamps within half a day's walk. Only the largest shops also sold suitcases, hoes, bicycles, ploughs, simple pharmaceuticals or the full range of clothing articles. In the 1960s and 1970s, smaller stores expanded their range to include more textiles, toiletries and tinned foods.

Fresh produce was almost unknown in the stores; transport costs and the high risk of spoiling prevented the sale of fruit or fresh vegetables.[27] Smaller stores with low turnover often kept stock for months or even years before selling it.

Supplies came from the SWANLA/ BBK/ ENOK wholesale stores or from wholesalers in the Police Zone and South Africa. Buying in Tsumeb, Windhoek, Cape Town or Durban was cheaper, but only worth the expensive trip if you could buy large quantities. Most small traders could not afford to keep the necessary sums invested in stock and opted for buying at the local wholesalers. Richer traders often went to Tsumeb and frequently to the central Namibian towns. They had long-standing relationships with specific wholesalers, but both sides usually preferred personal transactions to distance sales. Goods usually had to be paid for in cash.

Evaristus Shipoh from Onhuno, for example, regularly drove to Tsumeb or Grootfontein on a two-day supply trip. He bought large quantities at once, and wholesalers sometimes had problems supplying more than one trader. If he met David Sheehama, Frans Indongo or Eliakim Namundjebo coming back from Tsumeb on the road, his son recounts, he changed directions and drove to Grootfontein; if the trader Induma from Rundu had been in Grootfontein, he drove on to Otjiwarongo.[28]

The social role of traders

Even poorer traders often played an important role in their village and gained considerable status. Before World War II, churches and chiefly courts had been the only regular public meeting places. People socialized in homesteads or while working on the fields. The slaughter of a cow or the brewing of a pot of *tombo* provided occasions for social exchange, and people met for church service or at the numerous life-course feasts.

---

[27] Most of the Europeans living in Ovamboland had standing orders with Wecke and Voigts in Grootfontein for fresh goods. Groceries were transported in cooling boxes in the back of the Railway Bus once a week, but nevertheless often arrived spoiled (personal communication Nancy Robson, Odibo, June 2006).

[28] Interview with Dr. Peingeondjabi T. Shipoh, Okatope, 28 September 2006.

Some homesteads saw more visitors than others, but just as homesteads were scattered across the landscape, social meeting places were decentralized and only rudimentarily specialized.

From the start, the new shops were conceived of as hospitable public places under the responsibility of an individual. They were simultaneously public places – everybody could go there and stay for some time – and private spheres closely associated with the person of the owner. One did not only visit a shop to make purchases. To visit a store was a social occasion, and shopping was often relegated to the second place. Many shops also served drinks; others had chairs and benches on a verandah or along the counter where people could just sit and talk. One came there to meet friends, to exchange the latest gossip or simply to pass some time in company of others. Over the years, many shops developed into nodes of the political sphere in the widest sense of the term: venues in which a society discussed its own future.

Most people had their favorite shops. If different shops were situated in an area, shops came to be associated with social circles. The more expensive ones (or those run by a well-respected individual) usually attracted the local elite; others were meeting-places for, say, young people, for migrant workers or for Christian women. The circles often grew around the shop owner as the central figure. He was in a position to extend patronage to his customers in the form of invitations, credit or transport facilities. As the host, he could participate in every group meeting at his shop; as a fellow trader, colleagues often welcomed him into their own circles. When a traders' circle expanded, so did his customer base and, with the necessary luck and know-how, his wealth. He could stock more goods and attract better-off customers, who again could become part of his social network. A traders' status was not merely defined by his wealth, but increasing wealth gave him better opportunities to extend patronage and increase his social status.

Throughout my stay in Namibia, when I asked people about successful traders, a few sentences came up in almost every story. "He was friendly to everybody, rich or poor"; "He drove people to hospital free of charge"; "She cared for the community"; "He gave money to his parish". These catchphrases denote typical elements of patron-client relationships. The trader is simultaneously described as different and as part of the community: (s)he is rich, converses with important people and has the resources to help the poor; but (s)he does not shun the common people and helps them whenever necessary. His or her status is thus well earned and rather a source of pride to the community than a threat to social cohesion.

I was very surprised not to hear more negative things about successful traders. Where traders live in peasant societies, the relations between both groups are often rather strained.

Peasants tend to see traders as greedy and rather unnecessary outsiders not doing any *real* work.[29] This tendency is much less marked in Ovamboland. This is certainly partly due to the moral code of public behavior in central northern Namibia, which defines criticism of people of higher status as disrespectful. But three other factors are more important.

Firstly, traders did not make a living from the peasants' agrarian production. The money spent in the shops usually came from outside sources: from migrant work of family members. Agriculture was mostly subsistence oriented, so traders and peasants did not compete for the same resources, and traders' profits did not clash with subsistence needs. Secondly, traders and customers came from the same social milieu. Successful traders were neither strangers nor bosses, but village people who had made it. Their success was a sign of social mobility rather than of class differences. Thirdly, no local trader could have been successful without being socially accepted. In order to gain enough customers, you had to be well liked. Joel David's colleague from Odibo had the nicer building, but as he did not treat his customers well, he had less success in a village society in which everybody knew him.

Rich traders thus typically were well seen and well integrated, but they differed in status from most of their customers. The ideal trader – typically male – had more money, and sometimes used it to support people in need; he had a nice car and transported people to hospital or to school; he was a church elder present at the same service on Sunday, but giving higher offerings. His house was modern and expensive, but he did not close his doors to the neighbors. Petrus Ndongo's manuscript characterization of Eliakim Namundjebo is archeteypical: "E.H.N. worked wonderfully. He was incorporated with everybody. He greeted big men at the same to poor men. He furnished the country with necessary they need. He helped all the Churches wonderfully. He made big feasts for all people. He made goodbye meetings to Missionaries who were going back to overseas. He helped many people with food, money etc. [...] He travelled a great deal to SA, Asia, Europe and the US where his daughter was studying."[30]

Credit and traders' networks

One very tangible aspect of the trust and status accorded to traders was that many people in their social environment used them as banks. Until the 1960s, the SWANLA stores were not allowed, in the words of the licence regulation, "to give credit to Natives".[31] The ad-

---

[29] See Dobler 2004, 257–264; for theoretical perspectives on the relation, see Foster 1965, Mintz 1967, Evers 1994, Verne 2006.
[30] Petrus Ndongo, notes probably for Namundjebo's funeral, 18 February 1991. Odibo Mission Archive.
[31] NAN SWAA 135-22, Regulations on Trading Licences in Ovamboland, October 1936.

Image 36: A pickup transporting people to town, 1972.

ministration feared that the usual practice of selling goods on credit would give traders the opportunity to exploit local people, who were often not used to bookkeeping and written registers. Before the first savings bank in Ovamboland opened in 1967 and a long time after, people usually either kept their cash at home or entrusted it to others. Giving money to somebody else for safekeeping protected one's savings against theft, against demands from the family and friends and against one's own temptations. Migrant laborers in particular often preferred to entrust their wages to somebody living in Ovamboland instead of keeping them in the workers' compounds, where theft was much more frequent. For the recipients, the relatively small risk of theft was outbalanced by the possibility to use the funds given to them until they were claimed back, and often by considerable inflation gains: as keeping money for others was perceived as a service rendered by the recipient, not as a credit by the giver, no interest was paid.

Respected traders were among the most favorite recipients of funds. They had a reputation to lose, so they were not likely to embezzle or lose the money; they needed money to work with and thus liked to receive credit; and they turned over enough money to mobilize resources if somebody claimed his or her money back.

In Petrus Ndongo's papers, two small credit books survive, one covering different lenders and borrowers through the 1950s, the other mainly noting the sums given by Ndongo to Eliakim Namundjebo for safekeeping.[32] Over the years, he entrusted more than R 5.000 to Namundjebo. When he asked for R 70 from Eliakim's son George in 1992, he called his deposits "my savings account", and they certainly functioned as such. Deposits and withdrawals were marked in both sides' books and countersigned by the receiver.

This credit relation between friends was the most extensive among Ndongo's, and the only one to last over more than thirty years. But he also marked debts and loans to 56 other people. About half of them were traders themselves. Often, the initial payment took the form of goods given on commission to each other, but the amounts remained in the books long after the merchandise had been sold. An extensive web of credit relations thus connected traders all over Ovamboland, and they often used these accounts to settle cash debts in a different region by correspondence.

Most of the remaining half of the sums had been entrusted to Ndongo by migrant workers during their absence. These sums, as well, often remained in Ndongo's safekeeping for several years. The percentage of well-known names we find among the 57 people in Ndongo's register is a measure of how small and how closely connected the new elite was in the 1950s. There is Herman Toivo ya Toivo, Rev. Gabriel H. Namuejah (the first Anglican Priest from Ovamboland), Joel David, Eliakim Namundjebo and their sister Elizabeth, Teofilus Tueumuna (teacher at Olukonda Mission School and the only Lutheran on the list), George Namoloh (at the time a young migrant worker, later Minister of Defense in independent Namibia), Emmanuel Haipinge (later Deputy High Commissioner in Zimbabwe) and Peter Kalangula (Anglican priest, founder of an independent Anglican Church; as a politician chairman of the Owambo Executive Committee, delegate to the Turnhalle Conference and President of the DTA coalition).

---

[32] Ndongo, who often proudly used his byname "father of the children", had left his village to attend school at Odibo mission as a ten-year old child in 1928. After two years with the Native Military Corps from 1942 to 1944, he became a well-known teacher and opened a small trading store in Odibo in the mid-1950s.

It is not surprising that most of Ndonga's contacts were Anglican Ovakwanyama who knew him from his work in Odibo. Traders' networks were often centered on mission stations, schools and parishes, where the members of the new elite first came into contact with each other and established relations of friendship and trust. A few individuals occupied central positions linking two networks by virtue of different social roles. Herman Toivo ya Toivo, for example, was connected to Anglican Ovakwanyama circles through his schooling and denomination, and to Lutheran circles further South by both his military service and his political work. Toivo Ndevaetela from Engela was an important member of the Lutheran parish and schooled in Oshigambo, but through his later work as school inspector and his role in the Ovakwanyama traditional authority he became well connected in Odibo, too.[33]

Traders' networks were one of the ways by which the ethnic organization in homelands (in this case, within a homeland) was translated into everyday practices. Whithin Ovamboland, they were not primarily ethnic in origin. Exchange between the Lutheran parishes of, say, Elim in Uukwambi, Ohangwena in Oukwanyama and Oniipa in Ondonga was livelier than between Anglicans from Odibo and Lutherans from Engela, both situated a few kilometers from each other in Oukwanyama. But ethnicity was one element underlying the networks, a different form of categorization that could be invoked at different times. In retrospect, one finds strong symmetries between the organization of elite networks in the 1950s and today's increasingly ethnicized cleavage between SWAPO and the breakaway party RDP (Rally for Democracy and Progress). Fractured by exile experiences and a long history of personal friendships and

Image 37: Petrus Ndongo.

---

[33] Ndevaetela was born in the late 1920s as the son of a hospital worker in Engela. He earned his first cash as a child, selling hand-woven mats to the Mission. After three years of schooling in Engela, he worked in a farm kitchen in the police zone from 1947 to 1950 and learned to speak Afrikaans. Back in Ovamboland, he worked as a builder when Ondobe and Okalongo schools were constructed and continued his schooling in Oniipa and at Ongwediva Teachers Training College. After three years as a teacher, he went to the new Oshigambo Senior Secondary School and was in the first class passing Standard VIII. He became principal of Engela Boys School in 1963 and went to the Paulinum in Otjimbingue with the aim of going to Finland to study theology. Instead, he returned to Ovamboland to teach at Ongwediva Teachers Training College and became Sub-Inspector, later Inspector of Schools for Oukwanyama and Uukwambi in 1967, a post from which he retired in 1992. He started trading in the 1960s, as well, opening a store at his homestead behind the Finnish Mission compound in Engela, which became a meeting place of the local elite. (Interview Toivo Ndevaetela, Engela, October 2006).

enmities, the old ties are still visible today, and former traders play an important role on both sides.

In the twenty years between 1955 and 1975, traders became the largest and most important professional group in the modern sector in Ovamboland. Only four European-owned shops had existed in 1952, all several days' walk from each other. In 1975, almost everybody in Ovamboland could reach a shop within one or two hours. For a great number of people in the area (more than 7000 in 1975, if one includes the unlicenced stores and cuca shops), trade became a way of earning a living and gaining a new place in society. The traders active in 1975 were all first-generation traders. They had not inherited a business, but had at one point in their lives decided to invest savings into a business.

Their previous life histories are varied, but they share common features: after some education at mission schools, they tried their luck in the South for several years and often in a multitude of jobs. The contract system encouraged such patchwork careers and discouraged advancement in a paid job. After settling down in Ovamboland and around the time of their marriage, migrant workers professionalized an activity which they had often previously pursued in their free time: investing disposable funds into trade goods. No other way of establishing oneself in a stable, respected and lucrative position in the homeland was as promising as trade, at least not for those whose education was not good enough to become a clerk, a teacher, a nurse or a priest. Many of the traders opened shops as one of several sources of income; they continued to grow millet and sorghum and to own cattle, and some left the store in the care of a relative while they went on further contract work. Only the more successful businessmen became full-time professional traders; many others, however, saw themselves foremost as traders, not as peasants.

This description already takes one character of traders for granted: almost all traders were men. Women had been prominent among the first people who opened trading stores in the early 1950s, but as the number of shops grew, the proportion of women traders declined. By 1969, only 30 of 484 shop owners whose first name was mentioned in the register were women – a mere seven per cent. 25 of those 30 women traded in Ondonga, which brings the percentage of women traders in the remaining polities to little more than one per cent. These figures, of course, only concern the official licencees, who were not always responsible for actual trade in the shops. The male owner almost always bought the supplies and represented the store in the local society. He rarely did the actually selling work, for which his wife, daughters or other female relatives were mostly responsible. So women were crucial for running many stores, and at least five of the thirty women traders were widows of male traders who had taken over the shop after their husband's death.[34] But single women usually simply lacked the funds to open a store, whereas single men could earn the seed capital by migrant labor,[35] and both the outward-oriented role of shop owners and the public status accorded to them was more compatible with male than with female roles in local society.

Male traders emerged as a new and closely connected social group in the 1950s and 1960s. They were mobile, enterprising and self-motivated, and they earned their living in the cash economy. This set them apart both from the old elite of headmen and from the modernist group of employed clerks and teachers. They were more critical of the government than the headmen, but in order to be successful, they had to remain socially much more embedded than the clerks. This made them much less radical than many clerks and teachers were, and it often brought them between the lines in the guerilla war, which would change their businesses and public lives for better or worse in the late 1970s and 1980s.

Before turning to the war, the next chapter will look at the spatial changes brought about by the new shops. Just as the ascent of traders changed the local society, the establishment of shops changed the physical landscape and had important consequences for social life.

---

[34] Interestingly enough, most shops seem to have been inherited through common law succession, which was still the exception in 1960s inheritance patterns. This is a further indication that shops were seen as a 'modern' economic activity substantially different from agriculture.

[35] This is, once again, an oversimplification. Although the number of male workers was substantially higher than the number of female migrant workers, not only men left Ovamboland for work. The history of female migrant labour remains yet to be written; they rarely figure in the sources, and their typical lifecourses are not well known. It seems that, while migrant work was a normal and culturally expected phase in masculine life, female labour migration rather had the character of an individual choice which could less easily be integrated into a typical lifecourse. Many female migrant workers married and stayed in central Namibia rather than returning to Ovamboland.

6   Stores and spatial organization after 1950

Namibia is not a country of big towns. Windhoek, the capital and Namibia's largest city, has around 315.000 inhabitants today; Rundu and Walvis Bay, the second and third biggest towns, are estimated at 81.000 and 67.000 respectively. The country's population has grown fourfold since 1950, when less than half a million people lived on South West Africa's entire surface of 824.000 square kilometers, but overall population density in Namibia still ranks as the second lowest in the world, right after Mongolia.[1]

In this sparsely populated country, the former Ovamboland stands out as the exception. At any time in the last century, almost half of Namibia's population lived on these mere 6.3 per cent of the country's surface, of which more than half is barely habitable due to lack of water. This brings population density in the central areas of Ohangwena region and some other settlement foci to more than 150 persons per square kilometer.

But high population density does not necessarily correspond to urban settlement forms. In pre-colonial times and well into the 1950s, Ovamboland had no towns. People lived in scattered homesteads usually comprising between one and twenty persons; in exceptional cases, large chiefly homesteads could be home to over a hundred people. Homesteads were not permanent; they were moved to a different location every few years when soil fertility for the fields surrounding the houses was depleted.[2] Several homesteads formed a sub-ward with a sub-headman as its political authority; several sub-wards comprised a ward under a headman, several wards a district under the authority of a senior headman. The homesteads of senior headmen and chiefs were larger centers of political activity, but even their venue changed when a new headman took office. Homesteads are usually thirty to several hundred meters from each other. Together, they form a large single settlement area covering the central areas of Ovamboland. One can walk long distances across the country and never come out of sight of homesteads, nor reach anything that resembles a village in the European sense of the term.

Since the 1870s, mission stations became the first permanent central meeting places, and the first architectural forms that fundamentally differed from a normal homestead. Missionaries usually started their work in improvised shelters under a tree, but wherever

---

[1]   This does not include Western Sahara, whose population density figures between Namibia and Mongolia. Namibia's population had grown to 750.000 by 1970, to an estimated 2.1 million by 2010 (Mendelsohn et al. 2002, 163).

[2]   Tönnies (1911, 52) puts the time before moving a homestead at three to four years; due to population pressure and the growing importance of external income, this time increased over the course of the 20th century. Today, homesteads are rarely moved.

Image 38: The Missionaries' living quarters in Oshigambo, ca. 1929.

possible, they built their stations by constructing large houses with thick clay walls and a high thatched roof. Converts began to settle in homesteads around the stations, and local mission workers often moved into European-style houses on the mission compound. Churches formed places of social exchange and community building, while schools and hospitals anchored the mission stations even in the minds of those who did not feel attracted by Christianity.

Compared to the rural settlements of scattered homesteads, even the mission stations had an "urban" character. Here, one found bigger houses, a higher concentration of people, a greater division of labor, a population segment which did not rely on agriculture for subsistence and social services which turned the station into centers for the surrounding area. Many new social institutions made their first appearance around mission stations – from strict monogamy and other moral codes sanctioned by Church discipline to schools and hospitals. But still, few people would have called mission stations towns. European visitors certainly did not, and the local population at least draws a strict line between the new towns which developed in the 1960s and the old village-like stations.

In African anthropology, there is an old discussion about the conditions a place has to fulfill in order to be called a town. Back in 1981, Ivan Karp criticized early studies for classing market towns or administrative centers as urban. "It is yet unclear either what is specifically urban about these centers or how most of the scholars who write about them define urbanity." Processes of community formation observed in "towns" often were re-markably similar to those of rural areas, and it was not clear enough what set towns apart.[3]

Almost thirty years later, I still see no accepted definition in anthropology of where the urban starts. The problem is not so much to define what lies at the core of the urban. High population density, high mobility, central functions for a hinterland, anonymous social relations, strong division of labor, a cultural scene that defines itself as avant-garde and celebrates urbanity – these are just a few of the largely consensual elements men-tioned again and again. The problem is to define how much urbanity a place needs in order to be called a town. Here, the perspectives differ very much in relation to the town on which a specific study focuses. For many researchers working on the large metropo-lises, Windhoek would not qualify as urban; but living in a rural homestead in northern Namibia, I very soon shared the locals' perception of even Ohangwena (a sleepy place of around two thousand inhabitants, including rural homesteads) as distinctly urban.

The distinction between urban and rural places I am using on the following pages is one of contrast. The most important local criterion for the definition of a place as a town – and I will elaborate on this later – is the degree of anonymity and individual freedom it affords to remake the rules of appropriate behavior. This is directly linked to what sociolo-gist Georg Simmel famously saw as the essence of the urban: an anonymity that allows people to freely chose their own way of life.[4] Even though anonymity was limited, the new towns in Ovamboland were frontier spaces in which people could experiment with new forms of social interaction. In the eyes of the rural population, this turned towns into unforeseeable and chaotic places – but also into new social spaces where individual self-realization was less bounded by authority than elsewhere.

Even a definition by contrast remains one of degrees. I think that most witnesses would agree to my descriptions of Ondjodjo in the early 1950s as a proto-urban space and of Oshakati of the 1970s as a town. Some might draw the lines differently, describ-ing Ondjodjo as a town or excluding from their own definition of urbanity anything less lively than the townships of Johannesburg, but the contrasts I describe would have been felt by everyone.

"Piccanins with guns" – Ondangwa in 1950

When South African troops occupied South West Africa in 1915, the first colonial out-posts were added to the mission stations as new permanent centers of power. In Ondan-

---

[3] Karp 1981, 220.
[4] Simmel 1903.

gwa and Namacunde (moved to Oshikango in 1927), the administration built offices and colonial style lodgings for the few white officials. They were rather modest at first. Even when they were expanded after colonial power had been consolidated in the 1920s, they remained smaller than most mission stations. The chiefly courts were the immediately relevant political authorities in the system of indirect rule, and ordinary people did not try to meet the white officials; so fewer people had reasons to visit the administrative centers than the missions. Some came to petition the Native Commissioner or to apply for miscellaneous permissions or licences; more simply passed through government stations because the railway buses stopped there. The only exception was the native labor compound in Ondangwa, which attracted large traffic in itself. Everybody who wanted to go on contract labor had to pass through the registration process at the SLO or SWANLA compound, had to pass a cursory medical examination and had to wait for his transport to the railhead in Tsumeb or Grootfontein.

When the Chamber of Mines stores in Ondjodjo and Omafo and Beersmann's store in Endola opened, they quickly became new points of attraction for parts of the local population (see Chapter 2). People walked from far to buy goods which were only available there, or they stopped on their way from the South to spend a part of their wages. But until roughly the 1940s, these white compounds (which usually comprised a few houses for local workers, as well) did not really change settlement structures in Ovamboland. They remained isolated stations: brick and roof sheet islands of European domination in a landscape of scattered peasant homesteads. Due to population growth mainly caused by the influx of migrants from Angola, the settled areas expanded during the 1920s and 1930s until the stretches of wilderness around the old polities vanished. Settlement in fertile areas became more condensed, with less free space between homesteads, but it was still organized in the old agricultural pattern, without any agglomerations and without any specialized buildings outside of peasant homesteads. The first proto-urban development in Ovamboland started in the late 1930s and early 1940s around the Native Commissioner's residence in Ondangwa and the neighboring SWANLA compound in Ondjodjo.

A large number of Angolans regularly crossed the border into South West Africa to be recruited as migrant laborers in Ondjodjo. They usually made up more than half of the workforce recruited by SWANLA in Ovamboland, and both SWANLA and the Namibian economy at large depended on workers' supply from Angola. Many of those who were rejected or had returned remained in the area and lived in Ondonga homesteads. Around 1940, a number of Ovambuela[5] men lived "in Nakathilo camp which they put

---

[5]   This, at least, is the designation given to them by Chief Martin; Eedes calls them Shimbundu (i.e. Ovimbundu). The Ambwela form one of the groups often classified as Ganguela pequena, western neighbors

up in Boy's area", close to Ondjodjo. They were soon resettled by Chief Martin, who reproached them to continuously break Ondonga laws, in Ombata ya Kakonya (Omusimani) – "close to the bush", as Martin's successor Kambonde called it.

> However, they did not want to move to this new settlement which was given them by Chief Martin. Very few of them went there with Kalungulungu [the Ondonga headman installed by Martin]. Those who did not go there, that is to Ombta, started making pondokkies for themselves in the neighbourhood of Ondangua station. These pondokkies are erected on the open country where the domestic animals of the country must feed.[6]

The first core of a resident urban population in Ondangwa thus consisted of Angolan immigrants, and their "pondokkies" (as informal houses from tin sheet, reeds or plywood were commonly called in Southern Africa) were the first informal squatter settlement in Ovamboland. Very soon, the usual conflicts between a peasant population and foreign squatters without land broke out. They were partly economic – grazing land in the central areas of Ondonga was already very scarce –, partly founded in life-style or simply in xenophobia. The mostly idle young men in the camp were accused of all kinds of misbehaving by the tribal establishment.

> I observed these things are bad. Many a time they appealed to me after having committed fornication with the wives of Ondonga people, and after they had fought among themselves and after they had stolen things from the kraals of the Ondongas. Owing to these things I became tired of their mode of living. Also many a time the Ondonga people came to me saying that they are tired of the life of the Ovambuela people and that if possible the Ovambuela must return to their domicile.[7]

Kambonde therefore asked the Native Commissioner Eedes to assist him in removing the immigrants. Rupert S. Cope, the SWANLA labor recruiter, perceived this as a machination against SWANLA set up by Eedes and wrote a strong-worded letter to his superiors. In his reaction to the Chief Native Commissioner, Eedes supports Kambonde's arguments and states that among the 402 extraterritorial ("E.T.") natives living in or near Ondangua area, only 78 were registered for the tribal trust funds and thus legal residents. The 402 men collectively owned only 216 head of large stock and cultivated only 159 small plots of land. For Eedes, this proved that "they must be regarded as parasites" who did not contribute anything to the common good, but asked for assistance in times of famine. On top of that, he argued, they "also introduce and practice certain evil customs which are detrimental to the tribe with which they live".[8]

---

to the Ovimbundu.
[6]   NAN NAO 51 3/2, Letter Chief Kambonde to Native Commissioner Eedes, June 1948.
[7]   NAN NAO 51 3/2, Letter Chief Kambonde to Native Commissioner Eedes, June 1948.
[8]   NAN NAO 51 3/2, Letter NC to CNC, 20 July 1948.

The figures on stock ownership and land cultivation and the reluctance to move to a new area show that only a minority of the Angolan squatters established themselves as farmers in Ondonga (even if over 130 of them were married to local women). We do not know if they had been given the choice to establish their own farms by the Ondonga headmen who controlled land distribution, but whether from inclination or necessity, many of them lived clustered around the SWANLA compound and earned an irregular income by giving shelter to arriving or returning migrant laborers from Angola. Some of them also worked as servants or day laborers for the administrative staff of the Native Commissioner's office.

In a large tribal gathering in 1948, Kambonde and his headmen decided to expel the Angolan squatters from Ondonga. They would be allowed to pass through the area in order to look for work, but they were no longer tolerated to settle in Ondonga after their return.[9]

The "evil customs", however, did not cease with their partial expulsion. Even without 'foreign' squatters, Ondjodjo remained a hotspot of social change. In 1950, the obviously embarrassed Lutheran pastor Efraim Angula wrote to the Native Commissioner and asked for an appointment without indicating any reason. When Eedes wanted to know what the appointment should be about, he wrote: "What is depressing us is that some of the young women from Ondonga, who get pregnant through prostitution, will do a second sin and murder the child in a gruesome manner before it is born."[10] Six weeks later, obviously after having made further inquiries, Eedes wrote to the Chief Native Commissioner:

> The local Missionaries have made representations in regard to the increase of prostitution in the Ondonga area, particularly in Ondangua, through which all labour passes. The matter was recently discussed with the Assistant Chief Native Commissioner who agreed that the Administration should take early steps to suppress it as far as possible. I shall therefore be glad to receive authority for the engagement of four special Native assistants. Their duties will be to patrol the Ondangua and Ondjondjo (store, labour compound, and embussing and de-bussing stations) areas, arrest all prostitutes and take them to the Chief for trial.

---

[9] It is not quite clear how many of them were actually expelled. After Cope took the matter before the Secretary of SWA, negotiations between Windhoek and Ondangwa resulted in a compromise: Eedes would ask Kambonde to consider allowing the Angolans to stay, with the exception of "those who have caused trouble and those who entered after Mr. Eedes took over as Native Commissioner". All others would have to accept to become Ondonga subjects (NAN NAO 51 3/2, Letter Secretars SWA to Administrator, 3 August 1948).

[10] "Wat op ons hart druk is dit dat sommige van die jongmeisies in Ondonga wat deur hoerery swanger word, weer 'n tweede sonde doen om die kind op 'n gruwelike manier te vermoor voor dat dit gebaare word." NAN NAO 72 32/13, Letters Efraim Angula to NC, 6 and 27 October 1950. Angula was one of the first local pastors; in 1956, he went to the theological seminary in Oskarsberg in South Africa for a year, together with Jason Amakutuwe and the future Bishop Leonard Auala.

Image 39: Crowd waiting in front of Ondjodjo Store, 1953.

In the margins, Eedes scribbled in January 1951, obviously after special assistants had been employed: "Lack of any form of control. [...] James complained 'vice squad' has arrested three women in his kraal." He also made a list of evils connected to Ondjodjo:

> Liquor ex Angola. Prostitutes, squatters, loose women, rejected recruits, rejected piccanins, beer sellers, 'Lambika' makers, piccanin traders, piccanin loafers at store, piccanins with guns.

In spite of the new police force, the problems seem to persist; three years later, Eedes writes to Kambonde "I send you women [NN and NN] who were found in the Swanla compound. When are your Headmen going to control the stray women in this compound please?"[11]

Prostitutes, squatters, illegal alcohol, a vice squad and kids with guns... In Eedes words, Ondjodjo sounds very much like one of the more lively quarters of a colonial capital. It wasn't, of course. The compound consisted of one store, a few offices and an open

---

[11] NAN NAO 72 32/13, Letter NC to CNC 5 December 1950; Letter NC to Chief Kambonde, 4 November 1953. The names were censored by me. – Lambika is locally distilled liquor, piccanin a derogatory term for a black child.

space in which migrant workers had to wait for their assignments. But while it had few of the architectural features of a city, the compound was the most urban social space in Ovamboland in the 1950s, and it differed fundamentally from the homesteads. Every year, between 15.000 and 20.000 young men passed through it on their way to and from labor contracts.[12] Many remained there for weeks or even several months. If the average leaving or returning worker stayed in Ondjodjo for just one week, between 600 and 800 young men lived in the area at any given moment. Half of them had money,

Image 40: Women selling beer and food near the Store, November 1953.

and most did not have anything to do but spend it. The presence of prostitution, illegal drinking and theft is hardly surprising under these circumstances, and the attraction the place had for squatters becomes understandable. The compound soon began to attract shops and other businesses. Women sold locally brewed beer between the store and the labor compound "nearly all the days of the arrival of the buses and Saturdays".[13] They were frequently chased away by the tribal police, but returned to the same place after a few days or weeks. In spite of the competition by the biggest store in the region, six of the twelve first licenced stores, restaurants and bakeries in Ovamboland were located in

---

[12]   For the official figures, see Notkola and Siiskonen 2000, 157f.
[13]   NAN NAO 71 32/3, Letter Tribal Secretary Ondonga to NC, 16 June 1953.

the immediate vicinity of Ondjodjo (see Chapter 3). Most of them specialized in food and drinks for migrant workers. In addition to the licenced shops, unlicenced cuca shops opened in the vicinity and hawkers offered their wares to the crowds or put up stalls near the compound.[14]

Ondjodjo became the first urban centre in Ovamboland in the early 1950s, but its urbanity was transitory. Only few people saw the place as their home; most just passed through on their way from home to the workplace and back. Their homesteads, their families, their workplaces, even the political authorities they had to follow were elsewhere. The 'town' was a place of entertainment and consumption, not a place of residence. This set a pattern for Ovamboland's urbanization.

The geography of stores, 1950–1965

In spite of the new social space that opened up in Ondjodjo, one cannot really talk of any formal urbanization process in 1950s Ovamboland. Almost everybody continued to live and work in peasant homesteads; even the newly founded shops were mostly opened in homesteads.

The following map shows that licenced shops were as much scattered across the landscape as the homesteads. Black dots indicate the places of shops licenced in 1959 and earlier. The dotted line shows the approximate boundary of continuous settlement areas.[15] The largest number of shops opened in the 1950s was located in Oukwanyama and

---

[14] Similar complaints as the ones cited here were again and again raised against shops in areas in which migrant workers gathered. In 1965, the acting and obviously still inexperienced Bantu Affairs Commissioner Burmeister gathered traders in Onengali to discuss the sale of Portuguese liquor and Otombo (which he thought "was a very potent and dangerous concoction, something like a mixture between Portuguese cognac and dagga", a notion of which the meeting soon disabused him). Especially, he asked the headmen to "take action against people who sell any kind of liquor at the bus-stops in Oshikango and Odibo" and to "see that your wives and daughters or sisters keep away from the bus-stop unless they have good reason to be there. I have received complaints about girls loafing about and getting themselves into trouble at places where large numbers of men returning from the Police Zone congregate. The doctor tells me that there is a high incidence of V.D. at these places." (KGO 1 N1/1 2).

[15] The maps are adapted from Republic of South Africa, Department of Foreign Affairs 1971, 10 and Google Inc. The data on shops comes from from NAN OVE. It is often difficult to locate the villages named in the licence. Orthography differs widely, many place names are only known to people in the vicinity, and there is no comprehensive list of place names available. Google Maps proved a very good resource for locating villages. Additional information came from the maps of schools in Ohangwena, Omusati, Oshana and Oshikoto regions produced by the Research and Information Service of Namibia and available at www.raison.com.na (last accessed January 2010). For 1959, 13 of 57 shops with known locations could not be located and are left out in the map. For Ombalantu, one sheet of information is missing in the archives; there should be 2 more dots there. Information about Uukwaluudhi and Ondangjera place names proved particularly difficult to find; the six grey dots could only be placed in the

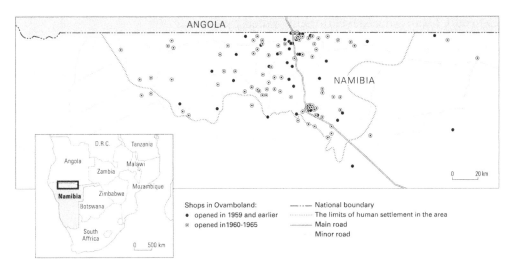

Image 41: Shops in Ovamboland opened in 1959 or earlier (dots) and 1960–1965 (ringed dots).

Ondonga. As many teachers or catechists were among the first storeowners, there is a certain concentration around mission and government stations, places which also often had a larger customer base. Businesses are more densely concentrated in two areas: around Ondjodjo and in central Oukwanyama.

Apart from these two centers, shops were evenly distributed across the land in the 1950s. They first became important in the lives of people in Ovamboland as distribution centers which made goods locally available, not so much as cores of urbanization or even as central meeting places. This began to change towards the end of the 1950s. The huts in which traders had first kept their wares became too small for the increasing turnover of the more successful stores, and the new licence regulation in 1959 made it obligatory to establish a more formal shop building. During the 1960s, a double process changed the role shops played in the social and spatial organization of Ovamboland: the larger shops in the rural areas turned into local meeting places and village centers, and clusters of shops contributed to the development of urban cores in a few distinct areas.

The ringed dots show shops licenced between 1960 and 1965. Not all stores could be located, but the pattern of shop distribution nevertheless becomes clear. The network of shops in rural areas became denser, but even more importantly, three centers of shop development became clearly discernible: Ondangwa, Oshikango and the central Okatana area, where Oshakati would be founded in 1965. These three centers experienced very different kinds of urban growth.

approximate vicinity of actual shops. For 1965, 35 of 137 shops had to be left out in the map, plus ten in the Ombalantu area for which information is lacking in the archives.

Central Ukwanyama: development stalled by the war

The area around Oshikango had been among the most densely populated areas in Ovamboland since at least the 1920s. Between the rural homesteads, cores of small urban centers developed, at first at the well-visited central places I have already mentioned: Oshikango was a small administrative center, with the Assistant Native Commissioner's office (from 1964 renamed Bantu Affairs Commissioner), a post office and the border post. Ohangwena, where the Oukwanyama traditional authority had its seat since 1949, attracted even more people who had business with the tribal authorities. Omafo, which is very close to Engela mission station with its schools and hospital, was the location of the second most important store in Ovamboland; Odibo was the main Anglican mission station in northern Namibia, and both the hospital and the English-language High School brought many people there.

A number of locally owned stores were founded around these centers in the early 1950s. Their customer base came from the surrounding rural homesteads, from visitors to the centers and, as the entire area is very close to Angola, from across the border. In the 1950s and 1960s, the 'urban' cores in this area did not develop into residential centers. The towns consisted of a few stores, often brightly painted brick buildings, and the living quarters of the few people employed by the administrative and mission centers who did not live in peasant homesteads. With its high population density and the concentration of political, economic and social centers, the Omafo-Oshikango-Odibo area seemed poised to grow into a locally organized urban center in the early 1960s. This did not happen; instead, the region lost much of its importance during the 1970s and 1980s. In part, this was due to the attraction of the new towns further South, but the war and the restrictions imposed by the South African occupation played a much bigger role.

After the first Swapo guerilla platoon had been engaged by the South African police in the skirmish of Omgulu gwOmbashe, a group of around ten guerillas attacked the administrative complex in Oshikango on 27 September 1966.[16] This was the prelude to more than twenty years of conflict in the border area. The central Oukwanyama region became a highly securitized potential combat zone. In 1975/76, a one-kilometer wide stretch of land along the border was evacuated, and frequent violent incidents made life in the area difficult for many.[17] Although Ohangwena village grew into a rural center with a

---

[16] Namakulu 2004, 10.

[17] Development at Odibo Mission can be taken as an indicator for the difficult situation. Staff and pupils of the High School and the Mission were among the people flogged by the tribal authorities in 1972/73, and a large number of pupils went into exile in the following years. In 1979, over one hundred pupils were abducted and taken into Angola by Swapo; as a consequence, the High School was closed and moved to Onekwaya further south in 1980. In 1981, the theological seminary was burned down, prob-

measure of formal urban development during the 1970s and the presence of the occupational forces balanced the economic losses to some degree, the area's urban development could not compete with the Ondangwa – Oshakati axis. The border region only recovered from the crisis after 1995, when trade into Angola picked up due to the country's reconstruction after the civil war.[18]

Small towns: New centers in the rural areas

Smaller towns developed in all parts of Ovamboland. In each tribal district, one place was chosen for the construction of a tribal office, around which other 'urban' institutions were established – usually a post office, schools, a clinic and a filling station. Private stores opened in the vicinity and further marked the place as different from its rural surroundings. Outapi, Okahao, Tsandi, Ohangwena or Eenhana are examples of this kind of small urban cores which developed between 1965 and 1985. They did not look very impressive to white experts. Gerhard Tötemeyer's assessment is typical:

> In theory, Ovamboland has ten towns, of which only two justify that description, while the rest, although represented by tribal offices, consist only of a handful of houses. In 1972, with two exceptions, a school and between one and eight businesses were located near each tribal office; in two instances, there was also a church. The only actual towns were Oshakati (606 houses) and Oluno, near Ondangwa (153).[19]

Tötemeyer's view is certainly correct in an urbanist perspective. It was partly shared by the local population who saw the "large" new towns of Oshakati and Ondangwa as essentially different from the emerging rural towns. But even the small cores brought new social forms and shaped life in a different way than rural homesteads alone.

Even at first glance, they were clearly differentiated from the homesteads by an architecture which marked their connection to the colonial world and at least partly detached itself from the local cultural economy. Homesteads were private areas fenced in by wooden palisades; the houses and shelters in them were built from clay and wood and usually thinly thatched with grass. The new houses built by the administration – schools, tribal offices and hospitals at first – looked different. Some of them were fenced in, as well, but

---

ably by the South African side. The local priests continued to be politically active and parish life went on, but the place lost most of its former importance during the 1980s. In 1989–91, the empty buildings served to house repatriates and refugees from Angola.

[18] See Dobler 2008(b) and 2009.

[19] Tötemeyer 1978, 126. In addition to the seven tribal offices, two sub-offices for Oukwanyama and Oshakati itself were counted as towns.

most stood on open ground and were immediately accessible. Brick walls, concrete floors and zinc roofs surrounded a higher, airier and more clearly defined interior.

From the start, the new buildings also represented claims to define a new center. Until the late 1940s, the political centers of the different polities had been the chief's (or the senior headmen's) homestead. When a successor was named after a chief's death, the center moved to a different place: the embodiment of power was not a palace in which a different ruler could 'take office', but the person of the ruler whose homestead by definition became the palace. When the chiefs became part of colonial indirect rule, the administration tried to strengthen those elements which were most compatible with the bureaucratic model of transferable political offices. The first step was the establishment of councils of headmen in the areas no longer governed by a chief – a measure to which the senior headmen, who were mostly glad no longer to have a chief above them, readily agreed, but which slowly transformed the headmen into office bearers under the control of the native commissioner. As a next step, all chiefs or councils of headmen were asked to employ tribal secretaries, who were responsible for the day-to-day administration and the cooperation with the native commissioner's staff. From the late 1940s, finally, these offices were housed in newly established tribal authority halls – permanent structures in which tribal courts and councils of headmen met and the chiefs held audiences. They no longer moved with the ruler; every new ruler moved into them. Parallel to the new offices, chiefly homesteads continued to play an important role as social centers, but most formal political institutions were concentrated in the new permanent buildings.

So even if these new centers could impress European observers neither with their size nor with their architecture, they brought a new structure into Ovamboland's social landscape. Around them, "a handful of houses" were built – shops, offices, schools or hospitals. None of them had the direct link to agriculture and very few housed living quarters.

Even the more successful businesspeople usually still lived in their homesteads in the 1960s. From the mid-1960s, the first brick buildings appeared within the palisades of homesteads, usually serving as living quarters of the household head (and his wife or wives, if the couple chose to have common rooms). The model of building in brick spread from Windhoek's township Katutura and from the countless smaller and larger building projects of apartheid's development plans in the area itself; bricklaying courses organized by the administration were one of the sources of inspiration for returning workers who looked for ways to earn a living in Ovamboland. The water department had constructed two-bedroom houses for local guardians of pumps, sluice-gates or boreholes in the 1960s, even before the formal quarters of Ondangwa and Oshakati were constructed. BIC's building branch occupied a large number of workers, and many of the more prosperous bricklayers started to make bricks and construct 'modern' houses when they moved back to their rural homesteads. But in the new central places, separate formal dwellings outside of homesteads only appeared in the 1970s. Most were built by the administration for teachers, nurses, clerks or the personnel of the army bases.

The absence of living quarters puts the new towns' size into perspective. Every building had some central function, and even the smallest of these towns indeed became a central place in Christaller's sense.[20] The shops which local businesspeople founded around the offices were a major element in their "charisma", as Thomas Blom Hansen and Oskar Verkaaik have recently called the way in which cities create distinct modes "of being in the world".[21]

I have already outlined in Chapter 5 how social circles developed around the stores of respected traders, how their stores became gathering places and venues of public exchange. The diaries of Petrus Ndongo once more offer a fascinating account of how much time a well-connected and relatively wealthy man who was engaged in the organization of village, school and parish life spent in the store of his colleagues. I will use three entries among many to illustrate this:[22]

> 29.6.1969 We visited Olunghono (store) & Ohalushu store, came back via Mukete store then proceeded home. Drove by Mr. E.H. David then by Mr. Joel David to Topland Store.

> 18.2.1978 Soon after 10am we drove to Onuno Store, at Omafo we went on shopping iron roof, we call Ohangwena and came to Mr. L. Nambala Store. I had refreshment. We then drove to Onuno and came at Mr. Shangadi Store, while here we missed Mr. E.H. Namundjebo who left Onuno for Okelemba. So we return to Olunghono for some articles and drove back. Brought the articles for Okatale people and Onengali.

> 25.2.1978 Mr. P. Heita, Mrs. L. Naimana, Mr. S. Hamola and I drove to Omafo and then to Firm Store Omafo. Here we found Mr. E.H. Namundjebo waiting for us. Mr. Namundjebo entertained us with good refreshments and meat roasted. After all these we drove back and came to Olunghono Store; here we found Mrs. Henry Marks of Onekwaya West. I talked to her. Then we came at Odibo, so we greeted Mrs. Lavinia Ndimufitu, then came back home.

---

[20] Walter Christaller's (1933) model for the distribution of services across space is not the most sophisticated of location theories, but Ovamboland in the 1950s is surprisingly well adapted to be described by it. Just like Christaller's model area, it is all flat, population was relatively evenly distributed across its central areas, and (as most income came from migrant work) purchasing power was more or less evenly spread. Unfortunately, however, apartheid's town planners had Christaller's model in mind when they thought about infrastructure development, which manifestly destroyed laboratory conditions.

[21] Blom Hansen/ Verkaaik 2009, 5.

[22] The diaries kept in English are extant for 1968, 1969, 1978, 1980, 1981, 1983 and 1988–1991. In them, visits to shops become much more frequent between 1969 and 1978, and the distances travelled daily become much longer. In 1968/69, Ndongo most often visited the stores of his close friends Eliakim and Joel David, or saw them at his own Topland Store in Odibo.

In these and similar entries, shops are much more than simply places of shopping. They are landmarks in the social and physical space of Ovamboland. When two people from different areas had to meet somewhere on the road, they chose stores as meeting place. When migrant workers came back from the South with a late bus, they spent a night at one of the shop compounds before walking on home. When somebody wanted to meet a shop owner, he walked or drove by the shop and waited for his or her return. Shops were also centers of local news; before walking to somebody's homestead off the road, most people inquired at the nearest roadside shop to hear if the friend had been seen leaving – and the friend in turn often called at the shop to tell people when he would return.

In his diary, Petrus Ndongo regularly marks afternoons or evenings spent at his own Topland Store, tending to customers or visitors and, as one of his favorite expression goes, "having strong talks" about Church affairs, the young people in Ovamboland or Odibo High School pupils who went into exile over the border to Angola. This, too, is typical for stores. They became an important venue of semi-public exchange. People met each other there and exchanged gossip, or they simple stayed a while waiting for something to happen.

As outlined above, different stores in the small rural towns had their own distinct public. A store was closely identified with his owner, and a certain ease of social exchange with the owner was a precondition for becoming a regular customer, so differences in status, age, political orientation or religion often led to a differentiation in store publics. But due to the economic function of shops, the differentiation was an open one. Everybody had access to every store to purchase things he or she did not find at his usual shop, and newcomers were often integrated into the rounds of gossip. In this, the stores and the small rural towns in general contributed to the supralocal cohesion of society. They were intimate and familiar enough that a meaningful exchange could emerge, and yet open enough to integrate newcomers or passers-by.

Just like in the 'large' towns which emerged slightly later, some of the most meaningful social activities outside of individual homesteads took place in small shops and cafés. Importantly, consumption and new public spheres were directly linked to each other through the stores. Most of the goods present in shops even in small towns came from outside of the reserve – from a world to which access could usually only be gained through migrant labor. The shops provided a link to this world, and thus contributed to the growing importance of consumption for self-assertion.

Shop owners could travel more easily, were better connected to people from elsewhere, and often drew others who had similar experiences to their shops. It was in the shops that news from the rest of the country was first discussed. Petrus Ndongo, for example, travelled to the Police Zone at least twice a year. As a teacher, trader and church elder, he found it relatively easy to get a pass for one or two weeks. Whenever he came back, he made the round of his friends' shops, greeted the owners and told his news.

But local stores also provided a conceptual link between the rural lived world and what people conceptualized as modern development, *ehumokomeho* (see below). This link was all the more important since it reached into the heart of rural Namibia. Moving to a 'real' town – Windhoek, Walvis Bay, later Oshakati – resulted in a certain detachment from the rural society. While many young people sought this detachment, the more established senior men and women often liked their own place in the rural society and did not want to move out of it. For them, shops in the new small towns provided an opportunity to participate in both worlds. They gave a link to developments on the national level and a place to meet people from other areas. But at the same time, the small central places remained closely linked to the rural world. The shops' customers, the councilors who met at the tribal offices and the teachers who taught at the mission schools continued to live in their rural homesteads and had no wish to move to the cities.

Where Ondjodjo was dominated by youth, elders dominated the rural towns. Senior teachers, businesspeople or clerks – the established elite which did not have to leave on contract work in order to spend money – were most at home there. It was in the shops in rural centers, just as in the parish councils, teachers' organizations or trade chambers, that this new rural elite found their own political sphere. In the 1960s, what political consensus existed among them stood midway between the headmen and the liberation movement.[23] It was modernizing, development-oriented and self-confident – but as this self-confidence was based on a local elite status with which the colonial administration rarely interfered, it was not militantly anti-colonial. With the war and the South African occupation, the consensus slowly changed. The nightly curfew, arbitrary violence and detentions and the army's and policemen's general mistrust and disdain of the local population, elite or not, were a reality check for those who had reckoned themselves to be leaders, not oppressed. Much of their change of attitude took shape in discussions in the small towns' shops, where people from different areas came together and traded experiences as much as goods.

Ondangwa and Oshakati: the new towns

Social and political changes in these rural centers were much slower than in the two places Tötemeyer acknowledges as real towns: Ondangwa and Oshakati. Ondangwa's develop-

---

[23] This is very well illustrated by the answers to Tötemeyer's (1978) questionnaires.

ment as a formal town started in the early 1960s. The Finnish mission stations surrounding Ondangwa – Oshitayi, Oniipa and Olukonda – and the Ondonga tribal office had a role in this, but the town's growth was mostly driven by the SWANLA compound and the number of people it brought into the area. The administration tried to regulate the town's development by formal planning. A new plot for the Administration's offices and the new European residential area (not including the SWANLA compound) was acquired from Chief Kambonde in 1955, and two additional residential quarters were established in 1965. The more luxurious one was meant for white officials and their families; it lay close to old Bantu Affairs office. The second residential quarter, Oluno, was conceived as native location. It is placed two kilometers to the southeast, close to the labor compound and separated from white Ondangwa and from Ondjodjo by the new main road. A new Ondonga tribal office was built in Oluno, and single quarters for labor recruits awaiting their departure were constructed for the first time. The reconstruction of Ondangwa was the first formal town planning project in Ovamboland, and it crucially shaped the town – most of the houses constructed after 1965 are still inhabited today, and the two new areas still form the core of Ondangwa's formal quarters.

Planned development, however, has only reshaped the town, not created it. This was different for Oshakati, which was centrally planned by the colonial administration as the new homeland capital. It quickly developed into the most important town in central northern Namibia.

Plans for the new capital go back to the late 1940s, when the first ideas about a state hospital were discussed between the Native Commissioner and Windhoek. The administration disliked the fact that all hospitals in Ovamboland were operated by the missions and partially subsidized by the state. The system was cheaper for the government than building up state hospitals, but it increased the missions' standing with the local population and put them into a strong bargaining position towards the administration. As a new hospital would have to be centrally placed, the Uukwambi, Oukwanyama and Ondonga borderland came into the administration's interest as its possible future location. In the early 1950s, these plans began to converge with ideas about a new capital for Ovamboland.[24]

---

[24] When Howard Eedes took over as new Native Commissioner, he quickly started to lobby the Administration's to find a new place for a capital, as Ondangwa, in his eyes, did not have sufficient water. A study by the Water Affairs Department found that the only places with enough water resources were Oshigambo and Ongwediva, and plans were made to take over Oshigambo from the Finnish Mission Society. In the face of their resistance and the high costs involved, and due to the fact that Eedes' successor Bruwer Blignaut favored Ondangwa, it was decided in 1954, to leave the Native Affairs Office where is was, but to replace the existing buildings. 34.700 Pounds for the new station (office block and housing for the Native Commissioner) were allocated in 1958 (see NAN SWAA 485, 50/222; NAN BAC 112,

In the eyes of some members of the Administration (most importantly Native Commissioner Howard Eedes), Ondangwa was rather unsuitable as a homeland capital. The Native Affairs office and later the SWANLA compound had been established there more or less by chance. In the words of the Bantu Affairs Commissioner in 1961, "Ondangua, at that time [in 1915] afforded the only solution in the form of a vacant mission station. Chief Martin Nambala Kadhikua of the Ondonga tribe was only too glad to have the conqueror of the then troublesome Ukuanyama neighbours housed in the Ondonga area, and in this manner, Ondangua became the administrative centre of Ovamboland".[25] It was relatively easy to reach and very close to the Ondonga Chief's residence. In the envisaged unified homeland, however, such closeness to one polity turned into a liability. Native Affairs officials felt that the future capital should be in the center of Ovamboland and as far removed from any one Chief's power base as possible.

The second and more important reason to look for a new site was insufficient water supply. The principal water source in Ovamboland is the annual flood of the Cuvelai river system. Ground water tends to be brackish and salty and is only of limited use for human consumption, so surface water has to be collected during the rainy months to provide sufficient supply for the dry season. Ondangwa lies outside of the central floodplain, in which the seasonal floods could be more easily collected. Local water harvesting systems and the dams constructed by the administration in the 1920s were largely sufficient to cover the needs of the local population, the government station and the native labor compound, but they were not able to sustain a larger urban population. They were upgraded in 1961 to make Ondangwa's expansion possible, but remained insufficient for a new capital.[26]

No place in Ovamboland had sufficient water for a larger urban settlement. Consequently, the plans for a new capital were linked to the establishment of a sustainable water infrastructure (see Chapter 4). The water projects concentrated on the Okatana area, where a reservoir and a surface dam were constructed in 1958 and connected to a 65

HN 5/2/3/7). The new Office was opened in 1961. Slightly later, this decision proved a waste of time and money, since the canal and reservoir scheme in Okatana made Oshakati the natural place for the new capital.

[25]   NAN BAC 112, HN 5/2/3/7 Letter Bantu Affairs Commissioner Ondangua to Chief Bantu Affairs Commissioner, 27 May 1961. After his arrival in 1915, Major Manning had built a small office which later came to be known as "Schettler's cottage", since the Rodent Officer Kurt Schettler occupied it during his stay in Ovamboland from 1932 to at least 1948. Hahn, in 1930, built three rondavels which served as administrative headquarters for more than 30 years. The Ondangua building close to the Post Office and Namcol which today is known as "Hahn's former residence" was inaugurated on 9 June 1961, 12 years after Hahn's death (NAN BAC 112, HA 5/2/3/7, Konsep toespraak by opening van die amptelike kantoor op Ondangua Ovamboland op 9 Junie 1961 deur sy Edele die Administrateur).

[26]   Hangula 1993, 14.

Image 42: Hahn's office in the early 1940s.

miles canal in 1964.[27] This provided enough water that the plans for a new capital could be engaged in earnest. The Odendaal Commission, which took up its work in 1962, had an important impact in this regard, even though it only linked and promoted existing plans and projects. The Commission incorporated the idea of a new capital into its recommendations. It suggested the establishment of a 350-bed central hospital at Okatana and recommended to go ahead with the Ruacana hydropower scheme, which included the extension of the canal system to the Kunene River.

These plans were among the first recommendations of the report put into practice by the Department of Bantu Administration and Development. From 1963, the inhabitants of five villages around the reservoir were forcefully removed to other areas of Uukwambi and to Ombuga, a former wilderness northwest of the Etosha Pan. Work on the new hospital started in 1964 and was finished in July 1966.[28] The following years saw the

---

[27] Bertelsmann 1959, 143. The dam was part of a five-year plan to improve Ovamboland's water infrasctruture, which saw the establishment of many dams and three reservoirs all over Ovamboland from 1953 to 1958. A second five year plan covered the years of 1959 to 1964. See also Davis 1964, 65.

[28] Hangula 1993, 20

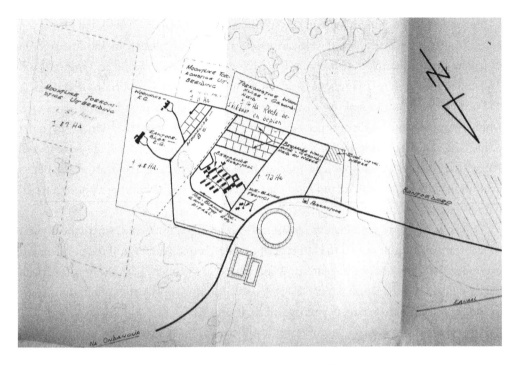

Image 43: Planning the new town: Oshakati as imagined in 1966.

establishment of many institutions the authorities deemed necessary for the future homeland capital (see also Chapter 4): a post office in 1964, a filling station in 1965, a radio
service in 1968, the first bank in 1969, a furniture factory and a building firm in 1965
and 1967, and a wholesale store in 1970. The office of the Commissioner General for
the Indigenous Peoples and the local headquarters of the Bantu Investment Corporation
moved from Ondangua to Oshakati in the mid- to late 1960s[29], and Parliament, Government and Administration of the new homeland were from the start established in the
new capital. Around these new institutions, separated black and white formal residential
quarters and a central business district were constructed. New migrants soon began to
establish informal settlements. In 1970, the new town already had 2.831 inhabitants,
among them 624 whites, surpassing Ondangwa/ Oluno, where 2.614 (including 191
whites) were counted.[30]

---

[29]   The Commissioner General had his office and residence there in 1966; see the Oshakati map in "Inter-
      departementele Komitee e Verslaag oor Ondersoek na blanke Beamptes te Ondangua en Oshakati se
      Belanges", NAN BON.

[30]   Thomas 1978, 168f. The overall census data give an indication of population changes, but they often
      only have a strenuous relation to empiric realities. In 1980, for example, the census included a break-
      down of urban and rural population into sex and age groups (Department of Economic Affairs 1990).
      Calculating urbanization rates from this set of data, however, I realized that the set produces a constant

But the town would only remain the administrative capital of Ovamboland for seven years. In 1975, when the South African Defence Force established its headquarters in Oshakati, the Legislative Assembly and the Executive Council moved to Ongwediva.[31] This town goes back to a Finnish Mission station and its schools and training centers; it had been laid out as a formal town by the first Legislative Council under guidance of the white administrators as yet another new capital.[32] The town was characterized by quiet residential areas for white personnel, administrative buildings and a large educational sector. The teachers training college opened there in 1968 became the heart of the Bantu Education system in Ovamboland (and, incidentally, one of the buildings photographed in every glossy brochure about apartheid's achievements).

Oshakati, however, remained the economic capital of Ovamboland, where the highest concentration of shops served the largest population cluster. And even if the government had moved out, the real power center was still placed in the town: both the South African Defense Force and the South African Police established their northern headquarters there, including the counter-insurgency units and their prisons.[33]

The town attracted a large number of in-migrants from the rural areas and from Angola. Employment in town gave an alternative to migrant labor, the fortified town of Oshakati offered some protection against the violence of the war, and the emerging urban life attracted many young people. Formal housing in Oshakati did not keep up with the influx of migrants; the "white" quarters in Oshakati East were only accessible with a special permit, and the "black" formal quarters of Oshakati West could only house a small part of the new urban population. Around these planned developments, in-migrants built informal houses from every available material. From 1980 onwards, the creation of the South West African Territorial forces and of the counter-insurgency police unit Koevoet (see Chapter 7) brought a further influx of men into the shantytowns of Oshakati.[34]

---

urbanization rate of 2.0% for males and 1.2% for females in every 5-year age cohort, with minimal aberrations due to rounding errors. It is obvious that an official charged with establishing the data preferred to infer them by calculation, using the 1970 urbanization rate, rather than by counting. In 1973, 553 people in Olunho lived in the 153 houses built by the South African Bantu Trust (151 of which were of type NE 51/6 with four rooms). In Oshakati, 2.642 people lived in 574 NE 51/6 with four rooms, 23 NE 51/9 (the slightly larger version with a bathroom) and 2 type 1/10 houses (NAN OVG G 7/2).

[31] Graefe, no date, 64.

[32] Tötemeyer 1978, 81.

[33] Leys 1989, 142. The SADF brigade commander in Oshakati commanded Sector 10, which comprised Kaoko and Ovamboland; the command for Kavango and Caprivi was in Rundu.

[34] The number of locally recruited soldiers is difficult to establish in the absence of official figures, but in 1989, 2900 black soldiers and policemen and 240 workers who had been employed by the security forces in Oshakati and Ondangwa lost their work (Tapscott 1990, 6).

The years between 1960 and 1975 saw the spatial organization of Ovamboland profoundly altered. In 1960, the entire area was characterized by scattered rural homesteads. Settlement was more compact in the core zones around Oshikango and Ondangwa, and the first proto-urban developments were discernible in Ondangwa and around some mission and government stations. In 1975, the northern core had lost much of its appeal, but the central area between Ondangwa and Oshakati had developed into a densely populated and distinctly urban region. The new towns did not grow out of existing peasant homesteads and the old village structure. Formal planning and informal settlement alike ignored and often eliminated old agricultural uses. Many peasant homesteads were forced to relocate to outlying areas; others could stay, but were cut off from the rural landscape by sprawling proto-urban developments. Life in the new towns stood in marked contrast to life on a homestead, and even if many new town dwellers still depended on food produced by relatives in the rural areas, the perceived gap in lifestyles increased the towns' attractiveness to many young people.

The structural changes did not just create a number of new towns. In two distinct ways, they created new realities. First, the process of urbanization left concrete traces in the landscape – traces which future generations will have to live with. Seen from 1960, many places could have developed into an urban core. But once the first towns took shape, a process of separation between towns and rural areas began. Zoning and urban master plans segregated rich from poor citizens, public from private spaces, formal from informal areas; houses built on formerly empty surfaces set limits to the ways in which a space could be used and imagined; roads, canals, pipelines, telephone cables or electricity lines constructed in relation to the new towns channeled people's agency into preconceived ways.

By 1975, the locations of Ovamboland's towns were fixed. New ones can and will emerge, but those towns which have become a reality can neither be undone nor unthought; their sheer material reality channels local agency into distinct paths which reproduce their relevance. Pierre Bourdieu has famously argued that all architecture is a condensation of social reality: it shapes the habitus of people growing up in it and thus influences future agency. In Oshakati's and Ondangwa's development in the 1960s and 1970s, local society and the apartheid administration jointly created a social form that had not previously existed in the area. Together with the architectural form, town life *as a social concept* emerged as a new local reality.

Many men and some women working in the South had of course long known the towns of central Namibia or of South Africa. But living in one's own town made a difference; there was more freedom for social creativity, less control and no danger of being expelled when a working contract expired. Town life could take on a new meaning. By passing through the new towns, visiting them, moving to and between them, people in Ovamboland for the first time developed local concepts of what it meant to live in towns, how towns differed from rural areas, and what social, cultural and political forms were appropriate for urban life.

Today, the Ondangwa – Ongwediva – Oshakati nexus is still the most important urban center in northern Namibia. It continues to grow very fast. New formal and informal settlement areas are developing around the old cores, but apartheid's town planning is still very visible in the towns' layout. Urban development planning, local agency and the specific situation of the war combined to create spatial and social structures which will shape northern Namibian life for a long time to come.

Frontier spaces: Social life in the new towns

What did people look for in the towns, and how is their experience related to shops and consumption? Urbanization is, of course, never caused by a single factor. But different towns attract people for different reasons. I will try to show in this section that, while economic opportunities and security concerns played an important role, the promise of a new way of life attracted people more than just economic chances. The new towns were characterized by a social and political situation very close to what Igor Kopytoff has described as "the frontier".

Kopytoff used Frederick Jackson Turner's famous conceptualization of Northern American history to identify factors driving historic change in pre-colonial Africa. He sees the fringes of existing systems of political order as the spaces in which social creativity had the best chances to generate new social and political movements. In a pre-colonial landscape characterized by islands of domination surrounded by stretches of wilderness, the frontier spaces between two polities gave room to experiment with new forms of order. They provided new actors with an area in which they could gain power resources without having to engage existing systems of domination first. Frontier spaces, Kopytoff argues, fuelled a dynamic of exchanges between center and periphery through which social creativity became politically relevant.[35]

Kopytoff's model certainly needs a number of differentiations to fulfill its original purpose of explaining change in pre-colonial African history. But the idea of the frontier as a creative marginal space has proven its value as a conceptual tool for a number of different

---

[35] Kopytoff 1986.

contexts, many of them far from Kopytoff's intent. It is in this sense that I want to use the frontier concept – as a tool for thinking about the attraction new towns had for migrants.

On the first glance, it might look odd to describe Ondjodjo, the first proto-urban core in Ovamboland, as a frontier town. Ondangwa was not located at the fringes of political power. It lay in the very center of the three most important systems of domination: colonial administration, contract labor recruitment and the Ondonga kingdom. But different systems of domination do not necessarily add up to tight control. It was precisely this triple sovereignty which made it possible to temporarily escape domination in Ondjodjo: being close to all three systems of domination, the area was under full control of none. Rupert Cope, the labor recruiter who ruled over the compound, was in rivalry with Hahn and especially with Eedes and had different aims than they had; the Native Commissioners delegated local rule to the Ondonga Chief and his headmen; and the Chief did not see the labor compound as his responsibility.

The discussion around the Angolan squatters and around prostitution in Ondjodjo illustrates this very well. The Ondonga Chief, even if he tried to settle the squatters elsewhere and had to sit in court over them, saw them as "Cope's people". He did not dare to move against them on his own, but held a large tribal gathering and sought cooperation from the Native Commissioner. Labor recruiter Cope, who had a vested interest in keeping the group in the area to host Angolan labor recruits, opposed the Native Commissioner and brought the affair to the attention of the Secretary for South West Africa. In the end, the three powers more or less levelled each other out – the squatters were warned to behave and allowed to stay.

In another case which left traces in the archives, two returning migrant laborers from Angola bought a goat for 10 shilling and slaughtered it on the SWANLA compound in 1947, eating some of it and selling a piece for 6 pence to a fellow worker. Headman Namadiko Abraham, who worked for SWANLA, confiscated the remaining meat and fined them £1.10/0 as, he argued, the sale of goat meat was forbidden according to Ondonga law. He then proceeded to eat the meat together with other SWANLA employees.

The Angolans complained to the Native Commissioner, who discussed the matter with Chief Kambonde. He argued that "Extra-Territorial Natives were encouraged by the Administration to accept work in the Police Zone, and that while they were en route they were under our protection". Kambonde agreed that the fine was unjust, as the Angolans could not be expected to know all Ondonga rules. He added that the respective headman had no authority to inflict fines on the compound – his own ward lay elsewhere and any authority he might have in the compound could only be due to his status as SWANLA employee. In this particular case, SWANLA stood by Kambonde and sacked the main responsible, an attitude which Eedes praised in somewhat ambiguous terms: "It might be mentioned that Mr. Cope co-operated fully." His stress on cooperation suggests that the opposite might have been expected.[36]

The three different systems of authority (with the occasional addition of the Churches as a fourth) worked together fitfully at best. When Namadiko Abraham used his status between two systems for personal gain, only a concerted action of the highest local representatives of the colonial state, the national economy and the traditional authority were able to rein him in. The uncertainties of jurisdiction increased the scope for individual actions that countered existing power structures and created the very situation which Kopytoff finds at work in frontier spaces.

'Boy', the man in whose area a number of Angolans had put up their squatter camp, is a very good example of how resourceful people were able to use the multiple sets of power relations to cut out a piece for themselves. 'Boy' was an Angolan-born oshiKwanjama speaker who became Native Commissioner Hahn's handyman in the 1930s or earlier. James Negley Farson, an American writer who stayed with Hahn for three weeks in January 1939, writes about him with a paternalistic fascination that probably is very close to Hahn's own:

> But when we had all my stuff on the 1-ton-lorry, we found that two of its springs were broken. [...] "You fix 'em", said Hahn to 'Boy'. Now 'Boy' – he had no other name – was a Portuguese Ovamba. He had never seen a town, much less a workshop – except the one he had patiently put together himself in Hahn's sheds. Yet, within four hours, 'Boy' had made and put in two perfectly good, serviceable spring leaves that he had made with some strips of steel, a vice, and a hack-saw.[37]

Even if neither Hahn nor Farson were interested in it, 'Boy' did have another name – and he did make quite a name for himself in the local society. Though he was a foreigner, Boy Shipandula managed to be chosen as local headman of the area on which the labor compound is located – a central position on the hinge of two systems of power for which familiarity with both was essential. Through his closeness to Hahn and his own skills, he became a middleman between Chief and Administration and between Angolan migrant workers and local authorities. In the 1950s, he owned a car repair workshop close to the Native Commissioner's office and was the only local mechanic who knew how to repair automobiles when Chief Kambonde and later some businesspeople bought the first cars in the 1950s.[38]

---

[36]   NAN NAO 71 31/7, Letter NC to Secretary SWA, 21 April 1947.
[37]   Farson 1944, 83.
[38]   His homestead was close to Ondjodjo (where Fysal's fruit market is today), his workshop north of the Native Commissioner's office, in the area now called Omwandi. – My information about 'Boy' comes

Ascents like 'Boy's' had not been impossible in pre-colonial times; strangers had always been incorporated into the local systems of leadership and could gain important positions at court. The crucial point is that Boy Shipandula's position was no longer at court. He was neither only the handyman to the Native Commissioner, nor was he only a local headman. He made his career at the intersection of both systems of power, in the uncontrolled spaces at their very center. In this way, his ascent is a symptom of the frontier situation around the labor compound.

Not only new careers became possible here, but also different ways of everyday interaction. The number of people passing through the compound and the lure of the returning laborers' wages made it difficult to control the compound. "Misbehaving" (as elders call youth culture today, just as their own parents called it in the 1950s) was easier when you were in a peer group of young people, many of whom would be away in a very short time and would only return after any sins they might have committed were forgotten by society anyway. Eedes' list of social evils is worth repeating here: "Liquor ex Angola. Prostitutes, squatters, loose women, rejected recruits, rejected piccanins, beer sellers, 'Lambika' makers, piccanin traders, piccanin loafers at store, piccanins with guns".

The young migrant workers and their local peers experimented with new forms of social interaction in the compound. At home, young men found it difficult to escape supervision and control by the household heads who had the economic power and the moral authority to keep dependents dependent – particularly since settlement fragmentation prevented any predominance by numbers. The fragmentation of authority in and around the labor compound, the number of temporarily idle young men and the prospect of leaving for contract work with its often harsh living and working conditions favored more reckless feasting than would have been possible in the homesteads.

Not all people in the compound 'misbehaved', of course, and not all who did spent their time feasting. The compound was also a place for politics. It brought people from different regions together, who would not have met otherwise, and created a climate in which political discussions were more freely possible than at home. Topics like labor conditions, control by elders, headmen and colonial authorities and the injustices of segregation lay close at hand and were linked to common experiences. Just like the mining compounds, the Native Labor yard in Ondjodjo facilitated a political exchange that made it easier to perceive the structural dimensions in individual experiences. Here, too, the frontier space at the fringes of existing power structures made new interpretations and new organizational forms possible.

---

from Denis Nandi, whom Nancy Robson was kind enough to interview while I was in Switzerland. He was sent to the workshop by his father Petrus Nandi to learn mechanical work.

Ondjodjo Store and the local stores, cuca shops and beer stalls surrounding it were an important ingredient in this proto-urban social climate. Cuca shops and beer stalls offered public spaces and alcohol as media of exchange, and the stores presented coveted goods which motivated migrant labor and provided possibilities for symbolic self-determination. In some cases, storeowners could use their position in the center of emerging networks for formal political organization. Toivo ya Toivo's "Cash Store" in Ondjodjo, for example, was not only a successful business; it was also an excuse for the constant presence of strangers and for frequent travels, and thus the ideal front for political work.[39] The shops formed an intersection between the transitional urban life on the labor compound and rural local society. Many people congregated at Ondjodjo Store. The interior was usually packed, and people often waited for entrance in long queues.[40] Many people had to walk long ways to reach the store and stayed in the area for one or several nights, also visiting other shops.

Ondjodjo was a special place due to its unusual residential patterns, but the new towns of the 1960s shared some of its characteristics. They, too, became frontier spaces in which new forms of social interaction and political organization was possible. Oshakati, the most important town, was deliberately built in the margins of existing local polities, and from the start, local headmen had very little say in the town. The forced removals of villagers from the area and the strong presence of central institutions of the homeland administration let the balance of power swing to the bureaucratic administration. Chiefs and headmen of course officially governed the country as members of the homeland government, but the factual power of administrators in the service of the South African Department of Bantu Affairs was much greater.

In their vision, the formal town spaces of Oshakati and Oluno should lack the hybrid and chaotic character of 1950s Ondjodjo area and be in the firm grip of the official institutions of law, order and economic development instead. In consequence of this strong component of urban planning and control, Oshakati differed considerably from Ondjodjo. The increasing securitization of the town in the 1970s further decreased the room for self-determined urban life.

In spite of this, Oshakati attracted many people from the villages of Ovamboland. They often came for employment opportunities: most of the new jobs created with state

---

[39] On the role of Toivo ya Toivo's store, see e.g. Namakalu 2004, Namhila 2005.
[40] Ruth Dammann's photos of Ondjodjo (Basler Afrika Bibliographien, Album D8) are a vivid visual illustration of the queues. Some of them were taken on 23 December 1953, when crowds probably were especially large before Christmas, but those taken on 18 November 1953 – an ordinary Wednesday – show almost the same number of people queuing up. Archival accounts give further evidence of the press of people in the store – see for example the obligation to take off glasses cited in Chapter 4, footnote 54.

166

money by the Bantu Investment Corporation were located in Oshakati's factories and in the building company based there. Other opportunities arose in formal businesses and in the town's infrastructure and service sector, mainly in electricity and water supply and in the central hospital. Oshakati West, the formal town quarter designated for the black population, very soon became too small even for the housing demands of formal sector workers. In 1980, the Army began to recruit local men, which brought a further massive influx of rural people and considerably increased local buying power.[41]

Many people settled in the informal quarters which developed around the formal cores of Oshakati West and Oshakati East, often in shacks made from every available material. To the relatively well-off employees in the formal sector came a large portion of poorer migrants, who looked for employment in vain or simply came for the greater physical security the town offered during the 1980s. Formal town development did not keep up with these dynamics. This created a constantly widening gap between the living conditions in different quarters, but it also opened up new possibilities for urban dwellers to transform the new spaces according to their own vision of town life.

The focal point of formal urban development and town life outside of white Oshakati East was Peefitola in Oshakati West, the area in which most the shops BBK rented out to local businesspeople were concentrated. It was the place most people from outside of Oshakati had reasons to visit, and it started to rival Ondjodjo as the liveliest business area in Ovamboland in the early 1970s. During the 1980s, Peefitola, which was surrounded by residential areas, became too small, and new shops were built along the main road directly north of Oshakati West. Gradually, and most prominently with the opening of the Omatala main market in 1986, the area along the main road developed into the new commercial center of Oshakati.

Apart from this business center, the formal areas of Oshakati were rather bleak. The town did not possess the same attractions as the townships of Windhoek, let alone Johannesburg or Durban. Bottle stores, bars and restaurants catered for the visitors by day, but night life was not very lively from the start and vanished almost completely after the curfew was imposed in Ovamboland in 1979, to be lifted only in 1989 in preparation of independence. From sunset to sunrise, nobody was allowed to leave their homesteads; soldiers and police patrols sometimes shot on sight and often intercepted people who visited neighbors, looked after their cattle or simply went to the toilet in the fields. Oshakati was slightly better off in this regard than the rest of the homeland, as the curfew

---

[41] South West Africans had been integrated into the South African units as volunteers even before 1980, when the South West African Territorial Force SWATF was formed. The establishment of this new 'local' force was meant to provide the South African military presence with local legitimacy and remove some of the odor of an occupational force.

was less strictly enforced in the Ongwediva and Oshakati agglomeration than elsewhere. Everywhere outside Oshakati East, bars closed before sunset for everybody but soldiers on free time.

In the shantytowns outside of formally developed Oshakati, life was organized differently than in the formal quarters. They were much less controlled by the security forces and barely reached by the official administration. As the war progressed, Army posts, earth walls and frequent patrols surrounded the entire area, but the informal quarters themselves were largely left alone. Those who lived in the formal town did not often venture into the shantytowns, where they felt insecure and threatened by violence. Especially the businesspeople of Oshakati West looked down on shackdwellers and largely kept to themselves, and social differentiation between different informal areas was sometimes as clearly marked. But in the absence of central control and the necessities of agricultural work, a distinctly urban culture developed within the informal areas. Once again, outsiders often saw it characterized by misbehaving youths, and once again, alcohol, sex and consumption played an important part in it.

All over town, unlicenced cuca shops opened since the mid-1960s. Their number multiplied during the 1980s, when local soldiers spent a large part of their pay on alcohol. I do not know of any statistics on their number prior to independence. In 1993, a survey found there were more than 500 cuca shops in Oshakati alone; most of my informants judged that their number had been even higher before the end of the war left many soldiers unemployed. As everywhere in Ovamboland, the cuca shops were "a cross between a local pub and a corner store".[42] They usually sold some groceries, but almost all of them made the bulk of their business with bottled beer and locally brewed *tombo*. Off-duty soldiers, youths and unemployed often spent their days in cuca shops; the evening hours saw brisker business, before most customers hastened home not to be met outside during the curfew. Few had far to walk. Cuca shops were, and still are, doing their best business with a small circle of neighbors and friends who use them as a regular meeting place.

Cuca shops took over the functions of the public spaces within rural homesteads. While a large part of a rural homestead is clearly a private space and will not be entered without prior permission by a household member, the gathering place near the entrance can be accessed by everybody and often sees meetings of smaller companies of friends and neighbors. These meeting places, however, were always under the authority of the respective homestead head, and clear rules of public conduct applied for young people in the mixed gatherings.

---

[42] Pendleton/ LeBeau/ Tapscott 1993, 69.

Cuca shops in town had a different public and much less clear an authority structure. They were dominated by young people, many of whom lived in their own shacks, earned their own money and had no reason to behave according to somebody else's standards. Of course, there were standards of propriety and rules of conduct enforced by moral pressure and sometimes by violence, but these standards could be relatively freely altered in an ongoing negotiation between peers.

Here, again, the town was a frontier space at the margins of existing authority structures. The fact that many shanty dwellers were army soldiers further increased the freedom within the informal settlements. Patrols largely kept out of the informal settlements in which most soldiers lived. Many young men had severed the ties to their families in the rural areas, who continued to suffer from army oppression and often had little tolerance for their sons' choice of work.

The majority of workers in the factories and of soldiers in the army was men, but many single women also moved to Oshakati. The rural population looked upon them with even greater skepticism. Housing was scarce, the lack of control could make life in the informal settlements dangerous, and friends made it easier to organize one's life under the new circumstances, so many women moved in with men without being married. People in the rural areas often regarded them as *iikumbu*, prostitutes, in the 1960s and 1970s.[43]

Differing moral and social codes, war-related enmities and the increasing securitization strained the links between the town and the rural areas to a degree that more than half of the urban dwellers in Oshakati stated in 1976 they had no ties left to their families in the rural areas. This again accentuated the differences between town and village life and stabilized the idea that town life was completely different from village life. Villagers who came to town found even Oshakati noisy, chaotic, dirty and dangerous. Many stories circulating in the villages told of the differences. Some stressed the dangers and disorder of the town and told of honest villagers who had been cheated by young thugs in Oshakati, or of women who had lost their lives due to attempted abortions; others stressed the opportunities by telling about traders or soldiers who had moved to town and earned a fortune, or by describing the consumption opportunities the towns offered.

A large part of Oshakati's attraction in the 1960s and 1970s actually was economic, but this is by no means the whole story. People moved to Oshakati in search of a new life. *Ehumokemu*, which Tirronen translates as "development" and Hangula as "self-realization through development", became the catchword of the era.[44] The new social forms which

---

[43] "Loose women" or "women living in immorality" would perhaps be better translations, as the term does not necessarily imply a commercial relationship. Tirronen (1986, 153) translates the word with "prostitute (in a township)".

[44] Tirronen 1986, 84; Hangula 1993, 23.

developed here were closely integrated with South African rule – much more so than life in rural homesteads, into which homeland policy came as an intruder at best.

BBK's development projects, the South African army and police and the homeland administration were the economic foundations of the new towns; their rules had to be accepted at the workplace. But in the shadow of these institutions (and under often precarious economic conditions), the town offered a social space that was relatively free from outside domination. While the workplace was strongly regulated and segregated, leisure time offered new opportunities to young people. "Self-realization through development" was thus delegated to leisure time, and consumption played an important role in it. This, in turn, makes shops and bars central to urban life and its attractions – a point to which I will come back in the conclusion.

7 Taking sides? Traders and politics during the liberation war

The twenty years between 1955 and 1975 form a crucial, but blatantly understudied period in Namibian history. It seems that the era is still too close to the present for historians to study, and too far removed for anthropologists to take an interest; but the social dynamics playing out during these twenty years still shape independent Namibia. If the period has been studied at all, the interest has mostly been focused on the large-scale political developments and the struggle between liberation movements and apartheid government. In that perspective, the homelands often appear as stagnant places in which apartheid and emergency laws stifled all social activities. But in the shadow of the large movements, people started to organize civil society activities in many domains.

Since it came to power in 1968, the new homeland government divided opinions in Ovamboland. Was it a mere puppet institution of the apartheid state, which served to fracture the country while quieting internal and external opposition by a travesty of self-government? Or was it an imperfect way forward that would finally lead to reforms, to the abolition of apartheid and to a peaceful transition to real independence? The international political discourse was shaped by Swapo and the global solidarity movement. Both denied the homeland institutions any legitimacy and boycotted the 'elections' in 1973 and 1975 (in which people could only choose from a list of pre-selected candidates). In Ovamboland, however, the choice whether to cooperate with the government, perhaps even to become a part of it, or to publicly voice opposition to it, was not an easy one. Even Swapo members or sympathizers temporarily became part of the homeland parliament, and for many people who wanted to remain in the country, reformist cooperation seemed a more plausible alternative than revolutionary opposition. The individual decision was complicated by ideological differences: many older Christians, for example, were influenced by the Missions' anti-communism, and the reorientation of Christian Churches towards the liberation movement in the 1970s led to frictions in a number of parishes.[1]

---

[1] The most visible expression of these frictions was the founding of the Ovamboland Anglican Church by Petrus Kalangula (renamed Ovamboland Independent Church after the Anglican Church successfully went to court). Kalangula (1923–2006) was schooled and passed two years of theological training at Odibo until 1945. He was a catechist from 1944 to 1947, while teaching at Anglican schools in Oukwanyama from 1945 to 1947. In 1948, he found work as a clerk at the Assistant Native Commissioner's office in Oshikango, where he stayed until 1954. Kalangula was fluent in English, Afrikaans, Portuguese, "all 5 Ovambo tongues" and Omasaka, and passed Standard VII by correspondence in 1955. While working as a Government Interpreter in Ondangwa in 1961, he started an Anglican congregation there. At first, he held services in the Court Room of the government buildings, but he soon was granted permission and a site to build an Anglican church – the first outside of Oukwanyama. In 1962, he went

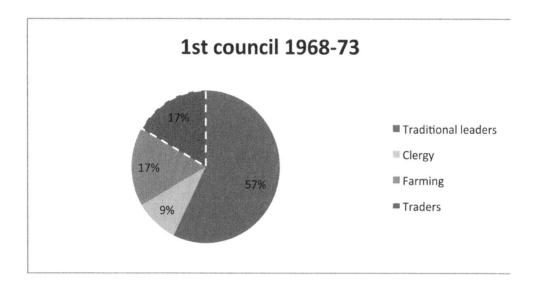

1st council 1968-73

- Traditional leaders
- Clergy
- Farming
- Traders

17%
17%
57%
9%

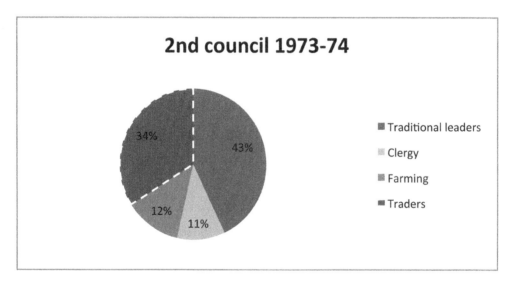

2nd council 1973-74

- Traditional leaders
- Clergy
- Farming
- Traders

34%
43%
12%
11%

Shop owners felt these rifts keenly. Some were staunch Swapo supporters, but overall, they were more likely than teachers or clerks to become part of the controversial administration. From the start, traders were overrepresented in the Legislative Council, even though the

on a one-year theological training course in South Africa and was ordained as a deacon on his return. His ordination as a priest was already scheduled when Colin Winter was made Bishop of the Diocese of Damaraland on Bishop Mize's expulsion, took a radical pro-Swapo stance and made very controversial decisions on St. Mary's affairs in Odibo. Among those who signed a letter of protest against Winter to the Archbishop of Cape Town were Eliakim Namundjebo and Petrus Kalangula. In consequence, Winter denied Kalangula the ordination, and Kalangula finally founded his own breakaway Church in 1970. He later became a Legislative Council member and a delegate to the Turnhalle Conference.

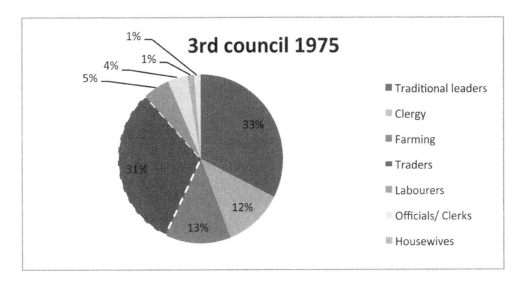

Images 44–46: Composition of Legislative Councils

first Executive Council only consisted of seven traditional leaders designated by the seven tribal authorities in Ovamboland. In the second and third Legislative Councils, an even higher percentage of shop owners were elected, and in 1975, Frans Indongo, one of the richest traders in Ovamboland, even became Minister of Economic Affairs. The graphs on the left and above show the composition of the first three Legislative Councils.[2]

Successful traders were in many ways ideal candidates for parliamentary representation. They were locally embedded and in need of local acceptance, but well connected and conversant with the modern economy; they were mobile and travelled frequently between the new towns and the countryside; they lived in Ovamboland on a permanent basis; and they were typically less fundamentally critical of the system than, for example, teachers, nurses or clerks (see below). Both sides profited from the traders' presence in the Legislative Council: some of them undeniably brought great energy and competence into the homeland parliament, but the political connections and the respect traders gained in it could also have very tangible advantages for their business.

Not all traders in the Legislative Council had sympathies with the homeland system, and many simply sought their way through the entanglements of public life in an unjust regime. Leonard Mukwilongo, for example, had joined Swapo in 1959, but he still became a member of the Legislative Council before going into exile in 1980. Thomas Nakambonde, another elected member of the third Legislative Council and, like Muk-

---

2   The data were taken from Tötemeyer 1978.

wilongo and many others, a very active member of the Lutheran Church, joined DTA instead and opted for a reform approach. "We did not see eye to eye politically, but as traders, we cooperated. He was a good man, we met in church and at other occasions. And whatever your political conviction: You had to live with everybody", Mukwilongo recalled.[3]

Chapter 5 has shown how traders were connected to each other by friendship, joint professional activities, Church membership or credit relations in the 1950s. In the 1960s and 1970s, first attempts were made by traders to give an institutional framework to these relations which they could use for networking and lobbyism. The first Ovamboland Businessmen Association I am aware of was founded in 1964 by, among others, Thomas Nakambonde and Leonard Mukwilongo. They organized fellow traders in a Church context, with the aim of helping each other, exchanging information and voicing traders' concerns towards the government. Similar informal associations seem to have existed in different areas of Ovamboland. Petrus Ndongo mentions attending "a meeting for all traders (business people) in Ukuwanyama held at Ohanguena" on 16 February 1968 and another one at Omafo on 7 May 1969.[4]

In 1969, the homeland government asked traders to form associations in the different tribal areas. In the context of BBK's increasing interest in trade activities and its planned acquisition of SWANLA's stores, the administration wanted to have an organized counterpart in order to channel information about training courses or business plans more efficiently. The traders' associations were indeed founded in 1969, and met since 1970 for a yearly "General Assembly of Owambo traders". In 1973, the Association was transformed in a "Trade Chamber" (Kamer van Koophandel) and gave itself regulations in Afrikaans and English.[5]

All of the few assemblies for which minutes have survived in the official archives were opened and closed with prayers by traders or local pastors. In their deliberations, the traders were not shy to criticize BBK and the administration. In 1970, the assembly sharply complained about the BBK wholesale in Oshakati, which "still had the manners of the bazaar", and asked for private wholesalers to be established in Ovamboland. The BBK wholesalers in Omafo and Endola should to be closed down altogether, as they continued to illegally retail goods. The traders also criticized the large profits the BBK garage

---

[3] Interview Leonard Mukwilongo, Elim, October 2006.
[4] Diaries Petrus Ndongo, Odibo Mission Archives.
[5] All NAN OVE 19/2/8/1. In 1971, the Executive Committee consisted of K. Amupolo (chairman), Henock David (secretary), Leonard Mukwilongo, E. Mbango, P. Jakob, S. Kaulinge, Oswin Mukulu and Thomas Nakambonde (NAN OVH 21, 5/1/3/2-1).

made and asked for it to be replaced by private enterprises.[6] In 1971, the traders asked for standing authorisations to travel to the police zone in order to buy goods, since they often had to wait for a month after sending a telegram to obtain a travel authorization. They complained about the behavior of the police in Oshivelo and asked for new laws regarding alcohol consumption. It was certainly a pity, they wrote, that so much beer from Angola was consumed in South-West Africa, since the territory's wealth should not leave the country in this way, and government should legalize local bars. Meanwhile, however, it was wrong to arrest people on the border who had bought Cuca beer in Angola – when they approached the police to complain about theft, the police sent them to the traditional authorities, so they should leave alone the smugglers, as well. The traders once again complained about BBK, stating that BBK had asked Windhoek wholesalers not to sell to Ovambo traders. "Since [BBK] came to bring development and help where help is needed, they should do so. But they have to be careful not to interfer in our business."[7] In 1973, traders complained again about the difficulties of obtaining travel documents to the towns of the Police Zone "to buy various articles which may be required in Ovambo stores and which are not obtainable always in wholesalers of Ovambo. They want to go down without sending telegrams first".[8]

Traders, in short, wanted to be free of regulations which hampered their business. They thought that competition would force private, non-monopolistic enterprises to offer better prices. They did not criticize the pass law system as such, which contained hundreds of thousands of people into narrowly defined areas, but they wanted to be spared the bother of writing telegrams. Seen from Swapo's point of view, these demands fell well short of what was needed. But in order to agree on a joint programme, traders' associations had to strictly argue from an occupational point of view. What aspects of the current public order were detrimental to their own advantage as traders? This was the common denominator for shop owners from different political sides. The Trade Chamber tried to avoid political polarization and to establish itself as a reformist organization instead. It was a civil society organization in the classic liberal sense of the word, an institution which contributed to the control of government and thus, out of self-interest, furthered the public good.

---

[6] NAN OVE 12 9/2/8/1/1, Vergadering van die Owambo-Winkeliers, Jaarlikse Vrystelling 16 October 1970.

[7] NAN OVH 21 5/1/3/2-1, Owambo Sakemense Vergadering, 3 June 1971.

[8] NAN OVE 12 9/2/8/1, Traders meeting of the Oukwanyama tribe at Ohangwena on 20 March 1973. 40 out of 320 trades in Oukwanyama were present at the meeting, a number those present judged insufficient to elect representatives into the homeland Trade Chamber.

It was, however, not very efficient in doing so. BBK and the homeland government largely ignored its 1970 demands. The Development Corporation was not keen on losing its profits from the wholesale operations to private competitors. It argued that the wholesalers acted in common interest, as the proceeds were reinvested into the economic development of Ovamboland. The Ovamboland Legislative Council, which largely depended on white civil servants lent to the Ovamboland administration from Windhoek or Pretoria offices, did not become active in the matter.

Traders between old and new elites

Traders were a politically and socially very active group which influenced public opinion and political decisions in pre-independence Ovamboland. But what were their political convictions, and what rifts became visible between different traders? In order to better understand this and to judge their role as an economically modern, but locally embedded and politically reformist elite, we have to go back once more to the late 1940s.

When, in 1946, The Witwatersrand Native Labour Association wanted to recruit workers from Ovamboland, Native Commissioner Hahn strictly opposed. He felt that SWANLA had already been given too much leeway for recruiting and that migrant work already formed a "disruptive element". Chiefs and Headmen, Hahn argued, were strictly against sending young men to South Africa.

> For years past they have expressed wishes as to the necessity of keeping foreign and disruptive elements away from Ovamboland, since, if not suppressed, these would undermine the present peaceful and progressive way of life and administration. They expressed these fears when recruits for the N.M.C. [Native Military Corps] were sent to the Union. Now that these men have returned they have fallen back into tribal life and have given no trouble, but it must be remembered that they were always kept under strict army discipline and had not the same opportunities and inducements to enter into, or take part in, the type of political activity, communistic, anti-European, anti-Government etc., in which the Rand Mine natives revel. [...] A most disquieting factor is that amongst all these labourers – the cream that Ovamboland and the Okavango can supply – will be included many young men of the old and traditional families who are the mainstay of Ovambo tribal life and tradition. These young men, it must be acknowledged, will play a leading role in Ovamboland in the future, and should they return from the Rand with anti-Government and communistic ideas, it can easily be imagined that the future trend of events, in a political sense, will be very seriously disrupted. [...] This can only result in disintegration, in other words the breaking down of ordered native life and a system of control which has set an example.[9]

---

9   NAN A450, Strictly confidential letter NC Hahn to CNC Neser, 10 May 1946.

Hahn was a biased, but perceptive observer. He might or might not have downplayed the role NMC members like Herman Toivo ya Toivo or Samuel Kaukungua played in political mobilization (the immediate postwar was indeed a rather quiet moment in Ovamboland), but he clearly saw the change ahead and the role that relations to the outside world played in an increasingly critical attitude towards tribal and colonial authorities. His attempts to stifle criticism by isolating the region appear in retrospect as a rather helplessly fought losing battle. They were doomed to failure, not least because the colonial economy's ongoing need for migrant labor made even short-term isolationism impossible. The system of indirect rule was built on hollow foundations. It could not exist without freezing "ordered native life", and could thus only react to social change by oppressive and reactionary social engineering.

Hahn clearly perceives migrant workers as one element of social change. One could, he suggests, to some degree control public life in Ovamboland by closing the borders to people and to information. This would not prevent criticism and topical political unrest, but it could partly hinder the development of a systematic critique of the colonial system – a modicum of control that slowly slipped away in the southern towns and on the mining compounds. There, people from very different backgrounds came together, compared experiences and jointly interpreted them. They eagerly discussed news of the outside world, from the ANC's struggle in South Africa to the UN debates on South Africa's mandate. Political movements which gave a common frame of reference to such experiences were hotly debated and experimented with, and the new interpretations quickly found their way home into Ovamboland. Returning migrants differed in their opinions about specific issues, but they acknowledged that such issues existed and that colonialism, wage labor and racial discrimination made social and political change inevitable. They found it difficult to accept their own social and political subjugation to headmen who did not share their experiences and had, in their eyes, a much narrower horizon. To the older generation who did not share the workers' experiences, the migrants' complaints often seemed just the usual restlessness of young people looking for their role in society.

The first traders came from the new social stratum: young men with some education, savings from migrant work and often experiences in a great many places and occupations. Trade, for them, was a way to settle down at home and to acquire income and status while escaping the experiences of domination intrinsic to wage labor in a racialized society. In the 1950s, future leaders of the liberation movement imprisoned in Robben Island and future homeland ministers cooperating with counter-insurgency police were all part of the same social milieu, and their differences to the established society were greater than those between both sides.

From the late 1950s, the two groups started to part ways. Many traders were success-ful in their march through the local institutions. They made it into the establishment of a transforming society: became economically successful, respected and often envied, were chosen as church wardens, as foster parents and sometimes as village headmen. In order to achieve this success, traders had to arrange themselves with the local establishment. They needed good relations to the political powers, to native administration and traditional authorities alike. And whatever their political convictions, they could not allow those convictions to spoil their relations to all social groups.

On the other side stood people who, step by step, turned into professional politicians. They became big men not by accommodation and cooperation with everybody, but by taking a stand and voicing concerns of others. Sometimes compassion, sometimes ambi-tion, sometimes a sense of dignity and freedom led them to oppose the colonial rule more actively and to centre their public life on that opposition. People like Eliaser Tuhadeleni or Teofilus Hamutumbangela put more and more energy into an increasingly organized political fight. They – and to an even higher degree the leaders of the liberation movement in Windhoek – became professional politicians.

They did not always do so out of their own will; imprisonment and forced exile gave no other choice to many among the first generation of political leaders. Since the mid-1960s, Swapo's political stance was defined by those full-time politicians who led the movement from exile and were closer to the international diplomatic and activist scene than to their followers in Namibia.[10] In their fight against an oppressive political system, they had to distance themselves as far as possible from that system and exclude any com-promise. Swapo's official documents and speeches increasingly described the homeland government as traitors, and cooperating with it as collaboration with the enemy.

The traders who remained in Ovamboland were often very critical of the apartheid system, but they took a much more pragmatic and less revolutionary stand. They did not orient their public life on political principals and binary oppositions, but on everyday compromises and a search for reforms. Some really collaborated; others refused to cooper-ate with the apartheid system. But it was scarcely possible to live open opposition without losing one's freedom or even one's life – or (like Mukwilongo) finally transforming into a professional politician in exile.

So in the 1950s and 1960s, the professional trader and the professional politician de-veloped from the same milieu into different roles and different life choices. Both groups' experiences were shaped by the repression of political opposition under apartheid. Some

---

[10]   The greater importance of the international community than the domestic political scene for Swapo's policies is argued, in my eyes convincingly, by Dobell 1997.

crossed back and forth between both roles. Toivo ya Toivo went back to his "Cash Store" near Ondjodjo when he was banned from Windhoek in the late 1950s; when Samuel Kaukungua went into exile in 1964, he had to leave both his store and his trading career behind.

But as apartheid transformed the political system, it became ever clearer that, in Leonard Mukwilongo's words, "business and politics are enemies".[11] If you concentrated on your business, you had to make political compromises; if you concentrated on politics, it could damage your business interests. Professional politicians were forced into exile and for better or worse had to concentrate on politics. A large percentage of post-independence Namibia's political class lived in Dar-es-Salaam, Lubango or Lusaka during the struggle, detached from everyday life in the country and from the political compromises it necessitated.

In the absence of these professional opposition politicians, professional traders took over important functions in public life. But politics often played the second role in their lives; they were first and foremost traders. This was mirrored in their values and opinions, as well. For his work on "Traditional and modern elites in Ovamboland" Gerhard Tötemeyer conducted a value survey of elite representatives in 1977. On almost all accounts, traders represented the middle ground between the "traditional" elites of headmen and the "modern" elites of pastors, nurses, teachers and clerks. All in all, they were "satisfied" with the political development in Ovamboland.[12] It is not very clear how Tötemeyer chose his sample, and the figures are too small to be statistically representative, but the coherence of the values expressed by traders is impressive. In Tötemeyer's account, traders appear as rural petty bourgeoisie. They are politically rather conservative, but moderately critical of the old nobility. They prefer to live in rural areas instead of towns and seek status through consumption. Money and large cattle herds appear equally alluring to them. They would like to see some reforms, but they shy revolution.[13]

Traders saw apartheid as unjust and unjustified, but they had invested rather a lot into their own place in apartheid society and had much to lose by a revolution: status, moderate wealth, success in that given society – and their living. They suffered less from state interventions than, for example, teachers did under the Bantu Education system, and apartheid's development policies created a much more favorable environment for them. While teachers, pastors or nurses carried their professional skills with them and could start at a new place or in a new society, with relative ease, traders were bound to their

---

[11]   Interview Leonard Mukwilongo, Elim, October 2006.
[12]   Tötemeyer 1978, 69 ff., 112.
[13]   Tötemeyer 1978, 57ff., 174ff. Most traders in the 1970s owned fields and cattle herds and were part-time peasants.

shops and made vulnerable through them. Many traders still chose Swapo and revolutionary change, but the threshold to do so was higher than for other professional groups.

Instead, traders more and more moved into the centre of the local establishment. In a general survey on the status accorded to different groups, traders equally took the middle ground. The most prestigious occupations were the teacher, the clergyman and the doctor; they were followed on place four and five by the chief or headman and the trader. Traders' status was significantly higher in Ovamboland than in other countries where similar surveys were conducted.[14]

Of course, far from all traders were successful. But the percentage of successful traders and their overall status in society were probably higher than in the South African homelands described by Leo Kuper in 1965. In his work on the new African bourgeoisie in South Africa, Kuper stresses the difference between publicized success stories of black millionaires and the rather bleak realities of "petty trade conducted by amateurs". Most of the traders, Kuper states, were on the verge of bankruptcy. Kuper blames this partly on the traders' own inadequacy, partly on the political system.[15] In Ovamboland, the absence of white or Indian competition – who were not allowed to enter the homeland, let alone trade there – in combination with a working agriculture providing the means of subsistence made the market situation much more favorable. In the early 1970s, many businesses were indeed on the verge of bankruptcy, but most of them survived and thrived

Image 47: David Sheehama's House near Outapi in 2006. The damage done by the 1979 bomb blast is still visible. The house was renovated in 2012.

---

[14]   Tötemeyer 1978, 148. For comparisons, see Kuper 1965, 278.
[15]   Kuper 1965, 278ff., 287.

after this. The relatively high standing of shop owners in Tötemeyer's survey is all the more significant if seen in relation to their mixed success.

A few traders, however, were very successful. Everybody knew their names, and stories about both their success and their embeddedness in community life were widely told. 'Aupa' Frans Indongo (*1936) was the emblematic 'black millionaire'. He had started as a cattle herder and a migrant laborer; by his fortieth birthday, he owned a supermarket chain and was Minister of Economic Affairs in the homeland government.[16] One typical story about him is that, in the late 1970s, his car broke down in Mariental in Southern Namibia. He went into the local Mercedes dealership; when the white owner eyed him suspiciously, he bought the most expensive Mercedes available, paid cash and drove it home to Ovamboland.[17]

In many of these stories, rich black men confront white bosses with their own expectations and show them a different reality. Envy, respect and pride intermingle in the way people talk about the few really rich traders, but the most important component is the wish to succeed at least by proxy. Where the real world was characterized by exclusion, marginality and injustice, the few black millionaires embodied the possibility of coming on equal footing with the white masters who would be shamed by the experience. So freedom fighters were not the only new role model in 1970s and 1980s Ovamboland. Traders' success was less heroic, but it impressed many people just as much, and it too offered a possibility to find some pride in one's identity.

Traders did their best to fuel the admiration by showing their success. The first generation of traders were among the first people in northern Namibia who owned cars, and many men who grew up in the 1950s and 1960s still recall the brands and types of their vehicles. Most traders always dressed in suit and tie, and many built large brick houses at a time where the chiefly homesteads were still mostly constructed in wood and clay. David Sheehama from Ombalantu, one of the three richest traders in the 1970s, erected the

---

[16]   On Indongo, see the rather hagiographic biography by Shiimi yaShiimi 2004, which, among other things, fails to mention his political career. Indongo worked as teaching aid for three years (1952–55) after finishing primary school. During this time, he started sewing and selling clothes. With his wages from a contract with Walvis Bay municipality, he bought a sewing machine and slowly expanded his business. – His Okatana store was first licenced from 22 December 1962, when he was 29 (NAN OVG 3, G9/5/2/2 Gronsake: Handelsterreine, Frans Indongo).

[17]   I have heard several versions of this story; one of them ascribed it to a different trader from the same generation. In one of the more plausible variants, Pastor Peter Pauly told me that a car dealer from the South he knew called him and asked whether this black man who wanted to buy a car really had the money. "I told him", Pauly concluded, "that this black man could buy his entire shop if he wanted to." – On the importance of success stories, see also Kuper 1965, 268. Kuper sees the success of a few as the necessary spurn to keep traders in line and shift their attentions away from the political struggle. "There are now no limits to the ambitions of the trader and, the making of money being defined as a morally praiseworthy enterprise, he acts with a ruthless disregard for the interests of others."

first two-storey house in Ovamboland in 1972, employing a Portuguese architect from Luanda for the planning. He inaugurated it with a large feast at which his fellow traders (if they paid 10R entrance fee) were seated in a special V.I.P area.[18] More than twenty-five years after his death, almost every talk about him still mentions the impression of achievement and pride this made on a society in the grip of apartheid. If traders took part in community life, the new houses were also favorite places to receive high outside guests. When the Anglican Bishop came to Odibo, for example, he was usually received and served food at church warden Eliakim Namundjebo's house before driving the last six kilometers to Odibo.

Profiting or dying: Traders in war

So some traders had a comfortable living, were well known and respected and had wide networks of social relations. They were less revolutionary than the poorer teachers, nurses and pastors and liked to take a middle ground in politics. But by the mid-1970s, this became increasingly difficult. The guerilla war and the military occupation split the society apart, and whoever tried to remain neutral between the clearly established fronts only became a potential target for both sides.

When South Africa ignored the UN decision to revoke its mandate over South West Africa in 1966, Swapo decided to launch armed attacks on South African institutions in South West Africa. In the following years, guerilla platoons led local surprise attacks and retreated immediately. Their local knowledge, the possibility to hide in the dense bush at the fringes of inhabited areas and not least widespread support by the population (motivated partly by fear, partly by solidarity) made it difficult for the South African police to find a successful strategy against these attacks. When Swapo intensified its military actions in the early 1970s, South Africa reacted with a massive increase of its army and police troops in the area.

In 1975, Angola became independent. Throughout most of the ensuing war which only ended in 2002, the MPLA, which was allied to Swapo, controlled South-Western Angola. This made it possible for Swapo to establish its exile headquarters in Angola and to keep up guerilla bases in proximity to the South West African border. In an effort to keep its buffer zone against "communist" black Africa and to crush the guerilla, South Africa fortified the border region, brought more troops in and frequently led military expeditions against Swapo camps and MPLA bases in Angola. In 1975/76, a one-kilometer wide strip along the international border to Angola was forcefully cleared of houses and

---

18   Interview with Sheehama's daughter Rose-Mary Kashululu, Outapi, 2 September 2012.

homesteads, and the existing border fence was replaced by a 450 km long, two-meter high border fence topped with barbed wire.

The South African Army concentrated troops in heavily armed and fortified bases all over the homeland. The militarization of Ovamboland reached its highest point in the early 1980s, when probably more than 100.000 South African troops were on active service in Namibia.[19] As the presence of troops did not end guerilla attacks, a counter-insurgency strategy was devised and often brutally executed. Paramilitary police units and special army battalions concentrated on "hunting the terrs" and on demoralizing the population by incalculable violence. The most notorious police unit was called "Koevoet", crowbar, and mostly consisted of white officers and black ordinaries. It was founded in 1979 by Brigadier Hans Dreyer of South African Police's security branch; one of its colonels was Eugene de Kock, who later became head of a South African secret police unit systematically and illegally executing political opponents.[20] Koevoet units often operated under cover or used captured PLAN uniforms and weapons. The population could never be sure whether a platoon asking for shelter or food in the night really consisted of PLAN fighters, or whether South African units merely tested their reactions. In areas suspected of guerilla sympathies, many homesteads were burned down or simply bulldozed, and many civilians were arrested and tortured. Under emergency laws, the police could summarily imprison people for up to six months without any judicial procedure.

Not all political violence was directly linked to Swapo or PLAN actions. In the hot climate after the general strike of 1971/72, for example, several gangs of contract workers drove through the country on bicycles to "do justice". Their actions were partly aimed at the institutions of colonial rule; they cut the border fence to Angola, attacked Senior Headmen Silas Isak and Timotheus Muunda with pangas and finally decapitated the wife of Ondobe Senior Headman Samuel Kaulinge, seriously injuring Kaulinge as well. This

---

[19] Official figures were never released, so the numbers are rather unreliable. Rotberg (1983, 16) estimated the number of soldiers in 1977 at 47.000; solidarity movement publications often speak of 120.000 in the early 1980s. A UN Report in 1983 equally puts the number of South African troops in Namibia at over 100.000, whereas 400.000 soldiers could be mobilized on short notice (United Nations Council for Namibia 1983, 4f.; see also MacGill Alexander 2003, 34. A high proportion of the troops were stationed in Ovamboland.

[20] Much has been written on Koevoet, but there is still no systematic scientific account of its history and actions. One of the best first-hand accounts of Koevoet interrogation techniques and brutality is found in Goodman 2002, 89ff.; for other aspects see Hinz/ Leuven-Lachinski 1989, Battistoni 2009 and the more problematic accounts by Hooper 1988 and Stiff 2004. – De Kock was sentenced to 212 years of prison for his crimes in South Africa, but due to the policy of 'national reconciliation' in Namibia which proscribed the persecution of crimes from both sides, his exact role in Koevoet remains unclear. On his time at "Vlakplaas", the way he rationalized and justified his actions, and the never-quite-outspoken commands by the political leadership to eliminate opponents, see Pumla Gobodo-Madikizela's (2003) account of interviews with him after his imprisonment.

last act only partly seems to be motivated by politics; the group also executed people accused of witchcraft.[21]

Due to the episodic character of guerilla attacks and counter-insurgency actions, many peoples' daily routines went on largely undisrupted by the war. Military occupation and emergency measures certainly made life much more difficult, and a nightly curfew hampered social and institutional activities. If one could still live for years in Ovamboland without ever witnessing any actual violence, the war spread a climate of fear, and no one knew if the uneasy normality would be disrupted by unforeseeable violence in the following night.

If people experienced acts of violence, they were often unable to tell who the perpetrators were. Armed groups coming at night looked very much alike, and both side's guns and bombs left the same wounds. Police inquests routinely ascribed acts of violence to "unknown persons – terrorists". If the police was informed and an inquest opened, corpses were usually taken to the morgue at Oshakati hospital, but often, the victims were silently buried in improvised graves by villagers who preferred not to attract the authorities' scrutiny. The graves were often marked by an earth mound or a small cross. They are sites of memory to many villagers, and different explanations of the same violent event often still compete with each other today.[22]

In travelogues by outside activists, local people during the war often appear as staunch supporters of Swapo and enemies of the government – the well-known waters in which guerilla fighters could vanish like fish. Reality was much less clear-cut. Far from everybody supported Swapo; in Oukwanyama in particular, many people were suspicious of the liberation movement. But even Swapo supporters hid their opinions. In the closely-knit local society, every move people made was suspiciously watched, and gossip flourished. Political activities had the potential to break the society apart by pitting family members against each other as political and military opponents and transforming neighborly relations into enmity. These fissures existed, but people tried to contain them by not openly acknowledging them. Even to a village public, only the political convictions of a few activists were clearly known in the 1970s. The fear of repressions by the authority had their

---

[21] See Weidlich 2008. The National Society for Human Rights NSHR, on whose information Brigitte Weidlich's article is mostly based, however confuses two incidents. The mass grave at Epinga contains the bodies of the victims of the Epinga shooting mentioned in footnote 13 (see above) and has nothing to do with the 'Bicycle gang'. The confusion is symptomatic for the heavy silences and the lack of public information about the war era in central northern Namibia.

[22] In April 2006, a building project uncovered a mass grave dating from the last days of the conflict in April 1989 in Eenhana. A very engaged dispute about the responsibility for the killings broke out in the national media, and a number of similar graves were 'discovered' over the next months. All of them had all along been known to people living in the vicinity.

share in creating a culture of secrecy. In many families, sons or daughters who crossed the border into Angola and joined Swapo were no longer spoken of openly.

Traders were public figures who could not avoid coming into contacts with both sides. "PLAN soldiers bought here, SADF soldiers bought here. The money was the same."[23] In consequence, traders were under continu suspicion to cooperate with the respective enemy. "You were selling things to everybody – after all, you had a business, and that's what shops do. But when SADF soldiers came and drank at my shop, the next night Swapo would come and ask about them. Who were they? Why did they come? I told them they only came to have a few drinks, but they would not believe me. And the next day, a white officer would be in the shop and ask about last night's visit."[24]

Many traders were actually supporting Swapo, giving food and shelter to PLAN soldiers or serving as link between exile and home organizations. But it is very difficult to know for sure which trader actually worked for the liberation movement. Almost everybody today claims Swapo sympathies and recounts experiences of repression. But even without being politically active, traders could get between the lines and become a target for one or the other side.

Many shops were burned down or attacked by grenades – ten in 1975/76 alone.[25] Today, these attacks are invariably ascribed to SADF or UNITA units by the local community. The following list only covers a fraction of the attacks on shops and murders of businesspeople between 1975 and 1985. Sadag Kristian's first small shop at Eshoke was burned by UNITA the day after Joel David's murder in 1976.[26] SADF soldiers burned down Alfeus Hamukoto's store in Ohangwena in 1979, after his eldest son had joined Swapo in exile and a brother had been arrested by the SADF giving supplies to PLAN soldiers.[27] In the same year, a petrol bomb destroyed the roof of Evaristus Shipoh's store in Okatope.[28] Stepanus Zacharias from Okatope was killed in 1981 by SADF soldiers who came to arrest him. He started a fight and stabbed one of the soldiers with a knife before being shot dead by the others. His daughter witnessed his killing and the subsequent burning of the shop.[29] Reuben Nicodemus from Omafo, who had opened a shop in the early 1960s, was killed by either Swapo or SADF after becoming headman of Okwalondo in the 1980s. Toivo Shiyagaya from Uukwambi, a trader, tribal secretary of Ongandjera

---

23 Interview Sara Hamutenya, Ohangwena, 18 September 2006.
24 Interview IlenaiShangadi, Onhuno, 28 September 2006.
25 Tötemeyer 1978, 99.
26 Interview Sadag Kristian, Omafo, 3 October 2006.
27 Interview Mathias Hamukoto, 22 September 2006.
28 Interview Dr. Peingeondjabo Shipoh, Okatope, 18 September 2006.
29 Interview Sara Hamutenya, Ohangwena, 18 September 2006.

and Minister of Health and Welfare in the Ovambo government, was assassinated in February 1978, his assailant shot dead by the security forces.[30]

In June 1980, the white opposition newspaper *Windhoek Observer* published a death list of people allegedly targeted for assassination by the South African security police. The list, which brought Koevoet into the limelight for the first time and sparked a lively controversy about its authenticity, had previously been published by *Omukwetu*, an important church magazine in Northern Namibia. It was headed by two dead businessmen: David Sheehama from Ombalantu and Matheus Elago from Oshakati. Elago had been killed by a car bomb, Sheehama was shot dead on 14 March 1980 with automatic rifles and his house partially burned down.[31]

The third person on the death list was Eliakim Prins Shiimi, a son of Uushona Shiimi, Uukwambi senior headman and first Chairman of the first Executive Council for Ovamboland. Shiimi had opened a furniture store in Ondangwa in 1976. While his father was a central pillar of the apartheid homeland administration, he became active in the liberation movement. Under the guise of church meetings, he organized opposition groups and gathered support for Swapo. He was arrested in 1980 and held in prison for three months without official charges; he only came free after a human rights group in Ongwediva intervened. While he was in prison, his two shops were burned down. When his name was published on the death list, friends urged him to leave the area and hide in Windhoek until things had calmed down. He did not want to leave, but when children found a bomb mounted under his car, he gave in. A Finnish missionary brought him over the Police Zone boundary at Oshivelo in the trunk of his car. He escaped physically unscathed and could rebuild his stores after returning to Ovamboland in 1983.[32]

Thomas Nakambonde, one of the richest traders in Oshakati, was killed when the largest service station in Oshakati was blown up by a bomb in 1984. From the start, South Africa authorities and Swapo blamed each other for the bombing, and the real culprit was never found. Nakambonde was a chance victim; he had wanted to fuel his car on his way back from Church Service. Nakambonde had been in the third Legislative Council and was a DTA supporter. (His daughter Alina in the meantime went to school in Cuban exile. She had crossed the border into Angola with friends as a child and was brought to Cuba after being injured in the South African attack on the Swapo camp in Cassinga in 1978.)[33]

---

30   Interview Prins Shiimi, Ondangwa, 4 October 2006; interview Rose Kashululu, 2 September 2012.
31   The police docket is found at NAN LON 6/50 301/80. The cause of death is given as "veelvuldige skietwonde", the perpetrator as "onbekende persone – klaarblyklik terroriste".
32   Interview Eliakim Prins Shiimi, Ondangwa, 10 July 2006.
33   Interview Alina Nakambonde, Oshikango, 8 May 2004. In 1974, Thomas Nakambonde bought sup-

These few names stand for many more. There were civilian war casualties in all ways of life,[34] but traders were targeted more frequently and more systematically than others. They were well-known people whose businesses attracted notice, and they often had contacts to all sides. As their businesses were public and vulnerable, they tried to keep their official neutrality – but attempts to remain neutral often made them all the more suspicious. If traders took sides, their activities did not remain hidden very long, and could be 'punished' by one side or the other by hitting their economic base. In addition to this, stealing the victim's money seems to have been a further incentive for violence against traders.

But while the war brought suffering to many, it also led to an unprecedented business boom. Tens of thousands bored young men concentrated in army bases and receiving regular pay enormously increased the local buying power. All traders I asked stated that the 1980s were the best time for their business. Some said the boom started in 1980, other only saw it in 1983, but all agree that war was good for turnover. "The 1980s were the best time for shops. It was a bad time for Ovamboland, but the shops became bigger and bigger. There were so many soldiers in the area, and they had nothing to spend their money on but beer. You know, soldiers are always good for business", one of the major war profiteers told me.[35] The expansion of shops into supermarkets and the founding of ever new branches only really took off in the 1980s. It was not only due to the money flowing into the area with the occupation army; South African development policies and a larger wage labor sector in the area played their role, too (see below). But the backbone of trade in the time was the beer the soldiers drank. A large percentage of the oppressors' wages was injected into the local economy in bars near to the army bases. "Here was my bar, and just across the road were the SADF barracks. The soldiers always came here. They drank until they had to return to the base. Often, they started to fight. The next morning, their boss would come and ask who had started the fight. If you told him,the

---

plies for R2.456 and sold goods for R4.042 in an average month. (NAN OVE (2) 9/2/5/7/141.)

[34] The history of the liberation war is still only very incompletely written. A public memory project is currently collecting eyewitness accounts. A first list of more than 600 names of civilians killed during the war has been published in the Namibian in 2006.

[35] Interview Jairus Shikale, Ondangwa, 22 August 2006. 'Punyu' Shikale, who died in October 2009 aged 59, was one of the most successful businesspeople of his generation. He founded a shop in his natal Etilyasa, a small place south of Okahao, in the late early 1970s, and rented a store from BBK in 1976. His business began to expand quickly, and he established branches since 1983. In the late 1980s, there were rumors that he used UNITA contacts for smuggling. In addition to the Punyu supermarket chain and several specialized stores, Shikale owned a hotel complex at Onethindi near Ondangwa, a stone crusher near Tsumeb and several filling stations.

culprit would come back later and beat you up. It was difficult, but you had to live with everybody, and at least business was good."[36]

Beer consumption was officially legalized in 1973, but it remained a concessional commodity distributed by breweries' exclusive wholesale partners who sold it to retailers. At first, BBK had the only concession in Ovamboland. In 1977, the homeland government urged South West African Breweries to increase the number of agencies in Ovamboland, as demand was growing quickly. The Breweries complied and granted four licences to four of the most important traders: David Sheehama in Ombalantu, Frans Indongo in Uukwambi, Thomas Philips in Ondonga and Eliakim Namundjebo in Oukwanyama.[37] This decision can be justified by the volume these businessmen could turn over in their important stores; but Frans Indongo also happened to be Minister for Economic Affairs in the homeland government, and his authority had asked for the agency expansion in the first place. The new concessions made those four men really rich and allowed them to expand their web of social relations. Every trader who wanted to sell beer had to pass through them or their middlemen.[38] Indongo started to support Swapo shortly before independence and invested his considerable fortune in real estate, farms and fisheries in Central Namibia; today, he is one of the wealthiest and most respected businesspeople in the country, with a road in the central business district named after him.

Traders as development partners for a modernizing administration

Overall, the war showed two faces to traders in Ovamboland. The sporadic violence and the continuing brutal securitization disrupted the lives of many traders. Shops were burned down and more than a few traders killed. Even those who escaped the destruction of their shops unharmed did not always have the energy or the capital to make a fresh start.

But the background for these individual experiences was an unprecedented trade boom equally triggered by the war. Next to the sheer buying power of the soldiers, transport infrastructure was crucial, too. The main roads were tarred and the network of gravel roads extended with money from Pretoria to facilitate troop deployment and control. The third way in which the war profited trade was through South Africa's efforts to "win the

---

[36] Interview Ileni Shangadi, Ohangwena, 28 September 2006.
[37] NAN OVE 9/5/1, Letter South West Breweries Ltd to Economic Affairs Department Owambo, 18 January 1978.
[38] Beer was usually marketed through local agents of the four major representatives. In Ohangwena, for example, Usko Nghaamwa, a supermarket owner and Swapo activist who became Governor of Ohangwena Region in 2004, had started as an agent for Indongo.

hearts and minds" of its black subjects. This new counter-insurgency policy was designed in the late 1970s to balance the oppressive security regime and to dry out Swapo support among the population.[39] In some parts, it was compatible with the old development policies of the late 1960s and early 1970s. A prosperous population, Pretoria reasoned, would be less likely to support 'communist' liberation movements. In addition, successful homeland development was perceived as an asset on the international diplomatic front. In consequence, new money was poured into development programs.

The parastatal development corporations tried to foster industrial economic development. They succeeded to some degree, but only through big corporations in direct ownership of the development agencies. Local entrepreneurs were only successful in trade or, from the 1980s, in small services like car repair outfits or barbershops. To change the structural conditions which channeled economic energy into retail trade would have been outside of the scope of most development agencies; it was all the more difficult for an official institution of the apartheid state whose core policy was to keep up these very conditions. Instead, BIC and ENOK chose the easier way for Ovamboland and targeted potential traders as development actors.

When more money was put into "winning the hearts and minds" in the 1980s, it became very easy for traders to tap into these funds. Shop premises for rent were cheap and readily available, and licenced traders could obtain short and medium term credit from BIC or ENOK. At the official wholesalers, most traders were allowed payment targets of between 30 and 120 days for trade goods. "They just came and had a look at your shop. If it had a roof and you did not shout any Swapo slogans at them, you got your credit."[40]

This partly solved one of the most serious obstacles to the growth of stores: small traders in the 1950s had started with very little capital. As all goods had to be paid in cash, traders had to sell their entire stock before reinvesting the profits. Very often, they needed the cash for other things before selling enough goods to pay for a renewal of the stock. Small shops thus could only expand when they found external cash or credit. This favored stores owned by teachers or catechists who had an additional income. In order to overcome that difficulty, many traders had relied on each other during the 1950s. The credit networks described in Chapter 5 were also means not to spend one's money too early, and to establish relations of trust with potential creditors.

---

[39] Charles Lloyd, the commander of the joint forces in South West Africa, was quoted in 1981 with words which could have come from a guerilla handbook: "The source of power in an insurgency war lies with the people. The population is the battlefield." (Time Magazine 1981). On the "WHAM" strategy, as solidarity groups started to call it, and its failure, see Herbstein/ Evenson 1989, 113ff., Silvester 2009, 192ff.

[40] Interview Ileni Shangadi, Ohangwena, 28 September 2006.

Growth of shops financed by reinvesting profits or securing loans from friends was slow, but it was also sustainable, and only very few stores outgrew the demand. The external funding of business expansion by BIC and ENOK produced quicker and easier growth. More people could profit from the trade boom of the late 1970s and 1980s, and businesspeople were less hampered by lack of funds. But ENOK was so eager to finance potential success stories that it was not very selective in its expenditure of public money. A number of small businesses founded in the 1980s could not repay their credits and quickly went into bankruptcy. I have not found any reliable statistics on business failure, but from all accounts, the percentage of failing shops increased in the 1980s.

Surprisingly, all traders active in the 1980s also agreed that there was much less red tape before independence than after 1990. The security police might have murdered traders and burned down shops, but they did not bother with controlling trading licences. The homeland government and administration, which were officially responsible for trade control, did not function very well in the 1980s. Everybody waited for an independence which seemed imminent without ever arriving, and many regulations not immediately related to security concerns were never fully enforced.

All in all, apartheid's attempt to develop the homeland economy crucially helped individual traders to establish and run their businesses. But in doing so, it contributed to the creation of an entire sector that only thrived during the protectionist homeland regime and very quickly became uncompetitive after 1990. The real boost for trade in Ovamboland in the 1980s had been the result of the war economy and the highly protected economic environment, not of South Africa's development policy.

Civil society or uncivil despotism?

So from the modest beginnings of the 1950s, trade developed into a mainstream economic activity, and traders became the most important professional group in Ovamboland's market economy. With the help of their wealth and their networks, they became local or regional patrons. By necessity or choice, many of them sought contacts to the homeland administration and were sometimes able to influence local politics. The central administration (if not necessarily the homeland government dominated by chiefs and headmen) became more and more sympathetic towards traders. In the 1960s and 1970s, the administration saw traders as a non-radical group combining political moderation with social and economical modernism.

Simultaneously with the traders' ascent, chiefs' and headmen's legitimacy declined. Many local people saw them as puppets of the apartheid regime. Doubts increased when headmen, whose material basis lay in agriculture, were less successful than many traders in channeling new economic resources into their communities through patronage.

The administration still needed the headmen for practical and for ideological reasons. On the practical side, their integration into the apparatus of domination endowed the regime with traditional legitimacy and solved the problem of effectively establishing foreign control without the necessary local resources. On the ideological side, the architects of apartheid believed in tribal traditions embodied in chiefs, and the obvious injustices of apartheid could be justified by referring to tribal self-government. But when it came to establishing a modern homeland administration, let alone to the developing the area economically, headmen were not the ideal partners. Many of them had never been to the Police Zone, had never worked for wages and had never seen an account book, and administrators sent by Pretoria to oversee homeland administration sometimes had a hard time co-operating with them.

Traders were more compatible to the administration's modernist ideas. They were also more critical of the administration, as their exposure to the modern economy brought a sharper sense for the injustice of the system. Traders were less radical than teachers or nurses, but if their ascent should not question the entire system, they had to be kept satisfied. Economically and politically, traders thus gained influence on the administration.

How can we understand their political role in a more theoretical perspective? Mahmood Mamdani has argued that apartheid combined a decentralized despotism in the homelands with a centralized despotism in the urban areas. In the homelands governed through traditional authorities, repression was organized by proxy; in the urban areas, it was more centralized and direct. This, in Mamdani's analysis, led to a bifurcation of power along urban-rural lines. An increasingly organized urban civil society took shape in opposition to the common enemy of central despotism, while the rural society became fragmented and remained politically stagnant, as no common analytical framework and no joint interests could serve as focal points around which civil society could organize. Apartheid left South Africa with a fragmented society, whose key challenge today lies in linking the rural and the urban.[41]

Seen from Ovamboland, Mamdani's much-debated analysis seems inspiring, but also rather simplistic.[42] The consequences of indirect rule were not as clear-cut as both its proponents and Mamdani believed, and his analysis of rural politics shows a clear urban bias.

---

[41]   Mamdani 1996, 101; 61; 297.

[42]   I suspect that a closer look at South African homelands would allow similar criticism there. Ovamboland was exceptional in some dimensions, but it was not the exception that proves the rule; see, for example, Hart 2001.

First of all, civil society in Ovamboland was rather well organized. Until roughly World War II, the decentralized despotism of indirect rule through local headmen was more or less successful in maintaining a social cohesion which was one of the foundations of its legitimacy. No system of domination is without opposition and uneasiness, but overall, chiefly rule under the 'guidance' of the native commissioner seemed the normal state of affairs to most people in Ovamboland. The system of traditional authorities also had the aspect of grass root representation from below – headmen were expected to bring their subjects' qualms to a larger forum –, but by its very nature, it was fragmented into hierarchical patronage systems and prevented rather than created social movements across village boundaries.

From the 1940s onwards, however, migrant workers and educated clerks began to voice opposition to the system as such, not only to aspects of it. Political divergence was underpinned with sociological differences: young migrant workers were materially well off and increasingly self-conscious, but they lacked social status and a political voice – both in their own society and in the colonial system at the workplace. As their criticism of the system of indirect rule and of the industrial relations linked to it was based on common interest and shared experiences, migrant workers could easily find claims around which to organize. Strike committees on the mines and civil society movements like the Mandume Movement were forums of political experimentation and precursors of the institutionalization of a liberation movement in the late 1950s.

Parallel to and often intertwined with these movements, the Mission Churches formed centers of political and social organization of particularly young men and women. Generational conflict was one of the major experiences expressed by religious conversion, and the young people who felt underrepresented in the political system found a new forum in the Churches.[43] Many local pastors were very critical of the old establishment of headmen, too, and increasingly expanded their enmity to the colonial system of which chiefs' rule was but a symptom. As the apartheid administration was at first reluctant to act against the Churches, both from fear of their relations to a global public and from an often deeply engrained respect towards religious leaders, Church groups became a major element of political organization.

In the 1960s and 1970s, finally, the first contours of civil society groups organized around joint professional interests were visible. Traders' associations are a good example of this new form of civil society organization. In Trade Chambers, shop owners organized a representation of their interests across political opinions, across internal tribal boundaries and to some degree even across class differences. Similar organizations existed

---

[43]   See MacKittrick 2002.

for nurses, teachers and government clerks. Ovamboland was perhaps the ideal region to organize such groups. It was small enough that elites often knew each other's families, were members of the same Church, had been to school together or worked on the same mines. In this close-knit society under external pressure, people tried to avoid frictions by acknowledging each other's public role rather than his or her political convictions. In an ethos very close to what Richard Sennett has described as the courteous exchange between public personae in European cities, even enemies showed respect for each other in public and tried to avoid open fissure.[44]

So, to sum up the first point, there were strong elements of horizontal civil society organization in Ovamboland. Secondly, all these organizations were closely linked to urban movements; or, to be more precise, they were simultaneously urban and rural. People moved back and forth between Cape Town, Windhoek and small villages in rural Ovamboland. Virtually all older political leaders in Namibia have a rural background and still keep up links to their home villages. Like Mamdani argued, pass laws made the exchange difficult for rural villagers, but the contract labor system also forced many people to frequently move between the towns of central Namibia and the reserve. New ideas were discussed in the mining compounds and easily found their way into remote villages. The best expression of this rural-urban exchange is the founding of the Ovamboland People's Congress in, of all places, Cape Town.

This link between towns and homeland, however, became more strained in the 1970s, when young people left South West Africa in large numbers for exile. They had had no time to develop social networks in the rural areas and quickly became detached from their families and from activist networks at home. For them, none of the civil society institutions mentioned above was particularly meaningful; what counted were their colleagues in professional politics living in Lusaka, Lubango or New York. The real rift in Namibian politics until today is not between rural and urban areas, but between exile politicians and those who remained at home. As the older generation anchored in their pre-exile experiences starts to leave politics and the exile generation concentrates its political and social life in Windhoek, this rift is more and more felt as an urban-rural divide today. But this is not the consequence of indirect rule, but of a liberation fight which had to be fought in exile and forced an entire generation of politicians to lose touch with the rural areas.

---

[44] See Sennett 1977. One could link this ethos of courteous exchange to the principle of honor John Iliffe (2005) sees at work in most African societies. It is still prevalent today, and I see Swapo's insistence on Unity as one of its expressions. Its flipside is the total exclusion of those who do not respect the dignity of the leaders, which can be seen in the treatment of political pariahs like Phil ya Nangoloh, the leader of the National Society for Human Rights, and his reactions to the exclusion.

When Mamdani analyzes the consequences of indirect rule – and this is the third point in which my analysis of Ovamboland differs from his findings – he privileges the colonial perspective from above. He sees Chiefs as powerful patrons and as efficient rulers backed by the full weight of colonial authority. But indirect rule did not achieve its aims so easily. In Ovamboland, chiefs were by no means the powerful decentral despots Mamdani describes. Being politically powerful, but economically weak, they started to lose status as early as in the 1950s. Trade was an important factor in this. Chiefs had gained much of their power by controlling trade goods and monopolizing access to firearms and horses in the nineteenth century. They lost control over trade in the early twentieth century, but cooperating headmen gained the backing of colonial armies instead and could stabilize their power. As long as trade was monopolized by white companies and migrant workers' wages partly channeled into the headmen's coffers, the loss of control over trade did not affect them too severely as a class. But migrant workers and traders started to become better off economically in the 1950s and asked for political representation, as well. Headmen looked for new resources outside their old domains and increasingly resorted to violence to keep young men in line. For example, senior headmen started to sell sub-headmenships to the highest bidder[45] and began flogging political opponents with the backing of the native affairs department in the early 1950s. In consequence, they were criticized and sometimes ridiculed by young men who had better schooling and often more income than they had.

When the liberation movement gained momentum, their association with the colonial regime turned from an asset into a liability. By the 1980s, Chiefs who for many had become hated symbols of the apartheid system hid away behind earth walls and armed bodyguards. More than a few were killed, most prominently Ondonga King Filemon Elifas who was murdered in 1975.[46] The system of decentralized despotism was much

---

[45] Expert witness report for the Odendaal Commission by Arthur MacDonald, Odibo, undated (probably 1961/62), Odibo Mission Archives.

[46] Filemon yElifas lyaShindondola (*1932) became Ondonga King and Executive Councillor in the Homeland Government in 1970 and was elected as Chief Minister of Owambo after Uushona Shiimi's death in a car accident in 1972. After his murder in 1975, the South African authorities accused Swapo of the killing and applied new emergency measures. Four Swapo members were convicted in the first instance, but released by the South African Supreme Court in 1977 due to irregularities in the court proceedings. (Among the four was Aaron Mushimba, brother of Sam Nujoma's first wife, who became one of the richest and best connected businessmen in post-independence Namibia and profited enormously from Black Economic Empowerment deals.) – Other famous representatives of traditional authorities murdered during the liberation war were Oukwanyama senior headmen Elia Weyulu from Okongo (1976), in whose homestead Eliaser Tuhadeleni had been held under house arrest in 1960, and the tribal secretary for Ongandjera and Minister of Health in the Owambo government, Toivo Shiyagaya (1978). Toivo Shiyagaya was also the husband of a trader; his wife Taimi had opened a shop and a bakery in Okahao in 1966.

more controversial and contested than Mamdani suggests, and by the 1970s, probably everybody in Ovamboland was conscious of its links to the central despotism in the urban areas.

However, Mamdani is right that the homeland system was a direct continuation of British-style indirect rule and that it fragmented political organization to some degree. Close ties connected urban and rural areas, and an organized civil society confronted the government on all levels, but links between different homelands were much weaker. The liberation movement and the Churches tried to overcome this fragmentation. They could build on the joint experiences of migrant labor, but most people's daily experiences and the social networks anchored in that everyday life were still confined within homeland boundaries.

Traders were present in all domains of political organization. Many first-generation Swapo members had a trading background, but those who turned into professional politicians or were jailed had to leave their businesses behind. Those who continued to work in their shops were by definition less radical and more focused on compromise. Where politics became the focus of everyday life for the exile generation, people who stayed in Namibia had other things to occupy them. "Human life everywhere is never totally a matter of politics; [...] even where political activity is forcibly suppressed, life still goes on in its rich variety, [and] under a rigid system of control people preserve their sanity – though, to some critics perhaps, postpone their ultimate relief – by busying themselves with their non-political interests."[47]

Still, many traders continued to be politically active, both as a professional interest group and as members of different organizations on both sides. As the largest and most successful professional group in the modern sector who was not forced to leave the homeland to earn money, traders became an important constituent of a local elite; their economic status, their social integration and their political role fed into each other. They partly suffered from the apartheid system, partly profited from it, but they were rarely passive victims of a decentralized despotism.

---

[47]   Marwick 1971, xvi

Conclusion

In the introduction, I claimed that Ovamboland's trading stores were a prism which refracts and renders visible the major social and political developments in twentieth century Namibia. I hope that the main part of the book has made good on this claim. It is now time to revisit some of its major themes and sum up its findings. From the many threads which run through the history of trading stores in twentieth century Ovamboland, I will concentrate on three points: on the links between changes in colonial domination and local elite formation, on the way in which homeland development policy has shaped economic structures and on the relation between consumption, trade and social order. Before that, however, I start with an overview of trade development in the former Ovamboland after Namibia became independent in 1990. The failure of most existing stores to remain competitive under the new political regime sheds light on pre-independence business environment and thus can sharpen the analysis in the remaining parts of the conclusion.

Trade in central-northern Namibia after 1990

Namibia became independent in March 1990 after more than a hundred years of colonial rule. The first general democratic elections in November 1989 ended a drawn-out period of political and social stagnation and insecurity in the country. 57% of the electorate voted for Swapo, and the former liberation movement turned into a political party that has been in power ever since, continuously augmenting its share of votes to more than 75% in the 2009 elections.

With independence, peace came to northern Namibia after almost 25 years of guerilla war and military occupation. More than 40.000 persons returned to the country from exile, many of them seeing their relatives for the first time in twenty years. Peace and the newly won political freedom brought a climate of hope and social awakening. Swapo pursued a policy of national reconciliation and ruled off the past by a general amnesty for crimes committed by both sides during the liberation war. In economic policy, the party left behind its socialist rhetoric and adopted a liberal stance.

Many traders in Ovamboland placed high hopes into the new freedom from the restrictions which apartheid and the South African occupation had imposed on them. They soon realized, however, that only few businesspeople could earn the economic dividends of democracy and liberalization. This had several reasons.

First of all, the war-related transfer payments from South Africa ceased. The army and police units were pulled out of Ovamboland, the South African personnel repatriated and the local troops laid off. Peace left thousands of local soldiers unemployed. Most of them had earned higher wages than teachers or nurses and spent a good part of it on consumption. Overall purchasing power in the area sank dramatically, and many shop owners felt the decline in turnover.

As homeland boundaries, pass regulations and emergency laws were abolished, shop owners realized that apartheid regulations had not only curtailed their freedom and dignity, but had also protected them from outside competition. The homeland's closure had kept money within the area and competitors out of it. With independence, a new move into the larger cities of Windhoek, Oshakati and Ondangwa set in. Wage earners typically were the first to move, as the abolishment of old injustices brought better job opportunities in the towns for many trained workers and employees. This led to a further slump in purchasing power in the area. Many shops, especially in the smaller towns and villages, had to face a decline in the number of customers. As running costs were very low, most shops were kept open, but many no longer provided a sufficient family income.

Around 1991, when the region had regained a certain normality after the radical changes which independence had brought, more competitive companies from South Africa began to expand into the region. The first were medium-sized fruit and vegetable businesses, all owned by South African Muslim families of Asian origin.[1] They imported fresh produce, which had not been available in most local stores, from South Africa. Due to the quality of their goods and the comparably low prices, they had a huge success and quickly gained an important market share.

As collective taxis provided an easy and relatively cheap means of transport on the regions' major roads, lower prices and better choice in the urban stores formed a more and more serious competition for the shops in the smaller rural towns. The larger locally owned supermarkets in Oshakati and Ondangwa profited from the better market, as well, and could match South African competition for some time. Frans Indongo's Continental group, the Namundjebo family's supermarkets in Oshakati or Jairus Shikale's Punyu stores did good business in the first half of the 1990s. But all in all, more shops competed for first declining, then stagnant purchasing power, and the turnover of the average village store shrank. Traders had to reduce the choice of goods in their shops to cut costs and

---

[1]   Fysal's Fresh Produce ("The poor man's friend"), owned by a family with Pakistani roots, was the first such business in Oshakati and Ondangwa, Dirk Fruit and Brenner Fruit followed slightly later. All three companies also opened stores in Oshikango in the late 1990s. Dirk Fruit is owned by the family of Cape Malay musician Taliep Pietersen's wife, who notoriously had her husband murdered in a staged robbery in December 2006.

to avoid spoilage and write-offs, which made the larger shops in town seem even more attractive in comparison.

After the South African transition to democracy in 1994, a new type of store expanded into the region: South African retail chains began to open branches there. They gained an ever-increasing market share in clothing, furniture and household goods since around 1995 and in foodstuff and electronics since the 2000s. A large assortment, low prices due to bulk supply, professional organization and highly visible marketing make the chain stores very attractive to local consumers. As the larger stores need a broader customer base, they can only survive in the population centers, which again increased business concentration in and consumer migration to the urban areas.

The 1990s thus saw a fundamental shift in the relations between Namibia and South Africa: indirect economic control replaced direct political domination. The end of apartheid brought political freedom to Namibia's people and economic opportunities to South Africa's companies. Local traders, well adapted to the conditions of colonialism, were ill prepared to benefit from the new liberty. The first half of the 1990s saw a steady decline of the old locally owned stores. Many closed down or were relegated to a side business.

When new demand from the neighboring Angola reversed the trend in the mid-1990s, only few local shop owners still had the capital and the energy to profit from it. Angola had been at war since before independence in 1975. In a particularly devastating phase of the war after the aborted presidential elections in 1992, many towns and a large part of the country's infrastructure were destroyed. When reconstruction started towards 1995, the southern parts of Angola could barely be reached from Luanda harbor (the only deep-sea harbor in Angola and the country's main trade hub). Northern Namibia was closer and much more easily accessible. From Durban or Walvis Bay, trucks could reach northern Namibia on excellent tar roads, so that transport costs were much lower than via Luanda.

Angolan demand created a new trade boom in Oshakati in 1995. Again, the larger stores could profit most, as the majority of Angolan customers were wholesalers who preferred to buy goods by truckload. Wholesale firms from Windhoek first opened outlets in Oshakati, but from 1996, the first warehouses were established in Oshikango, as close to the Angolan markets as possible. The town experienced an unprecedented growth exclusively based on export to Angola.[2] The boom attracted new international companies. From around 1999, Pakistani-owned used car dealers who had earlier established businesses in Durban or Cape Town founded branches in Oshikango and sold used Japanese or American cars to Angolan customers. Chinese migrants based in Windhoek opened

---

[2]   For the following, see Dobler 2008b, 2008c, 2009a, 2009b.

wholesale businesses there, and their success attracted an ever-growing number of new migrant entrepreneurs from China. A large Lebanese-owned company established the biggest wholesale warehouse in Oshikango, selling furniture from Brazil and electronics from the Far East. Families of Portuguese extraction who had moved from Angola to South West Africa in 1975 established a supermarket and another large wholesaler. Businesspeople from all over the world participated in the boom. Most of them are newcomers, either international investors or Namibians who used the opportunities to build a business from scratch. In this area which had known a boom of local entrepreneurship thirty years earlier, the only two local businesspeople who had substantial shares in Oshikango's boom were Frans Indongo, who owned one of the larger warehouses in Oshikango until he sold it to a Portuguese competitor in 2004, and the Namundjebo family, who had a ten percent share in Northgate Trading, a warehouse depot for Namibian Breweries' trade into Angola, before running into financial difficulties and selling the share in 2000.[3]

If we look at Namibia at large, only a handful of the most successful shop owners still play an important economic role today. These few have been able to expand into the nationwide economy and have used their connections and their business reputation to find a place in independent Namibia's politicized economy. Frans Indongo started early to invest in companies with a nationwide importance. In 1982, he acquired shares in Cohen motors, then the largest car distributer in South West Africa, in African Electric and in a small airline. After independence, he invested in the property market, in a large sugar importer and in three fishing companies.[4] Among his most important investments was the Frans Indongo Gardens Building in Windhoek's central business district, a 16-floor office building opened in 1996 in which some of the country's major companies have their headquarters. In 2005, the street on which the building lies was renamed "Frans Indongo Street".[5]

The Namundjebo family equally moved into real estate. United Africa Group, the company run by Martha Namundjebo's husband Haddis Tiluhan, bought several large hotels and business complexes, among them the Kaiserkrone and Gutenberg Plaza complexes in Windhoek. The group's highest-profile development is the "African Pride Eli-

---

[3]   The Namibian 17 August 2009.
[4]   Aaron Mushimba, brother to Sam Nujoma's first wife and Black Economic Empowerment kingpin, was the CEO of CATO fishing company. At the occasion of the christening of a newly bought ship in 1992, President Nujoma held a speech in which he called Indongo "a Namibian businessman and prominent SWAPO member, Mr. Frans Aupa Indongo" (yaShiimi 2007, 70) – an indication of both Indongo's quick integration into the new political mainstream and Nujoma's version of reconciliation.
[5]   It is somehow fitting that an intersecting road was, at the same occasion, named after Werner List, the chairman and majority owner of the breweries as whose distributer Indongo made a large part of his fortune.

Image 48: Once a huge supermarket, now empty: Punyu Depot, Onhuno, 2008.

akim Namundjebo Plaza Hotel" in central Windhoek, a five-star hotel run by the Hilton Group after its opening in 2011.

Eliakim Prins Shiimi no longer owns his furniture stores, but he still mostly lives in Ondangwa where he built up a paint factory after independence, "because you have to do something for local production", as he says. He has a share in Komsberg Farming, a 330 km² commercial farm and vineyard along the Orange River, and has served as board member of some of the largest Namibian companies – First National Bank Namibia, Pep Stores Namibia, Metje & Ziegler and Barloworld Namibia, as well as the non-profit Roessing Foundation. In spite of his national connections, he continues to be an active organizer of local Church circles and development groups and tries to represent "the ordinary people" in national political and economic circles, whom he reproaches of living detached from everyday realities in the country.[6]

These three are notable exceptions rather than the rule. Their continuing success in independent Namibia built on their capability to diversify. They were able and willing to act as entrepreneurs who centered their strategy on economic success, not on a specific profession; and they had the funds to do so successfully.

On the other side of the spectrum, a great number of young businesspeople were able to carve out a place for themselves in the early 1990s. Many who had opened a shop, gained business experiences and made some savings in the urban centers of Ovamboland

---

[6] I cannot put a date on these quotes; he repeated the words on several occasions during our many interviews and informal talks in 2006.

in the 1980s could capitalize on these beginnings, but were still flexible enough to react to the political and economic changes. Rather than retail stores, these young businesspeople typically operated garages, spare parts warehouses buying salvage cars, barbershops or public phone cabins. While their companies are not the main protagonists in the new trade boom, some of them have come to considerable wealth in it. Less affluent, but equally dynamic are self-employed actors in the informal sector, from day laborers in the cross-border trade to the owners of small cuca shops or street and market vendors.

The quintessential owner of a medium-sized trading store of the 1970s and 1980s, however, has completely lost his or her economic role. Most of the stores very slowly went out of business, and their owners lacked capital, energy, skills or simply the will to move into a different field of business. They had learned to see themselves as shop owners and were reluctant to give up both the everyday life the profession brought and the steady income it produced. Many of them perceived declining turnover as a temporary crisis, until they no longer had the funds to invest in a more lucrative business. Today, the vestiges of the 1980s trade boom can be found all over the area – as supermarkets in the rural towns in which the few shelves filled with merchandise slowly gather dust, or as closed-down buildings whose walls still advertise the beer brands now sold by South African-owned chain stores. The reasons for their decline can be found in pre-independence structural decisions and in the way they influenced post-independence agency. To analyze them, I have to go back to some of the major themes of earlier chapters.

Image 49: George Namundjebo with tills remaining from his father's supermarkets. Omafo 2008.

Colonial domination and local elites in Ovamboland

Ovamboland between 1915 and 1954 was one of the classic territories of indirect rule. The area was almost completely closed to outsiders, and its inhabitants at least officially were not allowed to leave it without a pass. In that way protected from undesired outside interference, Native Commissioners Hahn and Eedes governed the country as a personal fiefdom. They made up for their very limited resources of domination with a government by proxy through the local chiefs and headmen. The potential of military intervention which the colonial government proved in 1917 and 1932 helped to keep local rulers in line, but common interests, the integration of the native commissioners as new overlords into the local system of legitimacy and an often cunning power-play by Hahn and Eedes were much more important.

Both native commissioners, but especially Hahn, saw their role in preserving 'traditional society' from outside influences. Given that they simultaneously had to secure a steady flow of migrant labor for the colonial economy, this attitude appears rather schizophrenic in retrospect. But Hahn seems to have honestly believed that integration into the modern society could be confined to the migrant labor phases in the life courses of young men. If they found an intact and economically sound local society at their return, they would reintegrate into it and happily live under an essentially unchanged system – at least as long as both communist agitators and capitalist leeches could be kept out of the area.

This attitude shaped his trade policy. He was skeptical of independent traders who could exploit his subjects. Instead, he looked for ways to integrate new consumption opportunities into the local life without changing its power structures. His favorite solution would have been a cooperative store under the control of headmen, but as his superiors opposed the idea, he decided to give as much leeway as possible to emerging local traders, in whose efforts he saw no danger of exploitation.

In the eyes of most members of the local society, colonial indirect rule in Ovamboland at first did not differ much from the pre-colonial political system. There was a new supreme chief above one's headman; but just as ordinary people did not have many dealings with the king, they rarely saw the native commissioner except at ceremonial occasions.[7] In some situations, the new power in the land even provided the opportunity to look for help in conflicts with one's own ruler. Migrant workers frequently appealed to the native commissioner if they felt unfairly treated by their headmen. The headmen

---

[7]   Though the usual address of letters to Hahn was "Master Shongola" ("whip", his local name), some letters actually call him "Ohamba Shongola", "King", a title reserved for the supreme chief of an ethnic group. Officially, the supreme chief of all South West African 'natives' was the Administrator for South West Africa, or, from 1954, the South African State President.

themselves were not always happy with decisions imposed upon them by the native commissioner, but they generally appreciated the stabilization of their own rule – most of all in Oukwanyama and Uukwambi, the areas which had previously been ruled by kings. Here, the senior headmen had actually gained in power by the regime change, as the native commissioner interfered less frequently and in a more predictable manner than the King had.

Even though it was comparatively well accepted and never characterized by spectacular excesses of power, colonial domination in Ovamboland profoundly changed the local economy and society by integrating it into overarching colonial structures. The most important avenue of change was migrant labor. What had started as the individual decision by young men to seek their luck in the south (in itself rather an act of emancipation than of oppression) slowly changed its character. It turned first into a normalized cultural choice and then into an economic necessity, and it set Ovamboland's economy on a path which it would have become difficult to leave by the 1950s. To use the conceptualization of domination sketched in the introduction of this book: Like no other institution in twentieth century Namibian history, the institutionalization of contract labor set data which inevitably framed local agency.

The motivation to accept the conditions of migrant labor rested in the economic security and status ascent contract work promised. These, in turn, are linked to the freezing of social structures that indirect rule brought to Ovamboland. The reinforcement of the chiefs' rule by the colonial overlordship and the ban on intertribal warfare closed earlier routes of social ascent. The expansion of settlement due to population influx after the colonial border demarcation further diminished the scope for alternative strategies, as it brought the internal frontier zones between the polities under central political authority. In this more rigid societal situation, contract labor offered an alternative strategy to young men. At the same time, mission schools and hospitals opened up new career paths for educated Christian men and (to a lesser degree) women, who could find both an income and a social role as teachers, nurses or pastors. These two new options were not mutually exclusive; most mission employees spent some time as migrant workers before settling down in Ovamboland.

Slowly, a new elite group developed which challenged first the exclusive status, then the political authority of traditional leaders. The world outside of the reserve gained greater relevance in the lives of migrant workers, teachers or pastors, and they learned to interpret conflicts with their headmen, conditions at the workplace and the pass laws as a feature of one and the same colonial system. When the headmen reacted strongly to the new challenges of their authority, this only stressed their association with the colonial regime. So in a paradoxical manner, the group which was least exposed to the colonial regime and least compatible to its economic system, the headmen, became the local embodiment of colonialism and the main partners of the colonial administration, while migrant workers and educated elites – groups who had much higher skills in the colonial frame of reference and played a more important role in the colonial economy – came to be opposed to it.

At a decisive moment during this historical shift, the early 1950s, the South African regime change increased the association between chiefs and colonialism, and the rift between migrant workers and colonial administration. The National Party began to integrate South West Africa more closely into the South African political system and to replace segregation with apartheid.

Gradually, a new ideology of economic development supplanted the old one of preserving traditional society. Separate development of black and white living spheres, this utopia of apartheid thinking, could not become a reality until the reserves, now renamed homelands, provided sufficient subsistence for the black population. Development and apartheid were thus ideologically (if not practically) inseparable.

The problem was that in order for the apartheid development project to be successful, the state needed migrant workers, who opposed apartheid, and it needed headmen, who were not very much interested in development. The consequence was that homeland development could only take place under increasingly rigid social control. Economic changes had to be framed by social engineering and tight supervision, which became all the more crucial as the ideologically driven separation of living spheres constantly clashed with the real economic integration.

All this made the political regime increasingly oppressive. Its interference in all areas of private life, from sexuality to consumption, increased the modernist elites' political antipathy against it. At the same time, the modernist economic impulse which governed policy in the homelands made the new administration more and more incompatible with the old elites of headmen and chiefs. When Ovamboland was given its 'independence' as a homeland, this looked like a new summit of the system of indirect rule; in reality, however, the old rulers were turned into mere figureheads of a technocratic direct rule by white civil servants.

Between a modernist elite integrated into the colonial economy but opposed to colonial rule and a traditionalist elite which did not oppose the regime, but was not very compatible with its development plans either, Ovamboland traders occupied a middle ground. They were both integrated into the modern economy and in favor of the government's development, and their outlook on planning was compatible with the administration's; but they were also still part of a village society, did not want to lose their own status and looked for reforms rather than for a revolution.

This turned them into ideal partners for the apartheid administration's development plans. Their economic success could be presented to the outside world as proof of the beneficial aspects of apartheid. No brochure of the 1970s or 1980s lacks an image of a trader proudly standing in front of his business in suit and tie. Even more importantly, traders were the only social stratum administrators could really target in their efforts to find groups to be developed. All other projects of the apartheid state's development agencies were established top-down; shop owners as the only existing local entrepreneurs provided the ideal mirror for the development experts' self-image.

This does not mean that traders always accepted the role the regime had conceived for them. Most of them readily took advantage of the credit facilities, shop premises and political protection they received from the regime, but few agreed to all of its politics. Traders became a politically active group that gradually replaced the headmen as the most important supralocal political elite. They organized their interests in trade organizations and lobbied the administration, capitalizing on their importance for homeland development. Compared to traders' political role in the homeland administration, headmen's influence steadily declined.

So traders could have turned into an active civil society group, criticizing the government without fundamentally opposing it, and in the long run contributing to democratic reforms and perhaps one day to a passage to independence. This did not happen – simply because apartheid's combination of economic integration and social exclusion of the majority could only be upheld through a degree of pressure that made compromises increasingly difficult. In Ovamboland, the experiences under military occupation did not leave the traders unaffected. Many were opposed to Swapo in the 1970s, but the brutal counterinsurgency tactics of military and police troops gradually changed their political convictions. For the first time, this local elite experienced the indignity of being subject to arbitrary violence in their own persons – and they were all the more affected by this proof of the system's injustices as they had been used to being treated with civility and respect.

I would like to quote one last time from Petrus Ndongo's diaries. His experiences were not spectacular, but his first-hand accounts illustrate the changing attitude all the better. The first direct contact with military occupation is recorded on 20 April 1978:

> Troops came surrounded St. Mary's Odibo area. They took Mr. [illegible] with them. There came another troop and their Capt and entered my classroom and at the same time he asked me to go with him to our store. There they began to search our store and the next room. After these they accompanied me to our school, and here the Capt asked my shot gun licence and agreed with it.

Over the following years, he reported many such small incidents. His most demeaning experience came relatively late, on 10 September 1988. While he was sleeping, South African troops broke into his house. "As I thought that these gang must be the Botsotsos [criminals], I shout to my wife and to our boys at their sleeping huts". The soldiers pulled him out of the house,

> where I found a white man who began to clap me at my chicks [cheeks] and pulled me away from the house door. They then began to ask me many questions […] [I told them] I am a teacher […] and I don't know the terrorists. The other three men entered in my bedroom they took my petty cash book with R350 in it, my case with its eyeglasses, other articles were Tomato Sauce, bottle wine.

Ndongo was fundamentally shaken by this experience, most of all by the fact that his elite status and his good will ("I am a teacher and I don't know the terrorists") did not protect him, and that his complaints with the headman, the Bishop and the military authorities ultimately remained without success.

His was a very harmless experience compared to the violence, cruelty and torture many of his colleagues were subjected to, and it came rather late. The sum of these experiences changed many traders' attitudes towards the apartheid administration. The homeland parliament opposed the central government and the occupational forces ever more openly, and immediately before independence, many high-profile traders who had played an important role in the homeland regime could change into the Swapo camp without looking too opportunistic.

Political power in post-independence Namibia, however, was taken over by returning exiles. The leading Swapo cadres had become professional politicians during their decades in exile. Many of them had no other life to turn to and saw it as a matter of course that their struggle would be rewarded with a political office. Friendships and networks grown in exile (and sometimes enmities, too) decided over political participation in Windhoek. Only the best placed former homeland traders gained access to these political circles and were able to capitalize on their connections; most could only play an economic and political role on the regional level of, ironically, the former homeland.

Homeland development and economic structures

I have argued that development played a crucial role for the self-definition of apartheid administrators, and that they regarded traders as natural allies for homeland development. I will now look more closely at the structural consequences of this cooperation for Ovamboland's economy.

The apartheid era changed many things in Ovamboland, but it did not alter the fundamental importance migrant labor had for the economic integration of the region into the national economy. The continuous flow of labor power from the homeland into the white mining and farm economy was the one precondition no development policy in the region would be able (or allowed) to alter. Even if one was willing to accept the premises of apartheid, the white economy's need for labor was the fatal flaw in the idea of separate development, and it affected even the most honest attempts to better economic conditions in Ovamboland. The trade boom which the area experienced in the 1950s and 1960s was nothing but the reverse side of its integration into the global economy through the export of labor power.

Apart from saving them or spending them on consumption, surplus wages could of course also be invested into agriculture. Emmanuel Kreike has shown the high degree to which wages from migrant labor have been invested into a local agriculture that faced increasing ecological problems due to overpopulation and overgrazing.[8] While migrant labor had to be subsidized by the household economy, as the low wages could not cover reproduction costs, the wages at least allowed to sustain the household economy under ecological stress. But this, too, was a closed circle. Instead of leading to a market production which could have replaced migrant labor, it only allowed to keep up the export of young men's labor power.

Investing wages productively outside of the homeland was next to impossible. In the absence of industrial development in the area, there remained only one way to re-invest one's savings outside of agriculture: opening a trading store. For those who had saved sufficient capital, this was indeed a very promising investment. Running a store allowed the owner to settle down and still earn a regular cash income. The steady flow of outside resources into the region secured demand. Wages for migrant work were relatively low, but even low wages cumulated to a very significant purchasing power in an economy that relied on household farming for everyday subsistence.

For many people in Ovamboland, trade thus provided a way to better their own personal situation. A successful store gave access to a steady income, higher social status and extending social networks, together with all the comparative freedom of self-employment. Trade was attractive as a permanent profession in much the same way migrant labor had been attractive as a temporary employment, and it had fewer negative aspects than contract labor.

---

[8]   Kreike 2004, 81–101.

So trade appeared to many in the 1950s as a way out of economic dependence on contract labour. Andreas Shipanga, when looking back on the founding years of Swapo in an interview with Lauren Dobell, sums up their early aspirations:

> Our plan was simple – get rid of the Boers. Our strategy comprised two things: first, economic self-reliance, by which we meant that blacks would establish their own businesses, so that we would not have to buy from the SWANLA monopoloy. [...] Part two was that eventually, with economic strength, people would work for fellow blacks and not for the contract system.[9]

The major flaw in this argument was, of course, that success in trade was only the flip side of migrant labour. The money people spent in shops owned by fellow blacks came from work for the contract system (and, incidentally, a large part of the stores' supply came from SWANLA's wholesale stores or other white-owned businesses). So while trade empowered black traders, it could not be a pathway towards economic self-reliance of the black population. Rather, it exacerbated economic differences between ordinary workers and the new elite.

Structurally, then, trading stores set conditions in much the same way as migrant labour had. Prospective entrepreneurs relied on trade for their own economic emancipation just like individual young men had, in the early 20th century, relied on migrant labour. The sum of individual emancipatory decisions set conditions that narrowed the scope of future agency. Once migrant labor, and trade, had become the normal economic activity for a specific social group, that normality was not only reproduced in social practices and societal structures of relevance, but also in so concrete phenomena as spatial organization, roads, passports or tax laws.

Social scientists and political activists alike have often stressed how its integration into the colonial economy in a dependent position underdeveloped Ovamboland. Both groups usually assume that this was done on purpose, as a strategic element of first colonial, then apartheid policy. As far as the homeland development agencies are concerned, I do not think this is true. Experts within the Bantu Investment Corporation really tried to foster sustainable development in Ovamboland. They believed in modernization and in industrial development, and they used the whole arsenal of 1970s and 1980s development cooperation to bring it about – which, as James Ferguson has pointed out long ago, did not include political change.[10] The framework of separate development and the imperatives of migrant labor were the two conditions which they could or would not

---

[9]   Dobell 1997, 29.

[10] Ferguson 1990.

question; in consequence, their efforts could not but fail, as they reproduced the very conditions of underdevelopment which they set out to change.

The Bantu Investment Corporation and its successors tried to foster industrial development and were to some degree successful in this. Almost all major factories in today's Ovamboland have been founded by the corporations and have operated for some time under a protected environment. They received state tenders and credit and generally were not allowed to fail, as their existence was a major political asset. This created jobs, but it did not create bottom-up industrialization. To the contrary: no competitor could be successful against these subsidized companies. None of these industrial ventures was export-oriented; they all relied on the internal market in Ovamboland. This again increased the region's dependence on transfers, either by government or by migrant workers.

If South Africa's development policy in Ovamboland was still more successful than in many South African homelands, this was partly due to the amount of money spent in the region. Pretoria wanted to show both to the world and to potential Swapo militants in the region how beneficial South African rule was. But due to the late arrival of colonial domination and the country's relatively integrated society, Ovamboland also had much better preconditions than many of the fragmented, depopulated and socially disrupted South African homelands.

The only sector in which bottom-up economic development indeed happened was trade. This, due to the region's externalized integration into the national economy, was simply the easiest and most lucrative investment. Whoever wanted to establish a business did well to open a store. Under the prevailing economic conditions, this was a logical choice, but in the long run, it prevented a change to a more diversified and more self-sufficient economy. In this, today's situation in northern Namibia is eerily similar to the trade boom of the 1960s. Many people, including the Namibian government, urge Chinese or Lebanese investors to diversify and to engage in manufacturing, but in the current trade boom, the opportunity costs of not opening a store are simply too high.

In retrospect, a development policy that looked comparatively successful during the homeland era can only be seen as failed. The massive sums of money that flowed into the area for development and for the war did not initiate any really sustainable development. What successes there were remained intrinsically linked to the homeland system and the protectionist environment it offered for businesses profiting from the wages of migrant workers. It is thus small wonder that only few shop owners proved competitive after Namibian independence.

Consumption, trade and social order

This book has concentrated on the supply side of trade: on shops and on traders. I have not systematically treated the changes in everyday consumption, changes that simultaneously lived on and nourished shop development. Just to write a detailed history of clothing, of architecture or of cars in Ovamboland would need much more space than could have been afforded in this monograph – and it would have necessitated a very different set of sources.[11] But consumption changes have always stood in the background of the developments I have written about. They contributed to a specific social formation in which the ascent of the traders as a new elite became possible and in which new forms of political and social exchange developed. In the following, I will use three examples to show how closely consumption changes and the political sphere were linked to each other: the attractiveness monopoly stores gained in the 1930s, the place of local stores for village-level social exchange in the 1960s and the role shops played for the frontier space in the new towns during the 1970s and 1980s.

The monopoly stores quickly became important landmarks for the local society. They were the only places where people could buy an appreciable choice of European goods without leaving the reserve. Their main importance, however, was not their contribution to the region's integration into a consumer society. European goods had been appropriated into the local lifestyle for almost a century, and their relevance had further increased with the hike in contract workers' numbers after 1900. Rather, the shops were important because they made contract workers' wages more attractive. A good part of the European goods brought by returning contract workers had long served as means of barter. Without local stores and in the absence of trade caravans, many trade items were difficult to obtain locally and thus had a high exchange value. The new shops made it easier for returning workers to convert their wages into trade goods – one did not have to carry them home on one's back for weeks. As the shops only sold goods for cash which was almost only obtainable through migrant work, they did not greatly affect the exclusivity (and hence the value) of European goods.

The social ascent of the groups who had some cash at their command – migrant workers, teachers, slightly later nurses and clerks – was thus directly connected to consumption changes. As long as cash income was relatively exclusive, at least to World War II, the new shops increased the value of wages and allowed wages-earners to transform them more efficiently into social status. They did so partly in the established ways: by acquiring cattle, founding a household, taking on foster children or organizing cattle

---

[11] Vilho Shigweda's monograph on pre-colonial costumes gives a very good overview, but also shows the practical, often source-related problems of such an undertaking (Shigweda 2006).

feasts. But the status of wage earners was also expressed in new forms of consumption. European-style clothing, new pieces of furniture, later new architectural designs of one's living quarters became markers of identity which distinguished the new elite.

The ascent of these new elites was thus linked to consumption in a twofold way: their relative wealth was based on their exclusive access to consumer goods on which they could capitalize, and their status was enhanced by conspicuous consumption of these goods. Both factors increasingly moved into the center of local images of 'modernity' and contributed to the emerging rift between headmen on the one hand, migrant workers and wage earners on the other.

In the 1950s and 1960s, a similar connection between consumption and political transformations emerged in the local village stores. The stores were the first emphatically public places under the authority of local individuals. They became meeting places in which local news, gossip and political opinions were exchanged. This was important in itself as it created a new kind of village public connected to the new central places. But the venues in which this exchange took place were also spheres of consumption. New trade goods and the public sphere were linked in practice, all the more so since only those who could afford to buy things were regular visitors to the larger stores. One did not have to shop to participate in the gossip in a store, and one did not have to gossip in order to buy goods there. But consumption and public exchange became linked to each other among the wealthier segment of local society. This, again, contributed to the role of shop owners as new social elite. They were central persons in the networks of public exchange, and they earned money on the other participants. Both factors influenced the political stance they took towards colonialism and towards the liberation movement. While migrant workers experienced alienation and oppression on a daily basis, shop owners were largely their own masters and less inclined to seek revolutionary change.

When Ondangwa and Oshakati grew into towns in the 1950s, 1960s and 1970s, their attractiveness to a part of Ovamboland's population was due to the social creativity they made possible. Again, public exchange in the new towns was largely connected to consumption opportunities. Employment opportunities of course had their role in attracting migrants, but the specific urban formation in Ovamboland was much more characterized by consumption than by production. Bars and cuca shops, dance halls and stores were new public meeting places, and personal styling was more and more used to differentiate between social groups.

In the 1980s, these new consumption spheres became increasingly insular. They were largely financed by the wages of local soldiers in the occupational troops, and due to embarrassment, indoctrination and conflict, many soldiers had largely severed their connections to the rural areas. Established traders, on the other hand, partly profited from the new urban consumption by opening stores there, but mostly continued to live in the rural areas. In the occupied and fortified towns detached from their social environment, political liberation ceased to be a major concern for young people. It was largely replaced by the search for self-actualization through consumption.

All through the twentieth century, consumption, changing social structures and politics were closely interlinked in Ovamboland. In the closed reserve and homeland economy mainly connected to the colonial centers through the export of labor and the import of manufactured goods, consumption emerged as an important medium of social and political integration and differentiation. Shops provided the goods consumers used to express their social identity, and thus became venues for both social integration and social differentiation. Shop owners were active participants in the negotiation of status and group attribution, and, by importing and selling new goods, they provided the media through which both were expressed.

Entrepreneurship, dependency and economic structures

The history of traders and local shops in northern Namibia can be seen as paradigmatic for the relation between individual agency and longer-term structures. Traders were astonishingly successful entrepreneurs under apartheid; after the country's independence, they rapidly descended into irrelevance. This is not due to any change in their own attitude towards business, but to the narrowing of the economic niche they had found for themselves. This niche only existed because external actors had created it by economic power and strong political intervention. The colonial economy provided a steady income from migrant workers' wages; without it, entrepreneurs would have needed to find more productive sectors than trade and perhaps succeeded in creating a boom based on manufacturing. Segregation and apartheid made sure they only had each other's competition; without them, traders would have had to be competitive in a wider regional setting from the start. The framework of the colonial economy set their feet on a path it was easy to follow.

By following the path, however, the traders reinforced its pattern. Through their own actions, they translated the political framework into career plans, marriage arrangements or the cumulative reinvestment of profits over many years. Their decisions thus shaped economic and social structures in what could be called the 'medium durée': not the short horizon of everyday decisions, in which we can easily change plans, nor the long-term horizon of structural developments described by Braudel, happening over generations and fairly outside of the scope of human agency.

Unlike the longue durée, the medium durée can immediately be affected by revolutionary political decisions. Such a new deal, however, usually does not change the cards the players hold, but simply overturns the rules the game is won by. The conditions created by the old rules persist in the persons who were formed under them; in infrastructure created by them; in social and cultural choices made under their influence; in societal institutions that made sense under them. This makes it more difficult for some than for others to find a new place under new conditions. Political and economic freedom will not profit everybody, if everybody has not been allowed to learn to profit from it.

The structural consequences of Namibia's independence for local entrepreneurship were in the end surprisingly similar to those of Senegal's or Ghana's independence thirty years earlier. The established local business elite could only profit from independence in a very limited way. They either continued small-scale trade or moved their business interests into other sectors, often drawing on connections to the new political class. The gap that opened between these two groups was filled by minority entrepreneurs from third (and third world) countries – Lebanese in West Africa, Asians in East Africa.[12] Decolonization changed the rules of the game in a way that the links to external markets, the capital and the skills minority entrepreneurs brought into the country were more important than the local knowledge of established traders. In addition, it was easier for new actors to adapt to the new conditions than for established traders to radically change their existing business framework. In Namibia, Pakistani, Lebanese, Asian South African and Chinese expatriate investors played the same role and occupied the middle ground between declining village stores on the one hand, national shareholder capitalism on the other.

There is at least one important structural difference, however. If we follow Samir Amin's analysis of underdevelopment in Senegal, well-placed local businesspeople managed to profit from independence by connecting national markets to the former colonial centers in a way that served their own and the centers' interests.[13] Instead of developing into such a 'comprador bourgeoisie', well-placed Namibian businesspeople could transform political connections into economic gain by taking shares in Black Economic Empowerment deals and by taking over positions in parastatal companies. This has the same structural effect as a comprador bourgeoisie's share in external resources: it enables the best-placed potential entrepreneurs to reap rents of political connections, not of independent economic activities, and it decreases the chances of success for those entrepreneurs who are not part of elite circles. In the Namibian case, BEE policies favored former

---

[12] See e.g. Nugent 2004, 63 f.

[13] Amin 1971. The Marxian concept applied to South America and Africa by Dependence Theory in the 1970s is today taken up by scholars of post-socialist Europe – see Sampson 299ff. for a systematic example.

exile politicians, who had the best connections to the new political leaders and were convinced of their right to reap the fruits of decades of political struggle.

Some of the reasons for the decline of established traders in central northern Namibia are thus rooted in the country's post-independence economic and political development. But the relative incapability of former traders to profit from the new conditions is founded in the South African policies during the mandate regime, which had created economic structures that left the traders in an impasse when homeland conditions no longer existed. In this way at least, post-independence Namibia was created in the homelands, and analyzing the homelands' history might teach us more about the country's society of today than does the political history of liberation. I hope that, in thirty years' time, we can analyze the positive structural effects the country's liberation has had for people growing up under the conditions it creates.

Annex: Price List Ondjodjo and Omafo 1941

[NAN NAO 25 17/1. Items in Italics from price list 1940]

Oshindonga	Oshikwanyama	English	Unit	Lower Price	Upper Price
Omalapi	Omalapi	Shirting	2 yd	1/6	2/-
Omalapi	Omalapi	Baftas	2 yd	2/6	
Omalapi	Omalapi	Salempore	2 yd	3/-	
Omalapi	Omalapi	Ticking	2 yd	3/-	3/6
Omalapi Ijosali	Omalapi Ljosali	Shawls		6/-	
Osijata	Ositaja	Dressing Material	yd	-/9	2/-
Osijata ositokele	Ositaja ositoka	White Brocade	yd	-/9	1/-
Ositaja osizimine	Ositaja ituima	Khaki Drill	yd	1/6	
Oohema	Eehema	Shirts		2/-	11/-
Oombindja	Eembidja	Vests		-/6	2/6
Oombindja utaala	Eembidja outalal	Pullovers		2/6	5/-
Uuzolo	Eedolo	Waistcoats		4/-	
Oombaikisa	Eembaikifa	Jackets		7/6	24/-
Oombuulukueva ohupi	Eembulukueva dihupi	Shorts		5/-	8/-
Oombuulukueva onde	Eembulukueva dile	Trousers		8/-	20/6
Oombuulukueva ji kamasa		Breeches		8/-	
Oondolombruku		Pants		3/-	
Omagala	Omambale	Hats		4/6	12/-
Ukotili	Oikotili	Caps		2/-	
Ikausino jaalumentu	Ikaufino osilumenu	Socks	pr.	1/-	1/6
Ikausino jaakiintu	Ikaufino osikainu	Stockings	pr.	1/-	1/6
Oongaku za luumentu	Eenaku dosilumenu	Mens Shoes	pr.	15/-	20/-
Oongaku za kiintu	Eenaku dosikainu	Ladies Shoes	pr.	12/-	
Ikapute	Oikapute	Canvas Shoes	pr.	3/-	
Ikamasa	Ikamasa	Leggings	pr.	14/-	
Omapaja	Eemija	Belts		1/-	3/-
Oohanduka	Eehanduka	Towels		1/-	6/6
Ikumbersa	Omakumberfa	Blankets		6/-	12/-

Osali		Shawls		7/-	
Ikaiua	Ikaiua	Mufflers		-/6	1/6
Omasituka	Eenasituka	Handkerchiefs		-/6	1/-
Oondunda	Eenduda	Umbrellas		4/-	
Ombandi zo nguo		Buttons	doz.	-/6	1/3
Ombandi zo gosingo		Studs		-/6	
Omiti zu ongosi	Omiti de ongodi	Cotton	reel	-/6	
Ongozi jo kuhondja omia		Saddler-Twine	reel	1/9	
Ongozi jokumanga	Eengodi dokumanga	Ovambo Ropes		-7&	
Onane zo kuhondja	Eenguiga do kohondja	Sewing Needles	pk.	-/6	
Onane zo masina	Eenguiga do masina	Mach. Needles	pk.	2/-	
Onane zo kutunga	Eengumbo	Darning Needles	ea.	-/1	
Osipera	Eesipera	Safety Pins	pk.	-/6	
Omia jo gaku	Eemuiga deengaku	Shoe Laces	pr.	-/3	-/4
Ipa jo gaku	Oipa gengaku	Sole Leather		3/3	
Omuiti zo ongaku	Omiti deengaku	Shoe Polish		-/6	2/3
Ikombe jo gaku	Oikombe gengaku	Shoe Brushes		1/-	1/6
Ikamule	Eemendu	Combs		-/6	-/9
Ontalelo	Outengelelo	Mirrors		-/3	1/6
Uliinga	Oulinga	Finger Rings		1/-	
Utenda uomomakutsi	Outenda vomatui	Ear Rings	pr.	1/-	
Ugondo	Ouvela	Bangles		-/3	-/6
Imoma	Oilanda	Beads small	Bdl.	-/6	1/-
Omaue	Omamanga	Beads big	Bdl.	-&7	1/-
Uhumba	Oufilita	Mouth Organs		-/6	1/6
Oongongi		Concertinas		20/-	
Oseta zo kahumba		Guitar Strings		-/3	_76
Ohija	Osiva	Whistles		1/-	
Oseva somokoha	Eefeua domakosa	Washing Soap	bar	-/6.5	
			Tablet	-/5	
Oseva sismba	Eefeua dosidimba	Toilet Soap		-/3	1/-
Omagazi govaseline		Vaseline		-/9	
Omagazi gokuuaja	Omaadi okuvava	Brillantine		-/6	1/-
Omagazi gomea	Omaadi ameva	Hair-Oil		1/-	1/6
Omagasi gomasina	Omaadi omasina	Machine Oil		-/9	
Osize	Oside	Cinnober	kg	2/6	
Omuti uomi kumbersa	Omiti omakumberva	Baby Powder		1/-	

Okamfuli	Okamfuli	Naphthaline	lb.	1/3	
Omuele zombensi		Shaving Knives		2/6	
Esina ljo mbensi	Omasina endjedi	Safety Razors		-/6	1/-
Ukulule	Oumbi vokukulula	Razor Blades	pk.	-/6	2/6
Utegiso	Eendgolo	Fish Hooks	2 for	-/3	
Injoliso	Epena	Pencils		-/3	-/6
Injoliso	Eena dohinga	Penholders		-/6	
Oinga	Ohinga	Ink		-/6	
Embo hjo mbapira	Oifo geembapila	Exercise Books		-/6	
Embo hjo mbapira	Oifo geembapila	Writing Pads		-/9	2/3
Ondjato zo mbapira	Omakutu eembapila	Envelopes	25	-/6	-/8
Omakaja gofokata	Omakaja ofakata	Tobacco loose	lb.	1/-	
Omakaja umpunda	Omakaja oukutu	Tobacco in bags	Koodoo	-/3	
			Scots Mixture	-/6	
			Springbok	-/9	
			Silver Dollar	-/10	
Omakaja ondoha	Omakaja eendoha	Tobacco in tins	Boxer 1/4 lb.	1/-	
			Boxer 1/2 lb.	2/-	
			Boxer 5 lbs.	14/-	
Omakaja isalute		Cigarettes	Springboks 10's	-/6	
			Springboks 20's	1/-	
			Springboks 50's	2/3	
			C to C 50's	2/3	
			Loyalist 50's	2/8	
			Westminster 30's	2/8	
Ombiga somakaja	Eembiga domakaja	Pipes		-/9	2/6
Uparua	Ouparua	Matches	pk.	-/6.5	
Istroha	Oitolosa	Tinder Boxes		1/-	
Omakumba gikesa	Omakumba oikefa	Pad Locks		-/6	2/6
Omaljena	Omaljenge	Key Chains		-/3	
Ikonde	Eengonda	Scissors		-/6	1/-
Olusindo	Eenguto	Table Spoons		-/6	-/9
Omafoloke		Table Forks		1/2	
Imbere	Eembere	Table Knives		2/-	
Imbere	Eembere	Pocket Knives		1/-	1/6
Omakatana	Omakatana	Bush Knives			

217

Omakuja	Omakuva	Hatchets	2/6	
Omakuja omanene	Omakuva manene	Axes	9/-	
Omatemo	Omatemo	Kaffir Hoes	1/6	
Omatemo gombruru	Omatemo embruru	Kaffir hoes big	2/6	
Ihupolo	Oihupolo	Spades	7/6	
[unreadable]		Forks	5/-	
Iharaka		Rakes		
Ondrata	Eedalate	Binding Wire	Rll.	1/9
Ondungo	Eendungu	Nails	lb.	1/-
Ombiga zimagulu	Eembiga Domaulu	Kaffir Pots	7/-	12/-
Omaemele	Omavela	Buckets	5/-	6/-
Ikanjule	Oikangule	Sad Irons	7/6	
Olampa	Eelamba	Hurricane Lanterns	4/6	7/-
Omakente zo lampa	Omakende eelamba	Lantern Glasses	-/9	2/-
Omakente zu lampa	Omakende eelamba	Lamp Chimneys	-/6	2/6
Omalapi zo lampa	Omalapi eelamba	Lamp Wicks	yd.	1/-
Olampa zo patri		Torches 3 cells	6/9	
Omamanga go lampa		Batteries	-/6	1/-
Ekutu	Omakutu eembapila	New Grain Bags	2/-	
Ompunda zo meja	Omakutu omeva	Water Bags	3/-	
Isala	Omitumba dengambe	Saddles	87/-	
Itomo	Oitomo	Head Gears		
Omakopi	Eeneka	Mugs	-/6	2/6
Omatenga	Ouholo	Camp Kettles	3/-	5/-
Ijaha	Oijaha	Enamel Plates	-/9	
Ijaha	Oijaha	Enamel Washing Basins	1/6	4/6
Ikana omeja	Eekana domeva	Enamel Kettles	4/-	8/-
Ikana omahini	Eekana domasini	Engineer's Cans	4/-	8/-
Ombiga zo kutukela	Eembia dokuteleka	Kitchen Pots		
Omboli		Oval Bath	3/6	
Omblau		Washing blue	pc.	-/1
Osonda jokujoga		Soda	lb.	-/4
Osonda jokuminga oseeua		Caustic Soda	tin	1/6
Ondomo jetemba	Ondomo gomatemba	Axle Grease	tin	1/3
Omaholi go lampa	Omaholi eelamba	Paraffin	tin 4 Gall.	11/-

			tin 1 Gall.	3/6
			tin 1 Liter	1/-
Obedesina		Petrol	Case	29/-
Omalihita	Eekinteli	Candles		-/3
			pk.	3/9
Omungua	Omongua	Salt coarse	lb.	-/1
		Salt Table	pk-	-/8
Opepera	Ombepera	Pepper	tin	-/9
		Curry Powerd	tin	1/-
Osuka	Osuka	Sugar	lb.	-/5
Oluisi	Oluisi	Rice	lb.	-/5
Usila ombulumela	Oufila ombulumela	Boermeal	lb.	-/3
Usila ombulumela	Oufila ombulumela	Flour	5 lb. Bag	1/9
Usliauepungu	Oufila epungu	Mealie Meal	lb.	-/1.5
.ubisikiti	Oimbisikiti	Biscuits loose	lb.	1/6
Ulekenisa	Oulekenisa	Native Sweets	lb.	1/-
Onjama	Ondgema	Jam	1lb.	-/9
			2lb.	1/4
Oniki	Onjiki	Golden Syrup	tin	1/-
Onjama jo ondoba	Ombelela jo ondoha	Corned Beef	tin	1/2
Okusiua	Okafe	Coffee Mixture	2 oz.	-/3
			4 oz.	-/4
			8 oz.	-/8
		Coffee Ysendyk's	tin	1/10
		Coffee Kilimand-jaro	lb.	2/9
Otee	Otee	Tea	1 oz.	-/5
			2 oz.	-/6
			1/4 lb.	-/11.5
			1/2 lb.	1/8.5
			1 lb.	3/5

Bulk goods:

Goods	Price per lb	sh 7/-	-/6d	-/3d
Salt coarse	-/1	12 lbs.	6 lbs	3 lbs
Mealie Meal	-/1.5	8 lbs	4 lbs	2 lbs
Boermeal	-/3	4 lbs	2 lbs	1 lb
Sugar	-/5	3 lbs 6 oz	1 lb 3 oz	
Rice	-/5	2 lbs 6 oz	1 lb 3 oz	
Native Sweets	1/-	1 lb	8 oz	4 oz
Tobacco loose	1/-	1 lb	8 oz	4 oz
Naphthaline	1/3	12,75 oz	6.5 oz	
Biscuits loose	1/6	10,66 oz	5.33 oz	

Other:

Biscuits	Ass. No.1	1/1.5
	Marie	1/0.5
	Cream Crackers	1/0.5
Coffee	van Ysendyk's tin	1/10
Jam	1 lb tin	-/9
	2 lbs. tin	1/4
Matches	Small size pkt.	-/6.5
Ideal Milk	8 oz. tin	-/7
Paraffin	1 Gall. tin	3/6
	4 Gall. Tin	11/-
	8 Gall. Case	22/-
Rice	5 lbs or less. Lb.	-/5
	more than 5 lbs. Lb.	-/4.5
Soap	Sunlight 1 tablet	-/6
	Lifebuoy 1 Carton	1/4
	blue 1 bar	-/6.5
	yellow 1 tablet	-/5
	blue 1 c/s. 100 lbs.	37/6
	yellow 1 c/s. 90 lbs.	35/-
Soap Flakes	Lux 1 pkt.	-/8
Sugar	pocket 100 lbs	34/-
	Hulett's No. 1 100 lbs.	36/-

	1 lb.	-/5
Tea	1/4 lb.	-/11.5
	1/2 lb.	1/8.5
	1 lb.	3/5

For Europeans:

Tinstuff: Fruits, Fish, Sausages, Vegetables, Lard, Milk, Cream, Klim Milk, Quaker Oats, Baking Powder, Cury Powder, Custard Powder, Cocoa Powder, Dill Pickles, Ox Tongue, Roast Mutton, Jams

Bottleware: Lemos and Oros, Worcester Sauce, Salad Oil, Vinegar, Tomato Sauce, Mixed Pickles, Mango Chutney, Honey, Anchovette, Bovril, Marmite

Glassware: Water-, Beer-, Wine- and Portwine-Glasses

Chinaware

Brooms & Brushes: Hair-, Bass- and Hand-Brooms, Scrubbing- and Shoe-Brushes

Polish: Boot-, Floor-, Metal- and Furniture Polish

Paint and Paint-Brushes, Flit and Flit-Sprayers, Fly Swatters, Mosquito Gauze, Canvas, Stretcher

Iron-Mongery: Tools, Builder's and General Hardware, Corrugated Iron, Carpenter's Glues, Sandpaper, Linseed Oil, Strapazoid, Kitchen Pots, Torches and Batteries, Spareparts for Petromax Lamps

Foto-Articles

Toilet-Articles: Soap, Cream, Face-Powder, Dental Cream, Shaving Cream

Archival sources

As all archival sources are cited with their full shelfmark, I only list the archives and, if applicable, the abbreviations I used to designate them here.

BA   Bundesarchiv (German Federal Archive), Berlin-Lichterfelde, Germany

BAB   Basler Afrika Bibliographien, Basel, Switzerland

ELCIN   Archives of the Evangelical Lutheran Church in Namibia, Oniipa, Namibia

ELCRN   Archives of the Evangelical Lutheran Church in the Republic of Namibia, Windhoek, Namibia

NAN   National Archives of Namibia, Windhoek, Namibia

Odibo   Odibo Mission Archive (now Lukenge Archive), Odibo, Namibia

RMG   Rheinische Missionsgesellschaft, now in the archives of the Vereinte Missionsgesellschaft, Wuppertal, Germany

WCL   William Cullen Library, Historical Papers Collection, University of the Witwatersrand, Johannesburg, South Africa

ZBZ   Zentralbibliothek Zürich, Switzerland

List of Illustrations

Efforts were made to trace the copyright holders of illustrations used in this publication. We apologise for any incomplete or incorrect acknowledgments.

Illustrations

References

Allen, C. (1997), Who needs Civil Society? *Review of African Political Economy* 73: 329–337.

Allgemeine Zeitung (2006), *Damals war's. Land und Leute in Namibia*. CD. Windhoek.

Amin, S. (1971), La politique coloniale française à l'égard de la bourgeoisie commerçante Sénégalaise. In C. Meillassoux (ed), *The development of indigenous trade and markets in West Africa*. Oxford, pp. 361–374.

Andersson, C. J. (1856), *Lake Ngami; or, explorations and discoveries during four years wanderings in the wilds of Southwestern Africa*. New York.

Appadurai, A. (ed.) (2004), *The social life of things: commodities in cultural perspective*. Cambridge.

Asiwaju, A. (1988), Indigenization of European Colonialism in Africa: Processes in Yorubaland and Dahomey since 1860. In: S. Förster, W. Mommsen, R. Robinson (eds.), *Bismarck, Europe, and Africa: The Berlin Africa Conference 1884–1884 and the Onset of Partition*. Oxford, pp. 441–451.

Austin, G. (2008), Resources, Techniques and Strategies South of the Sahara: Revising the Factor Endowments Perspective on African Economic Development, 1500–2000. *Economic History Review*, 61(3): 587–624.

Banning, E. (1890), *Die politische Teilung Afrikas nach den neuesten internationalen Vereinbarungen (1885–1889)*. Berlin.

Battistoni, A. K., J. Taylor (2009), Indigenous identities and military frontiers: reflections on San and the military in Namibia and Angola, 1960–2000. *Lusotopie* 16 (1): 113–131.

Bauer, Gretchen (1998): *Labor and Democracy in Namibia, 1971–1996*. Athens.

Bayart, J. F. (1989), *L'Etat en Afrique: la politique du ventre*. Paris.

Beck, K. (2001), Die Aneignung der Maschine. In K.-H. Kohl (ed.), *New Heimat*. New York.

Beinart, W., S. Dubow (eds.) (1995), *Segregation and apartheid in twentieth-century South Africa*. London.

Beinart, W. (2001), *Twentieth-century South Africa*. Oxford.

Berman, B., C. Leys (eds.) (1994), *African capitalists in African development*. Boulder.

Berman, B. (1998), Ethnicity, Patronage and the African State: The politics of uncivil nationalism. *African Affairs* 97: 305–341.

Bertelsmann, W. (1959), Wasserbau im Ovamboland. *SWA Annual*: 141–144.

Best, A. C. (1971), South Africa's Border Industries: The Tswana Example. *Annals of the Association of American Geographers*, 61: 329–343.

Beuving, J. (2006), Lebanese traders in Cotonou: a socio-cultural analysis of economic mobility and capital accumulation. *Africa* 76 (3): 324–351.

Bley, H. (1971), *South West Africa under German Rule*. London.

Blignaut, B. (1965), Herinneringe oor Suidwes-Afrika. *SWA Annual:* 133–134.

Blom Hansen, T., O. Verkaaik (2006), Introduction: Urban Charisma. On everyday mythologies in the city. *Critique of Anthropology* 29(1): 5–26.

Boëtie, E. de la (1727), Essai sur la Servitude Volontaire, ou le Contr'un. In: M. de Montaigne, *Essais, Vol. V*. La Haye, pp. 74–136.

Bohannan, P., G. Dalton (eds.) (1965), *Markets in Africa*. Chicago.

Bollig, M., Power and Trade in precolonial and early colonial Northern Kaokoland, 1860s–1940s. In P. Hayes, J. Silvester, M. Wallace, W. Hartmann (eds.), *Namibia under South African Rule*. Oxford, pp. 175–194.

Bollig, M. (1998), The Colonial Encapsulation of the North-Western Namibian Pastoral Economy. *Africa* 68(4): 506–537.

Bonner, P., P. Delius, D. Posel (1993), The Shaping of Apartheid. Contradiction, Continuity and Popular Struggle. In: P. Bonner, P. Delius. D. Posel (eds.), *Apartheid's Genesis 1935–1962*. Braamfontein, pp. 1–41.

Boone, C., Commerce in Côte d'Ivoire: Ivoirisation without Ivorian Traders. *Journal of Modern African Studies* 31 (1): 67–92.

Boucher, M. (1981), Fogarty, Nelson Wellesley. In: *Dictionary of South African Biography IV*.

Bourdieu, P. (1979), *La distinction. Critique social du jugement*. Paris.

Bretton, M., *Civil Society and Political transition in Africa. IDS Reports* 11 (6).

Brincker, H. (1896), Bemerkungen zu Bernsmanns Karte des Ovambolandes. *Globus* 70 (3): 79–80.

Brincker, H. (1900), *Unsere Ovambo-Mission nach Mitteilung unserer Ovambo-Missionare*. Barmen.

Bruwer, J. P. van Schalwyk (1961), *The Kwanyama of South West Africa: A preliminary study*. Unpublished Thesis, Stellenbosch University.

Burke, T. (1996), *Lifebuoy Men, Lux Women*. London.

Chabal, P., J.-P. Daloz (1999), *Africa Works. Disorder as political instrument*. Oxford.

Charney, C. (1988), Janus in Blackface? The African petite bourgeoisie in South Africa, *Con-Text* 1: 5–44.

Chattopadhyaya, H. (1970), *Indians in Africa: A Social and Economic Study*. Calcutta.

Christaller, W. (1933), *Die zentralen Orte in Süddeutschland. Eine ökonomisch-geographische Untersuchung über die Gesetzmässigkeit der Verbreitung und Entwicklung der Siedlungen mit städtischen Funktionen*. Jena.

Clarence-Smith, W. (1979), *Slaves, Peasants, and Capitalists in Southern Angola 1840–1926*. Cambridge.

Clarence-Smith, W., R. Moorsom (1975), Underdevelopment and class formation in Ovamboland, 1845–1915. *Journal of African History*, 16(3): 365–381.

Cohen, J. L., A. Arato (1992), *Civil Society and Political Theory*. Cambridge.

Cole, P. (1975), *Modern and traditional Elites in the Politics of Lagos*. New York.

Comaroff, J. and J. (1991), *Of Revelation and Revolution 1: Christianity, Colonialism and Consiousness in South Africa*. Chicago.

Comaroff, J. and J. (1990), *Civil Society and the political imagination in Africa*. Chicago.

Cooper, A. D. (1999), The institutionalization of contract labour in Namibia. *Journal of Southern African Studies* 25(1): 121–138.

Cooper, A. D (2001), *Ovambo Politics in the Twentieth Century*. Lanham.

Cowley, C. (1980), Valombola. A Demonstration of Faith in the Future. *SWA Annual*: 123–125.

Crowder, M. (1964), Indirect Rule – French and British Style. *Africa* 34(3): 197–205.

Crowder, M. (1970), The white chiefs of tropical Africa. In: L.H. Gann, P. Duignan (eds.), *Colonialism in Africa, 1870–1960, vol 2*. Cambridge, pp. 329–336.

Daloz, J.-P (2003), 'Big men' in sub-Saharan Africa: how elites accumulate positions and resources. *Comparative Sociology* 2(1): 271–285.

Davies, R (1979), *Capital, State and White Labour in South Africa, 1900–1960: An historical materialist analysis of class formation and class relations*. Brighton.

Davis, S. (1964), Kunene River Dam. Ovamboland Canal and Hydro-Electric Project Promise End to Famine For Ever. *SWA Annual*: 64–67.

Delavignette, R. (1939), *Les vrais chefs de l'Empire*. Paris.

Department of Economic Affairs, Namibia (1990), *Namibia: Development Information Report*. Windhoek.

Dernburg, B. (1909), *Südwestafrikanische Eindrücke. Industrielle Fortschritte in den Kolonien. Zwei Vorträge vom 21./17.01.1909*. Berlin.

Dieckmann, U. (2007), *Haikom in the Etosha region: a history of colonial settlement, ethnicity and nature conservation*. Basel.

De Jongh, M. (1988), Bruwer, Johannes Petrus van Schalkwyk. In: *Dictionary of South African Biography, Vol. V*. Pretoria, pp. 99–100.

Dobell, L. (1997), *Swapo's struggle for Namibia, 1960–1991: war by other means*. Basel.

Dobler, G. (2005), Les élections en Namibie de Novembre 2004. *Politique Africaine* 98: 166–179.

Dobler, G. (2007), China in Namibia. In: H. Melber (ed.), *Transitions in Namibia. Which change for whom?* Uppsala, pp. 94–109.

Dobler, G. (2008a), Boundary-drawing and the notion of territoriality in pre-colonial and early colonial Ovamboland. *Journal of Namibian Studies* 3: 7–30.

Dobler, G. (2008b), From Scotch Whisky to Chinese Sneakers. International commodity flows and trade networks in Oshikango, Namibia. *Africa* 78(3): 410–432.

Dobler, G. (2008c), Solidarity, xenophobia and the regulation of Chinese businesses in Oshikango, Namibia. In: C. Alden, D. Large, R. Soares de Oliveira (eds.), *China returns to Africa*. London, pp. 237–255.

Dobler, G. (2009a), Oshikango: the dynamics of growth and regulation in a Northern Namibian boom town. *Journal of Southern African Studies* 35(1): 115–131.

Dobler, G. (2009b), Chinese Shops and the Formation of a Chinese Expatriate Community in Namibia. *China Quarterly* 199: 707–727.

Dobler, G. (2009c), On the border to chaos: identity formation on the Angolan-Namibian border, 1927–2008. *Journal of Borderland Studies* 25(2): 22–35.

Dobler, G. (2010), License to Drink. Between liberation and inebriation in northern Namibia. In: S. van Wolputte, M. Fumanti (eds.) *Beer in Africa. Drinking spaces, states and selves*. Münster, pp. 167–191.

Dobler, G. (2012), Private Vices, Public Benefits? Small-town Bureaucratization in Namibia. In: A. Peters, L. Handschin (eds.), *Conflict of Interest in Global, Public, and Corporate Governance*. Cambridge, pp. 217–232.

Drechsler, H. (1966), *Südwestafrika unter deutscher Kolonialherrschaft*. Berlin.

Dubow, S. (1992), Nationalism, Apartheid and the Conceptualization of 'Race'. *Journal of African History*, 33(2): 209–237.

Dumett, R. (1973), John Sarbah, the Elder, and African Mercantile Entrepreneurship in the Gold Coast in the Late Nineteenth Century. *Journal of African History* 14(4): 653–679.

Du Pisani, A. (1985), *SWA/ Namibia. The Politics of Continuity and Change*. Johannesburg.

Eirola, M., J. Bradley, A. Laitinen (1990), *Kavango, the Sambiyu Tribe. The Way of life of the Mupapama River Terrace community*. Rundu.

Eirola, M. (1992), *The Ovambogefahr. The Ovamboland reservation in the making: political responses of the Kingdom of Ondonga to the German Political Power, 1884–1910*. Rovaniemi.

Emmett, A. (1999), *Popular Resistance and the Roots of Nationalism in Namibia, 1915–1966*. Basel.

ENOK (1987), *FNDC – Bridge to the Future/ ENOK – Brug na die Toekoms*. Windhoek.

Epstein, A. L. (1958), *Politics in an Urban African Community*. Manchester.

Ellis, S., Y. Fauré (eds.) (1995), *Entreprises et entrepreneurs africains*. Paris.

Estermann, C. (1976), *The Ethnography of Southwestern Angola. Volume 1: The Non-Bantu People/ The ambo Ethnic Group*. New York.

Evans, I. T. (1997), *Bureaucracy and Race: Native Administration in South Africa*. Berkeley.

Evans-Pritchard, E. E. (1937), *Witchcraft, Oracles and Magic among the Azande*. Oxford.

Evans-Pritchard, E. E. (1961), *Anthropology and History*. Manchester.

Evanson, J., D. Herbstein (1989), *The devils are among us: the war for Namibia*. London.

Evers, H.-D. (1994), The traders' dilemma. A theory of the social transformation of markets and society. *In:* H.-D. Evers, H. Schrader (eds.), *The Moral Economy of Trade: Ethnicity and Developing Markets*. London, pp. 7–14.

Farson, J. N. (1944), *Behind God's Back*. London.

Fauré, Y., J. F. Médard (eds.) (1982), *État et bourgeoisie en Côte d'Ivoire*. Paris.

Ferguson, J. (1990), *The anti-politics machine. Development, depoliticization, and bureaucratic power in Lesotho*. Cambridge.

Forrest, J. B. (1998), *Namibia's Post-Apartheid Regional Institutions. The Founding Year*. Rochester.

Foster, G. M. (1965), Peasant Societies and the Image of Limited Good. *American Anthropologist* 67: 293–31.

Fumanti, M. (2002), Small Town Elites in Northern Namibia: The Complexity of Class Formation in Practice, in T. Fox, P. Mufune, V. Winterfeldt (eds.), *Namibia, Society, Sociology*. Windhoek.

Fumanti, M. (2003), *Youth, Elites and Distinction in a Northern Namibian Town*. Unpublished PhD thesis, Manchester University.

Fumanti, M. (2010), "I like my Windhoek Lager". Beer consumption and the making of men in Namibia. In: S. van Wolputte, M. Fumanti (eds.), *Beer in Africa. Drinking spaces, states and selves*. Münster, pp. 257–274.

Galton, F. (1890), *The Narrative of an Explorer in Tropical South Africa*. London.

Garlick, P. (1959), *African Traders in Kumasi*. Legon.

Garlick, P. (1967), The development of Kwahu business enterprise in Ghana since 1874 – An essay in recent oral traditions. *Journal of African History* 8(3): 463–480.

Garlick, P. (1971), *African Traders and Economic Development in Ghana*. Oxford.

Geschiere, P, (1993), Chiefs and Colonial Rule in Cameroon: Inventing Chiefs, French and British Style. *Africa* 63(2): 151–175.

Gewald, J.-B. (2002), Missionaries, Hereros, and Motorcars: Mobility and the Impact of Motor Vehicles in Namibia before 1940. *International Journal of African Historical Studies* 35(2/3): 257–285.

Gewald, J.-B (2003), Near Death in the Streets of Karibib. Famine, Migrant Labour and the Coming of Ovambo to Central Namibia. *Journal of African History*, 44(2), 211–39.

Gewald, J.-B. (2007), Chief Hosea Kutako. A Herero royal and Namibian nationalist's life against confinement, 1870–1970. In M. de Brujin, R. van Dijk, J.-B. Gewald (eds.), *Strength beyond structure: social and historical trajectories of Agency in Africa*. Leiden, pp. 83–113.

Gewald, J.-B. (Forthcoming), Beyond the Last Frontier: Major Trollope and the establishment of colonial rule in the borderland of the Eastern Caprivi, Colonial Namibia 1939 – 1954. Forthcoming.

Giddens, A. (1984), *The constitution of society: Outline of the theory of structuration*. Cambridge.

Gilliomee, H. (2003), *The Afrikaners. Biography of a people*. London.

Girvan, L. (1995), *FAO National sectoral report for Namibia – Women, agriculture and rural development*. Rome.

Gluckman, M. (1961), Anthropological problems arising from the African industrial revolution. In A.W. Southall (ed.), *Social change in modern Africa*. London, pp. 67–82.

Gobodo-Madikizela, P (2003), *A Human Being died that Night: A South African story of foregiveness*. Boston.

Goodman, D. (2001), *Fault Lines. Journeys into the new South Africa*. Berkeley.

Gordon, R: (1975), A note on the history of labour action in Namibia. *South African Labour Bulletin* 1(10): 7–17.

Gordon, R. (1977), *Mines, Masters and Migrants*. Cape Town.

Gordon, R. (1988), Apartheid's Anthropologists: The genealogy of Afrikaner Anthropology. *American Ethnologist,* 15(3): 535–553.

Gordon, R. (1993), The Impact of the Second World War on Namibia. *Journal of Southern African Studies*, 19(1): 147–165.

Gordon, R. (2005), The making of modern Namibia: A tale of anthropological ineptitude? *KLEIO* 37: 26–49.

/Gowaseb, M. (2007), *Triumph of Courage. Profiles of Namibian political heroes and heroines.* Windhoek.

Graefe, O. (1999), *Territoires urbain, pouvoirs locaux et gestion foncière en Namibie. Oshakati, Ongwediva, Ondangwa et Rundu. Des collectivités urbaines en gestation.* Thèse de doctorat de géographie. Paris X – Nanterre.

Green, F., C. H. Hahn, J. Rath: Account of an Expedition from Damara Land to the Ovampo. *Proceedings of the Royal Geographical Society of London*, 2: 350–354.

Grégoire, E. (1995), Commerçants et hommes d'affaires du Sahel. In S. Ellis, Y. Fauré (eds.), *Entreprises et entrepreneurs africains.* Paris, pp. 71–80.

Gregory, R. (1993), *South Asians in East Africa. An Economic and Social History, 1890–1980.* Boulder.

Gustafsson, K. (2005), The Trade in Slaves in Ovamboland, ca. 1850–1910. *African Economic History*, 33: 31–68.

Hackland, B., A. Murray-Hudson, B. Wood (1986), Behind the diplomacy: Namiba, 1983–5. *Third World Quarterly* 8(1): 51–77.

Hahn, C. H. (1981), *Erkundungsreise ins Ovamboland 1957.* Schwäbisch Gmünd.

Hahn, C. H. L. (1928), The Ovambo. In: *The Native Tribes of South West Africa*, Cape Town, pp. 1–36.

Hahn, H. P. (2004), Die Aneignung des Fahrrads. In K. Beck, T. Förster, H. P. Hahn (eds.), *Blick nach vorn. Festgabe für Gerd Spittler zum 65. Geburtstag.* Köln.

Hahn, H. P. (2005), *Materielle Kultur. Eine Einführung.* Berlin.

Hahn, H. P. (2008), Consumption, Identities and Agency in Africa – Introduction. In H. P. Hahn (ed.), *Consumption in Africa. Anthropological Approaches.* Münster, pp. 9–41.

Hailey, W. M. (1949), Obituary: Major C.H.L. Hahn. *African Affairs* 48: 74.

Hangula, L. (1993), *The Oshakati Human Settlement Project: The Town of Oshakati: A Historical Background.* SSD Discussion Paper No. 2. Windhoek.

Hannerz, U. (1980), *Exploring the city: inquiries towards an urban anthropology.* New York.

Hansen, K. (2000), *Salaula. The world of secondhand clothing and Zambia.* Chicago.

Harbeson, J. W., D. Rothchild, N. Chazan (eds.) (1994), *Civil Society and the State in Africa.* Oxford.

Hart, G. (1972), *African Entrepreneurship.* Grahamstown.

Haugen, H., J. Carling (2005), On the edge of the Chinese diaspora: The surge of baihuo business in an African city. *Ethnic and Racial Studies* 28(4): 639–662.

Hayes, P. (1992), *A History of the Ovambo of Namibia*. PhD thesis, Cambridge.

Hayes, P., J. Silvester, M. Wallace, W. Hartmann (eds.) (1998), *Namibia under South African Rule*. Oxford

Hayes, P. (1998), The 'Famine of the Dams'. Gender, Labour and Politics in Colonial Ovamboland 1928–1930. In P. Hayes, J. Silvester, M. Wallace, W. Hartmann (eds.), *Namibia under South African Rule*. Oxford, pp. 117–146.

Henrichsen, D. (1997), *Herrschaft und Identifikation im vorkolonialen Zentralnamibia. Das Herero- und Damaraland im 19. Jahrhundert*. PhD Dissertation, Hamburg University.

Henrichsen, D. (ed.) (2012), *Hans Schinz: Bruchstücke. Forschungsreisen in Deutsch-Südwestafrika. Briefe und Fotografien*. Basel.

Hinz, M., N. Leuven-Lachinski (1989), *Koevoet Versus the People of Namibia. Report of a Human Rights Mission to Namibia on Behalf of the Working Group Kairos*. Utrecht.

Hodder, B., U. Ukwu (eds.) (1969), *Markets in West Africa*. Ibadan.

Hooper, J. (1988), *Koevoet!* Johannesburg.

Hopwood, G. (2006), *Guide to Namibian Politics*. Windhoek.

Hudson, P., M. Sarakinsky (1986), Class Interests and Politics: The case of the urban African bourgeoisie. *South African Review* 3: 169–185.

Hummel, C. (ed.) (1990), *The Frontier war journal of Major John Crealock 1878*. Cape Town.

Hunter, M (1938), Contact between European and Native in South Africa. 1. In Pondoland. In L. Mair (ed.), *Methods of study of culture contact in Africa*. London, pp. 9–24.

Iliffe, J. (2005), *Honour in African History*. Cambridge.

International Court of Justice (1950), *International Status of South West Africa. Advisory Opinion of July 11th, 1950*.

Jauch, H., E. Shipki (2009), *Historic Strikes in Namibia: The Walvis Bay Fishing Strike of 1968 and the General Strike of 1971/72*. http://www.larri.com.na/files/Strike History.pdf. Accessed December 29, 2009.

Johanssen, P. (2007), *The Trader King of Damaraland: Axel Eriksson*. Windhoek.

Johnson, S. (2006), *The Native Commissioner*. London.

Karp, I. (1981), Review of Arens, Frontier of Change, and Hjort, Rural ties. *African Economic History* 10: 220–223.

Katjavivi, P. (1988), *A history of resistance in Namibia*. Paris and London.

Kiwanuka, M. (1970), Colonial Policies and Administrations in Africa: the myths of the contrasts. *African Historical Studies* 3: 295–313.

Kooy, M. (1973), The contract labour system and the Ovambo crisis of 1971 in South West Africa. *African Studies Review* 16: 83–105.

Kotze, C. E. (1984), *The Establishment of a Government in Ovamboland, 1915–1925.* Unpublished MA thesis, UNISA.

Kreike, E. (2004), *Re-Creating Eden. Land Use, Environment and Society in Southern Angola and Northern Namibia.* Portsmouth.

Kros, C. (2002), W.W.M. Eiselen: Architect of Apartheid Education. In P. Kallaway (ed.), *The history of education under apartheid 1948–1994.* Frankfurt, pp. 53–73.

Kuper, H. (1947), *The Uniform of Colour. A Study of White-Black Relationships in Swaziland.* Johannesburg.

Kuper, H. (1960), *Indian People in Natal.* Natal.

Kuper, L. (1965), *An African Bourgeoisie: Race, Class, and Politics in South Africa.* New Haven and London.

Labaki, B. (1993), L'émigration libanaise en Afrique occidentale sub-saharienne. *Revue Européene des Migrations Internationales* 9(2) : 91–112.

Lau, B., P. Reiner (1993), *100 years of agricultural development in colonial Namibia (Archeia 17).* Windhoek.

Laubschat, H. (1903), Bericht des Baumeisters Laubschat über eine Reise nach dem Norden des deutsch-südwestafrikanischen Schutzgebietes. *Deutsches Kolonialblatt* 22: 614–616, 641–646; 24: 678–682.

Lawson, R. (1971), The supply response of retail trading services to urban population growth in Ghana. In C. Meillassoux, D. Forde (eds.), *The development of indigenous trade and markets in West Africa.* Oxford, pp. 377–398.

Lazar, J. (1993), Verwoerd versus the 'Visionaries'. The South African Bureau of Racial Affairs (Sabra) and Apartheid, 1948–1961. In P. Bonner, P. Delius, D. Posel (eds.), *Apartheid's Genesis 1935–1962.* Braamfontein, pp. 362–392.

Lebzelter, V. (1934), *Eingeborenenkulturen in Südwest- und Südafrika.* Leipzig.

Leibrandt, V. (1976), Early days in Ovamboland. *SWA Annual*: 144–145.

Leichtman, M. (2005), The Legacy of Transnational Lives. Beyond the First Generation of Lebanese in Senegal. *Ethnic and Racial Studies* 28(4): 663–686.

Lempp, F. (1963), Ovamboland und seine wasserwirtschaftliche Erschliessung. In H. W. Stengel (ed.), *Wasserwirtschaft – Waterwese – Water Affairs in S.W.A..* Windhoek, pp. 51–62.

Leverton, B. (1987), Manning, Charles Nicholson. In *Dictionary of South African Biography, Vol. V.* Pretoria, pp. 88.

Leys, C. (1989), The Security Situation and the Transfer of Power in Namibia. *Review of African Political Economy* 45/46: 142–151.

Loeb, E. (1962), *In Feudal Africa.* Bloomington.

Löytty, S. (1971), *The Ovambo Sermon. A Study of the Preaching of the Evangelical Lutheran Ovambo-Kavango Church in South West Africa.* Tampere.

Louw, W. (1976), *Owambo.* Johannesburg.

Louw, W. (1979), Mangetti. Home of Cattle and Knowledge. *SWA Annual:* 43–45.

Lovejoy, P. (1980), Kola in the History of West Africa. *Cahiers d'Etudes Africaines* 20: 97–134.

Lubeck, P. (ed.) (1987), *The African Bourgeoisie: capitalist development in Nigeria, Kenya and the Ivory Coast.* Boulder.

Lugard, F. (1922), *The Dual Mandate in British Tropical Africa.* Edinburgh and London.

MacGill Alexander, E. (2003), *The Cassinga Raid.* MA Thesis UNISA.

Magyar, L. (1859), *Reisen in Süd-Afrika in den Jahren 1849 bis 1857. Erster Band* (=all). Pest and Leipzig.

Magyar, L. (1859), Die Reisen des Ladislaus Magyar in Süd-Afrika. Nach Bruchstücken seines Tagebuches, von A. Petermann. *Mittheilungen aus Justus Perthes' geographischer Anstalt* 1859: 181–199.

Malinowski, B. (1932), A Five-Year Plan of Research. *Africa* 5(1): 1–13.

Malinowski, B. (1938), Anthropology of changing African cultures. In L. Mair (ed.), *Methods of study of culture contact in Africa.* London, pp. vii–xxxviii.

Mamdani, M. (1976), *Politics and Class Formation in Uganda.* London.

Mamdani, M. (1996), *Citizen and Subject. Contemporary Africa and the Legacy of Late Colonialism.* Princeton.

Marris, P., A. Somerset (1971), *African Entrepreneurship: A Study of Entrepreneurship and Development in Kenya.* New York.

Marvick, D. (1985), 'Élites'. In A. and J. Kuper (eds.), *Social Sciences Encyclopedia.* London, pp. 243–254.

Marwick, M (1971), Foreword. In M. Brandel-Syrier: *Reeftown Elite. A study of social mobility in a modern African community on the Reef.* London, pp. xv–xx.

McKittrick, M. (2002), *To Dwell Secure. Generation, Christianity, and Colonialism in Ovamboland.* Portsmouth.

Meillassoux, C. (1971), *Development of Indigenous Trade and Markets in West Africa.* London.

Melber, H. (1996), *Urbanisation and internal migration: Regional dimensions in post-colonial Namibia.* (NEPRU Working Paper 48). Windhoek.

Melber, H. (2007), Poverty, power, politics and privilege: Namibia's black economic elite formation. In H. Melber (ed.), *Transition in Namibia. Which changes for whom?* Uppsala, pp. 110–129.

Mendelsohn, P., S. el Obeid, C. Roberts (2000), *A profile of north-central Namibia.* Windhoek.

Messiant, C. (2006), *1961, L'Angola colonial, histoire et société.* Basel.

Miers, S., I. Kopytoff (eds.) (1977), *Slavery in Africa. Historical and Anthropological Perspectives.* Madison.

Miescher, G. (2011), *Namibia's Red Line. The history of a veterinary and settlement border.* New York.

Miescher, G., D. Henrichsen (eds.) (2000), *New Notes on Kaoko.* Basel.

Miettinnen, K. (2005), *On the Way to Whiteness. Christianization, Conflict and Change in Colonial Ovamboland, 1910–1965.* Helsinki.

Migdal, J. (1996), *State in Society.* Cambridge.

Miles, W: (1994), *Hausaland Divided. Colonialism and Independence in Nigeria and Niger.* Ithaka.

Miller, D. (1995), Consumption and Commodities. *Annual Review of Anthropology* 24: 141–161.

Mintz, S. (1967), Pratik: Haitian Personal Economic Relationships. In J. Potter, M. Diaz, G. Foster (eds.), *Peasant Society: A Reader.* Boston, pp. 95–110.

Mitchell, C. (1969), *Social networks in urban situations. Analyses of social situations in central African towns.* Machester.

Moller, P. (1974), *Journey through Angola, Ovampoland and Damaraland 1895–1896.* Cape Town.

Moorsom, R. (1979), Labour consciousness and the 1971–72 contract workers strike in Namibia. *Development and Change* 10: 205–31.

Moorsom, R. (1980), *Underdevelopment and class formation: the birth of the contract labour system in Namibia, Collected Papers.* York.

Moorsom, R. (1997), *Underdevelopment and labour migration: the contract labour system in Namibia.* Bergen.

Moorsom, R. (1982), *Agriculture: Transforming a wasted land (A Future for Namibia 2)*. London.

Müller, E. (1912), *Report for the Year 1911 on the Trade of the Consular District of German South West Africa*. London.

Nafziger, E. (1977), *African capitalism: a case study in Nigerian entrepreneurship*. Stanford.

Namakula, O. (2004), *Armed Liberation Struggle. Some Accounts of Plan's Combat Operations*. Windhoek.

Nampala, L.: (2006), Christianisation and cultural change in northern Namibia. A comparative study of the impact of Christianity on Oukwanyama, Ondonga and Ombalantu, 1870–1971. In V. Shigweda, L. Nampala: *Aawambo Kingdoms, History and Cultural Change. Perspectives from Northern Namibia*. Basel, pp. 1–109.

Nas, P. (1993), *Urban Symbolism*. Leiden.

Nas, P. (1998), Introduction: Congealed time, compressed place; roots and branches of urban symbolic ecology. *International Journal of Urban and Regional Research* 22(4): 545–549.

Ngavirue, Z. (1999), *Political Parties and Interest Groups in South West Africa: A Study of a Plural Society*. Basel [originally PhD Thesis Oxford, 1972].

Nitsche, G. (1913), *Ovamboland. Versuch einer landeskundlichen Darstellung nach dem gegenwärtigen Stand unserer geographischen Kenntnis*. Kiel.

Notkola, V., H. Siiskonen (2000), *Fertility, Mortality and Migration in Subsaharan Africa. The Case of Ovamboland in North Namibia, 1925–1990*. London.

Norval, A. (1996), *Deconstructing Apartheid Discourse*. London.

Nugent, P. (2004), *Africa since Independence*. New York.

Nzimande, B. (1990), Class, National Oppression and the African Petty Bourgeoisie: The case of African traders. In R. Cohen (ed.), *Repression and Resistance: Insider accounts of Apartheid*. London, pp. 165–210.

Nzimande, B. (1991), *The Corporate Guerillas: Class formation and the African corporate petty bourgeoisie in post-1973 South Africa*. Unpublished Doctoral Thesis, Durban, University of Natal.

O'Linn, B. (1985), *The Attainment of an Honourable and Lasting Peace and the Obstacles in the Way. An analysis on the occasion of the opening of the 17th Session of the Third Owambo Legislative Assembly on 5th March 1985 at Ongwediva, Owambo*. Ongwediva.

Olivier, M. (1961), *Inboorlingbeleid en –administrasie in die Mandaatgebied van Suidwes-Afrika*. Unpublished PhD thesis, Stellenbosch.

Olivier, M (1961), Differensiële Wetgewing in Perspektief. In *Grense. ,n simposium oor rasse-en ander verhoudinge*. Stellenbosch, pp. 175–194.

Olivier, N. (1959), *Ons stedelike Naturelle-Bevolking*. Johannesburg.

Owambo Legislative Assembly (1985), *Debates of the Eigtheenth Session of the Third Legisslative Assembly, 23–30 July 1985*. Ongwediva.

Pendleton, W. (1974), *Katutura: A Place where we do not stay. The social structure and social relationships of people in an African township in South West Africa*. San Diego.

Pendleton, W. (1996), *Katutura. A place where we stay. Life in a post-apartheid township in Namibia*. Athens.

Popitz, H. (1999), *Phänomene der Macht*. Tübingen.

Posel, D. (1987), The Meaning of Apartheid before 1948: Conflicting Interests and Forces within the Afrikaner Nationalist Alliance. *Journal of Southern African Studies* 14(1): 123–139.

Posel, D. (1991), *The Making of Apartheid 1948–1961. Conflict and Compromise*. Oxford.

Powdermaker, H. (1962), *Copper Town: Changing Africa*. New York.

Pütz, J., H. von Egidy, P. Caplan (1986), *Political Who's Who of Namibia*. Windhoek.

Pütz, J., H. von Egidy, P. Caplan (1989), *Namibia Handbook and Political Who's Who*. Windhoek.

Putnam, R. (1995), *Making Democracy Work*. Princeton.

Randall, D. J. (1996), Prospects for the Development of a Black Business Class in South Africa. *Journal of Modern African Studies*, 34(4): 661–686.

Rautanen, M. (1903), Das Recht der Ondonga. In S. Steinmetz (ed.), *Rechtsverhältnisse von eingeborenen Völkern in Afrika und Ozeanien*. Berlin, pp. 326–345.

Reinhard, W. (1999), *Geschichte der Staatsgewalt*. München.

Report of the Commission of Enquiry into South West Africa Affairs 1962–1963 (1964). Pretoria.

Republic of South Africa (1964), Memorandum. Decisions by the Government on the Recommendations of the Commission of Enquiry into South West Africa Affairs. In *International Court of Justice. South West Africa Cases. Supplement to the Counter-Memorial filed by the Government of the Republic of South Africa*, pp. 5–30.
Republic of South Africa, Department of Foreign Affairs (1971), *Owambo*. Pretoria.

Rich, J. (2004), Troubles at the Office: Clerks, State Authority, and Social Conflict in Gabon, 1920–45. *Canadian Journal of African Studies* 38(1): 58–87.

Rizzo, L. (2007), The elephant shooting. Inconsistencies of colonial law and indirect rule in Kaoko (north-western Namibia) in the 1920s and 1930s. *Journal of African History* 48(2): 245–266.

Rogerson, C., K. Beavon, G. Pirie (1979), The geography of the Afrikaner Broederbond in Namibia. *Social Dynamics* 5(2): 13–17.

Rotberg, R. (ed.) (1983), *Namibia. Political and economic prospects.* Lexington.

Salokoski, M. (2005), *How Kings are made, how Kingship changes.* PhD thesis Helsinki University.

Salokoski, M. (1992), *Symbolic Power of Kings in Pre-Colonial Ovambo Societies.* Licensiate Thesis Sociology, Helsinki.

Sampson, S. (2001), Beyond Transition. Rethinking elite configuration in the Balkans. In C. Hann (ed.), *Postsocialism: ideals, ideologies, and practices in Eurasia.* London, pp. 297–316

Saunders, C. (2007), Michael Scott and Namibia. *African Historical Review*, 39(2): 25–40.

Schapera, I. (1938), Contact between European and Native in South Africa – In Bechuanaland. In L. Mair (ed.), *Methods of Study in Culture Contact.* London, pp. 25–37.

Schinz, H. (1891), *Deutsch-Südwest-Afrika. Forschungsreisen durch die deutschen Schutzgebiete Gross-Nama- und Hereroland, nach dem Kunene, dem Ngami-See und der Kalaxari. 1884–1887.* Oldenburg and Leipzig.

Schütz, A., Th. Luckman (1975), *Strukturen der Lebenswelt.* Darmstadt.

Sennett, R. (1977), *The Fall of Public Man.* New York.

Serfontein, J. (1979), *Brotherhood of power: an exposé of the secret Afrikaner broederbond.* London.

Shiimi yaShiimi, A. (2007), *The most successful African businessman in Namibia. The life story of Frans Aupa Indongo.* Windhoek.

Shigweda, V. (2006), The Pre-Colonial Costumes of the Aawambo. Significant changes under colonialism and the construction on post-colonial identity. In V. Shigweda, L. Nampala, *Aawambo Kingdoms, History and Cultural Change. Perspectives from Northern Namibia.* Basel, pp. 111–268.

Shiweda, N. (2005), *Mandume ya Ndemufayo's memorials in Namibia and Angola.* Master's Thesis, University of the Western Cape.

Shore, C., S. Nugent (eds.) (2002), *Elite Cultures: Anthropological Perspectives.* New York.

Siiskonen, H. (1990), *Trade and socioeconomic change in Ovamboland, 1850–1906.* Helsinki.

Silvester, J. (2009), "The Struggle is Futile": A short overview of Anti-Swapo visual propaganda. In G. Miescher, L. Rizzo, J. Silvester (eds.), Posters in Action: Visuality in the making of an African nation. Basel.

Simmel, G. (1903), Die Großstädte und das Geistesleben. In *Die Großstadt. Vorträge und Aufsätze zur Städteausstellung (=Jahrbuch der Gehe-Stiftung zu Dresden, Band IX, Winter 1902–1903).* Dresden, pp. 187–206.

Southall, R. (2004), The ANC and black capitalism in South Africa. *Review of African Political Economy*, 31: 313–328.

Spiekermann, U. (1999), *Die Basis der Konsumgesellschaft. Entstehung und Entwicklung des modernen Kleinhandels in Deutschland 1850–1914.* München.

Spittler, G. (2002), Globale Waren – lokale Aneignungen. In B. Hauser-Schäublin, U. Braukämper (eds), *Ethnologie und Globalisierung.* Berlin, pp. 15–30.

Spittler, G. (2008), Caravaneers, Shopkeepers and Consumers – the Appropriation of Goods among the Kel Ewey Tuareg in Niger. In H. Hahn (ed.), *Consumption in Africa. Anthropological Approaches.* Münster, pp. 147–172.

Strassegger, R. (no year), *Die Wanderarbeit der Ovambo während der Deutschen Kolonialbesetzung Namibias. Unter besonderer Berücksichtigung der Wanderarbeiter auf den Diamantenfeldern in den Jahren 1908 bis 1914.* Unpublished PhD Thesis, Graz.

Stengel, H. (1963), Der Cuvelai. Ein Beitrag zur Gewässerkunde Südwestafrikas. In H. Stengel (ed*.), Wasserwirtschaft – Waterwese – Water Affairs in S.W.A..* Windhoek, pp. 63–77.

Stiff, P. (2004), *The Covert War. Koevoet Operations in Namibia 1979–1989.* Alberton.

SWA Yearbook (1976), Economic Development in the South West African Homelands: The Role of the Bantu Investment Corporation. *SWA Yearbook*: 45–46.

Swainson, N. (1980), *The Development of Corporate Capitalism in Kenya.* London.

SWAPO (1981), *To be born a nation: the liberation struggle for Namibia.* London.

Tapscott, C. (1990), *The Social Economy of Oshakati and Ondangwa. An Overview.* Windhoek.

Tapscott. C. (1993), National Reconciliation, Social Equity and Class Formation in Independent Namibia. *Journal of Southern African Studies*, 19: 29–39.

Thomas, E. (2009), Mzee Simon Hafeni Kaukungua. *New Era*, 4 December 2009.

Thomas, W. (1978), *Economic Development in Namibia. Towards acceptable development strategies for independent Namibia.* München.

Time Magazine (1981), Namibia: a droning, no-win conflict. *Time Magazine, 2 March 1981.*

Tirronen, T. (1986), *Ndonga-English Dictionary.* Oniipa.

Tönjes, H. (1911), *Ovamboland. Land, Leute, Mission, mit besonderer Berücksichtigung seines größten Stammes Oukuanjama.* Berlin.

Tötemeyer, G. (1977), *South West Africa/ Namibia. Facts, attitudes, assessment, and prospects.* Randburg.

Tötemeyer, G. (1978), *Namibia Old and New: traditional and modern elites in Ovamboland.* London.

Tuupainen, M. (1970), *Marriage in a Matrilinear African Tribe. A Social Anthropological Study of Marriage in the Ondonga tribe in Ovamboland.* Helsinki.

Tvedten, I. (no date), *Oshakati Shanty Towns.* Unpublished manuscript.

United Nations Council for Namibia (1983), *The Military Situation in and relating to Namibia. Report of the UN Council for Namibia.* New York.

Van der Laan, L. (1975), *The Lebanese Traders in Sierra Leone.* The Hague.

Van Tonder, L. (1967), Obituary Johannes Petrus van Schalwyk Bruwer. *African Studies* 26(4): 247–248.

Van Wolputte, S. (2007), Cattle works: livestock policy, apartheid and development in Northwest Namibia, c. 1920–1980. *African Studies* 66(1): 103–128.

Van Wolputte, S. (2010), Beers and bullets, beads and bulls. Drink and the making of margins in a small Namibian town. In: S. van Wolputte, M. Fumanti (eds.), *Beer in Africa. Drinking spaces, states and selves.* Münster, pp. 79–105.

Verne, M. (2007), *Der Mangel an Mitteln. Konsum, Kultur und Knappheit in einem Hausadorf in Niger.* Berlin.

Vierke, U. (2006), *Die Spur der Glasperlen. Akteure, Strukturen und Wandel im europäisch-ostafrikanischen Handel mit Glasperlen.* Bayreuth African Studies Online.

Vigne, R. (1983), The Namibia File. *Third World Quarterly* 5(2): 345–360.

Vigne, R. (1998), The Moveable Frontier. The Namibia-Angola Boundary Demarcation 1926–1928. In. P. Hayes, J. Silvester, M. Wallace, W. Hartmann (eds.), *Namibia under South African Rule. Mobility and Containment 1915–46.* Oxford, pp. 289–304.

Visser, J. (1983), *Die Suid-Afrikaanse Weermag se bydrae tot die ontwikkeling van Suidwes-Afrika. The South African defense force's contribution to the development of South West Africa.* S.l., Military Information Office, SADF.

Warren, M. (2000), *Democracy and the Terrain of Association.* Princeton.

Weber, M. (1976), *Wirtschaft und Gesellschaft.* Fifth edition, ed. J. Winkelmann. Tübingen.

Weidlich, B. (2008), Bodies in 1972 mass grave identified. *The Namibian* 24 September 2008.

Weinrich, A. (1973), *Black and White elites in Rural Rhodesia.* Manchester.

Werner, W. (1990), 'Playing Soldiers': The Truppenspieler Movement among the Herero of Namibia, 1915 to ca. 1945. *Journal of Southern African Studies* 16(3): 476–502.

Widlok, T. (1999), *Living on Mangetti. 'Bushmen' autonomy and Namibian independence.* Oxford.

Wild, V. (1991), Black Competition or White Resentment? African Retailers in Salisbury 1935–1953. *Journal of Southern African Studies* 17(2): 177–190.

Williams, F. (1994), *Precolonial Communities of Southwestern Africa. A History of Ovambo Kingdoms 1600–1920.* Windhoek.

Wood, B. (1984), The militarization of Namibia's Economy. *Review of African Political Economy* 29: 138–144.

Wolfe, E. (1935), *Beyond the Thirst Belt. The Story of the Ovamboland Mission.* London.

Zimmerer, J. (2004), *Deutsche Herrschaft über Afrikaner: staatlicher Machtanspruch und Wirklichkeit im kolonialen Namibia.* Münster.

Index

du Preez, F.A. 57

Durban 120, 123, 126, 132, 167, 198, 236

Dymond, George 102 f.

E

Eedes, Howard XVI, XXV, 24, 26, 28 f., 46, 52, 57 f., 60, 65 f., 68–73, 77, 81, 84, 86, 101 f., 108, 143–146, 156 f., 163–165, 202

Eenhana 124, 151, 184

Eerste Nasionale Ontwikkelings Korporasie (ENOK) 32, 96, 98, 129 f., 132, 189 f., 229

Eirola, Martti XXV, 15 f., 20 f., 44, 228

Eiselen, Werner 88, 233

Ekandjo, Petrus 72 f.

Elago, Matheus 186

Elia Weyulu 194

Elifas, Paulus 119

Elim 137, 174, 179

Endola XXVII, 36 f., 39 f., 46, 51, 53, 55, 97, 99, 123, 143, 174

Engela 32, 76, 78, 137, 150

Epinga 107, 184

Eriksson, Axel 5, 11, 14, 232

Estermann, Carlos XXIV, 229

Eunda XIX, 44

F

Filemon yElifas lyaShindondola 194

Fogarty, Nelson 23, 58, 226

G

Galoua, Simon IX, XXVIII, 62–64, 66, 69

Görgens, H. 20

Grootfontein 15, 19, 24, 26, 30, 34, 48, 50, 55, 63, 74, 108, 115, 132, 143

H

Hahn, Carl Hugo (the elder) XXIV, 23

Hahn, Carl Hugo Linsingen XXIV, 22

Haipinge, Emmanuel 136

Hälbich family 22

Hamukoto, Alfeus 74, 112, 116 f., 120, 185

Hamuntenga, Philipusa 118

Hamutumbangela, Teophilus 103 f., 106, 178

Hamutumwa, Johannes 99

Hartmann, Karl 50, 226, 232, 240

Haukongo, Lazarus 104, 108

BASLER AFRIKA BIBLIOGRAPHIEN
Namibia Resource Centre - Southern Africa Library

Martha Akawa
The Gender Politics of the Namibian Liberation Struggle
Basel Namibia Studies Series 13
2014. 246 p., ill., map, index
CHF 32.00
ISBN 978-3-905758-26-9

Women's contributions against apartheid under the auspices of the Namibian liberation movement SWAPO and their personal experiences in exile take center stage in this study. Male and female leadership structures in exile are analysed whilst the sexual politics in the refugee camps and the public imagery of female representation in SWAPO's nationalism receive special attention. The party's public pronouncements of women empowerment and gender equality are compared to the actual implementations of gender politics during and after the liberation struggle.

"It is my contention that unless we rewrite history from a woman's perspective and by ourselves, we will not have a complete recollection of our past and be in a position to negotiate a space on the independence agenda. Martha Akawa has made us aware of this responsibility and asks of us what legacy we as women who fought in the liberation struggles will leave to future generations of women?"

Advocate Bience Gawanas, Windhoek

Martha Akawa obtained her PhD from the University of Basel (Switzerland) for the thesis which comprises this book. She is the Head of the Department of Geography, History and Environmental Studies at the University of Namibia in Windhoek.

Lightning Source UK Ltd.
Milton Keynes UK
UKOW06f0920310814

237810UK00005B/110/P